What Makes a Man?

MODERN MIDDLE EAST
LITERATURES IN TRANSLATION SERIES

What Makes a Man?

SEX TALK IN BEIRUT AND BERLIN

RASHID
AL-DAIF

JOACHIM
HELFER

TRANSLATED BY
KEN SEIGNEURIE
& GARY SCHMIDT

CENTER FOR MIDDLE EASTERN STUDIES
UNIVERSITY OF TEXAS AT AUSTIN

Cover art: *A Sacred Bird*, digital collage © Abraham H. Zeitoun,
original portrait © Randa Mirza. Printed by permission.

Cover and text design: Kristi Shuey
Series Editor: Wendy E. Moore

Library of Congress Control Number: 2014951951
ISBN: 978-0-292-76310-4

How the German Came to His Senses originally published in Arabic as
'*Awdat al-almani ila rushdih* (Beirut: Riad El-Rayyes, 2006).

The Queering of the World originally published in German as
Die Verschwulung der Welt (Frankfurt am Main: Suhrkamp, 2006).

Ken Seigneurie's article "Irony and Counter-Irony in Rashid
al-Daif's *How the German Came to His Senses*" originally published in
College Literature 37.1 (2010). Reprinted with permission.

CONTENTS

vii PUBLISHER'S NOTE

ix TRANSLATORS' NOTES

1 HOW THE GERMAN CAME TO HIS SENSES

55 THE QUEERING OF THE WORLD

Essays

171 KEN SEIGNEURIE
Irony and Counter-Irony in Rashid al-Daif's *How the German Came to His Senses*

198 REBECCA DYER
Colonial Discourse and Dissent in Rashid al-Daif's and Joachim Helfer's Contributions to the West-Eastern Divan

214 MICHAEL ALLAN
The Hermeneutics of the Other: Intersubjectivity and the Limits of Narration in *The Queering of the World*

228 GARY SCHMIDT
Writing, Reading, and Talking Sex: Negotiating the Rules of an Intercultural Language Game

241 ANDREAS KRASS
The Temple of Heteronormativity: Rashid al-Daif's *How the German Came to His Senses*, Joachim Helfer's *The Queering of the World*, and Navid Kermani's *Thou Shalt—* A Comparative Reading

PUBLISHER'S NOTE

In 2003, Lebanese novelist Rashid al-Daif was paired with German writer Joachim Helfer as part of the West-Eastern Divan, a Berlin-based initiative to promote dialogue between the Middle East and the West. Each writer spent time visiting the other's country and then returned home to write about the experience. With Helfer's approval, al-Daif wrote a piece focusing on a facet of his fellow novelist that he found particularly intriguing: his homosexuality. In 2005, al-Daif published in Arabic *'Awdat al-almani ila rushdih* (*How the German Came to His Senses*). Al-Daif's novelized account of his time with Helfer and Helfer's subsequent publication of *Die Verschwulung der Welt* (*The Queering of the World*), which includes a German translation of al-Daif's text with accompanying commentary, sparked a major debate among critics, both German and Arab.

The controversy focused on whether the "Rashid" and "Joachim" depicted in *How the German Came to His Senses* are meant to be seen as fictional characters and as a means to open a dialogue between East and West on homosexuality. In *The Queering of the World*, Joachim Helfer's commentary works to explain events as they occurred and expresses concern that the irony and fictitious elements in al-Daif's text might be lost on the reader and lead one to believe he is arguing for a heteronormative view of the world. Either way, the twin-text resulting from their honest effort to understand each other is strikingly bold and full of surprising turns and insights. Rarely have intercultural dialogue, gender, and sexuality been explored in such an entertaining way.

As Rashid al-Daif sees his text to be a "novelized biography," it is rendered in our edition in its original, uncommented form. As Joachim Helfer, on the other hand, considers it to be a realistic reportage on his private life, we also render al-Daif's text and Helfer's comments in the way they were published in German.

In order to provide some interpretation and background, we have invited five specialists in Arabic and German literature to provide essays on crucial aspects of this controversial but enlightening exchange.

Thanks go to Rashid al-Daif, Joachim Helfer, Gary Schmidt, Tarek El-Ariss, Wendy Moore, Kristi Shuey, and the German West-Eastern Divan program. Who would have thought that it would take so much work to achieve a modest dialogue? And yet it did, and does.

Only technical terms in Arabic are fully transliterated. Proper nouns and book titles are not transliterated except for 'ayn and hamza. Arabic words that have entered the English language are not transliterated.

Ken Seigneurie

Translating *The Queering of the World* has presented a series of challenges and raised essential questions about what it means to engage in translation. The reader may notice, for example, a number of discrepancies in wording and phrasing when comparing Rashid al-Daif's narrative with Joachim Helfer's commentary. In certain cases this is a direct result of the complexities involved with publishing a text consisting of two distinct parts written originally in different languages and rendered into English by two different translators. A further layer of complexity is added by the fact that Helfer's commentary is not a response to al-Daif's original Arabic text (neither Helfer nor I understand Arabic) but to the German translation published by Suhrkamp in the volume *Die Verschwulung der Welt*. The result is that in the current volume Helfer sometimes appears to misquote al-Daif—for example, when he distances himself from ever having stated that homosexuals were "persecuted like the Jews" by the Nazis. This jars with Ken Seigneurie's translation of what al-Daif reports Joachim to have said; namely, that the Nazis persecuted homosexuals "as they did the Jews." This difference of just a few words hints at potentially much greater misunderstandings. It would have been possible to eliminate such discrepancies by simply x changing my translation to conform to Seigneurie's rendering, which would indeed have a kind of logic, given that Seigneurie had access to the original Arabic, whereas, as far as these quotations are concerned, I have essentially translated a translation, operating at two levels of separation from the original. Such a move would, however, have veiled a crucial aspect of the intercultural exchange: the inevitable shifts in meaning that occur through the very process of translation, a process present at every level of the encounter between the two authors. Whereas Helfer and al-Daif's face-to-face discussions were conducted in a language that was native to neither of them (French), Helfer's written text is based on his native language of German, which in turn is wholly unknown to al-Daif. My hope is that the shifts in meaning and the misunderstandings that inevitably occur during such translingual and transcultural processes remain visible in my translation. A special thanks to Joachim Helfer, Ken Seigneurie, Wendy Moore, and Kristi Shuey for their collaboration in this unique and rewarding project.

Gary Schmidt

What Makes a Man?

HOW THE GERMAN CAME TO HIS SENSES

RASHID AL-DAIF

TRANSLATED BY KEN SEIGNEURIE

I met the German writer Joachim Helfer as part of the West-Eastern Divan program sponsored by the German government and administered by the Goethe Institute and other German foundations. This program provided for a writer from an Arab or Islamic country to visit a German writer in Berlin for a period of six weeks. During this time, the writers participated in various cultural activities, and afterwards the German writer returned the visit to the other writer's country for three weeks of similar activities. All these occasions provided ample opportunity for the writers to become well acquainted with each other and served the purpose of the program, which was to promote cultural dialogue, especially among writers.

Thomas Hartmann, the director of the program, called me from Germany to inform me he'd chosen the writer I would work with during my six-week stay in Berlin. Naturally, he told me his name, Joachim Helfer, his age, thirty-nine, and summarized his works, activities, and other such things—but the remarkable thing was that he insisted on informing me Joachim was gay. When I saw he was insisting, I told him this was something personal that didn't concern me. He responded, "Okay, but I saw it as my duty to inform you in order to complete the profile." His voice was uneasy as he addressed me on this one point whereas it leveled off with satisfaction when he affirmed that at last he'd found a suitable writer for me.

I was of course thinking about the reason for his insistence on telling me the writer, my future colleague, was gay. I wondered whether this might have something to do with my being an Arab, or that Arabs refuse to accept homosexuality as a human right whereas Germany has accepted it for quite some time now. Maybe he wanted to know whether I'd be opposed to this choice and request that the program find another writer. After all, it was among the conditions of the program that this writer would come to Lebanon to participate in cultural activities with me, and his homosexuality might be an obstacle to our working together. Or maybe he quite simply wanted to inform me about this writer's orientation because he felt it must be known and indicated, neither more nor less, especially if the person concerned was a man.

But to be quite honest, despite my response to Thomas Hartmann that the whole matter was the writer's business and not mine, I was pleased he'd told me. I said to myself, "It's a good thing he did!" because, frankly, the whole thing preoccupied me somewhat. I thought about it a lot and then said to myself, "Why not? Let him be gay!" This experience might be very instructive, especially since I'm interested in moral issues and sexual morality in particular. I've written about it and consider morality a battleground between Western modernity and our current situation in the Arab world. When my novel *Who's Afraid of Meryl Streep?*, which is related to the subject, was translated into French, I'd mention every chance I got in television, newspaper, and radio interviews that the bed was the site of the real battle between East and West. The bed is a frontline between Arab "tradition" and Western modernity. Something in this expression is not fully precise, but it does approximate a factual truth, that women have antennae that can pick up anything new faster than men can, and that women feel novelty more than men do. They smell it from afar and feel it as soon as it arrives, especially if it has anything to do with moral habits and practices—and sexual morality in particular. This is what creates tension in their relations with men. Women see, feel, and understand, and men don't realize they are like this. Sex is the "moment" that defines and exposes controversies.

The bond between a man and a woman, marriage and divorce, having children, celibacy, cohabitation, free love, the split between sex and sentiment, the connection between sex and sentiment, and so on and so forth—all these topics interest me a great deal. I observe their development in the world and stay informed as much as I can.

As for homosexuality, I follow the news on it in general but as one who is not directly concerned. I'm from an environment that honors and celebrates procreative masculinity; one that revels in it every chance it gets. The father in our culture is called "Abu" followed by the name of his eldest son, and the eldest son is named after his grandfather. The ancient Arab critics described the greatest and most creative poets as stallions. For us, the homosexual act is disgraceful, shameful, and must be suppressed. It's a crime punishable by law. Homosexuals are called perverts and their practices are considered sex acts against nature.

As a rule, I exercise constant vigilance to keep at a distance from the behavior and ideology of the society I belong to and count myself among those who reexamine at every turn society's convictions— and indeed my own personal convictions—yet many of my society's ideas have penetrated me and do their work in me without my realizing it. I remember feeling an overwhelming joy the first time my son and a girlfriend withdrew into his room. "Ahh!" I said to myself when I heard him lock the door. His masculinity was assured. Fulfilled. I myself was fulfilled and my fear vanished for good, unregretted.

He was fourteen years old at the time and staying with me in Beirut after having lived with his French mother in the city of Lyon and studying in one of its schools. I had been terrified for him about two things while he was in France: that he'd get mixed up in drugs and that he'd become gay. I'd keep a worried eye out for news about him and ask around in order to reassure myself he was free of anything to do with either of these calamities. From the age of three, my son lived in France with his mother, who returned to her country after our divorce. We agreed he'd live with her there because Beirut was witnessing a particularly dark period of the civil war. Later, when he was fourteen, he returned to Beirut in order to complete his secondary school studies. I was relieved by his return because it was easy for a young man to become gay in France, whereas it was very difficult in Beirut. That was my understanding and those were my feelings.

From the depths of my heart, I wanted my son to resemble me, but a much better version of me—a million times better. And maybe, at the same time, I wanted him to resemble us (and by "us" I mean we Lebanese Arab Middle Easterners) but without, of course, any of our inveterate faults.

4 I truly liked that girl, my son's girlfriend, and wished them to love each other and stay together for eternity. Without the slightest doubt, I still prefer—even as I write these words and without the slightest hesitation—that my son not be gay, but that doesn't mean I'd have let him down if he had been. I'd have stood by him, of course.

When Thomas Hartmann informed me about my colleague's homosexuality, I said, "Why not?" This would be an opportunity to become closely acquainted with openly lived homosexuality—and in Berlin to boot, the city where the largest gay pride demonstration takes place every year. Nor, to say the least, was this an exhaustively treated topic in our countries. When people hear about homosexuality in Europe or America, they laugh or smile ironically and look at the matter from a distance, considering it no concern of theirs. But I warned myself—and without the slightest compunction: I must be cautious from the beginning, clear from the beginning, dissuasive from the beginning, in such a way that boundaries are drawn from our very first meeting and that each of us stays within them! Because some gay men don't remain within their limits and don't hesitate to disturb others, especially when you consider I'm a hairy man—even if I don't have a mustache to show for it. I say this in all candor and without a qualm.

I'm afraid I'm locked into the cliché, the rigid stereotype of homosexuality, but what happened with me and with several of my friends permits me to say that hairy chests, arms, and mustaches are tempting for our rare gay friends. My friend M. told me his mustache aroused our mutual French friend, the Arabist J.B., who died of AIDS in the 1980s. J.B. was sharp-witted, deeply erudite, and at the same time he had an acute sexual desire that knew no limits when he felt the need for a man. Night and day, he ventured out into a West Beirut blackened out by the prevailing chaos and the law of the jungle, searching for prey or more precisely a wolf that would prey on him. I was astonished when I'd meet him afterwards and he'd tell me where he'd been the night before or over the past couple of days, which security checkpoints he'd crossed, and what dangers he'd faced. I couldn't believe it. If he spent two days without satisfying his desire, he'd explode! My thick chest hair aroused J.B. himself, but he had the wisdom to restrain himself.

F.Q., also French, worked with me on the translation of one of my texts into French. He was aroused by the hair on my hands and once pulled on it while blushing. I asked him firmly not to try that again. Another time he reproached me because I had scraped my wrist and left it exposed; he asked me to conceal the hair. Something similar happened with a Lebanese man, A.B., who told me hairy hands and chests excited him. When the matter between us settled down and he knew his limits, he confided to me that the sight of a mustache excited him the most, and he told me facial hair for him was an indicator of a man's body hair, his virility, and his animality.

Undoubtedly, these were special cases. I would not call them widespread tendencies that permit us to sketch an image of gay men based on them alone. I admit my understanding of homosexuality is not deep and my reading very limited. I also admit that much of the information I've gathered is marked more by the negative than the positive. For example, during the AIDS panic in the late 1980s, it was commonly said that homosexual practices increased the danger of the virus spreading. The virus spread among gay men in a frightening way, but, of the many reasons cited to explain this, what sticks in my mind is that the percentage of sexual encounters was much higher in the gay community than in others and that gay men changed partners much more often than heterosexuals did. Somewhere in my mind is also the idea that they hate men who don't return their affections. They also hate women although I don't know why. A thousand reasons.

In any case, I'm hairy even if I don't have a mustache. I was conscious of this when I met Joachim alone, face-to-face, for the first time. It was in Berlin in the apartment the Wissenschaftskolleg gave me for my six-week stay. At one point he rose from the sofa and sat next to me as I explained to him an Arabic expression written on a gift I had given him. I was somewhat surprised when he sat next to me. I got up to examine the gift and reflect on the inscription. I made a point of sitting on another sofa and told him my girlfriend in Beirut had chosen this gift for him, but the truth was I had chosen it, not my girlfriend. I claimed this to create a pretext that permitted me to talk about my girlfriend, and from there I proceeded to talk about my relations with women in general. The conversation between us began smoothly on these personal topics because, first of all, my colleague had an open disposition and also because each of us desired openness toward the other. It was in a way one of the "conditions" the program imposed on us.

I was in Germany to work, not to deal with such matters, so I was determined to fill him in from the beginning. I took advantage of every chance to make him understand how much I loved women, how life for me without a woman was unbearable, and how I smelled the odor of putrefaction and armpits when in the company of men without any women. I didn't want to be crude but was resolved to avoid any trouble. So let matters be clear from the outset. He was free to be himself and I was free in my desire to avoid finding myself in unpleasant circumstances that could jeopardize our work while it was still in its infancy.

In this atmosphere, I realized the meaning of being a girl or a woman, of being a source of arousal and a center of sexual interest. It had never before crossed my mind. Strange how a woman feels compelled to bring her legs together when she's seated in order to avoid revealing "more than she should" and how she must be careful about how she bends forward so as not to expose her breasts, which "should remain hidden." And that's in "liberated" countries, let alone others where women veil themselves in order to conceal anything that might arouse men's desires.

I didn't have to cover the hair on my chest because the weather in Berlin was cold, and I was wearing a woolen sweater that covered me to the neck. I surprised myself though by automatically pulling my shirtsleeves down from time to time to cover the hair on my hands as a seated woman pulls down her skirt to cover what she can of her thighs. It came to me as something of an epiphany that women are completely different from men. Men and women really lead two different daily lives. At one point I exclaimed to myself, "Oh my God! This can't continue." We were sitting together on the bus when he stretched his hand over the seat back where I was sitting without touching me, as if he simply wanted to relax while sitting and nothing more. I rose and stood in the aisle. He supposed that I thought we had arrived and that I was getting ready to get off, so he said, "We're not there yet."

I arrived in Berlin on a Friday in late October of 2003, and on the evening of that day, I met Joachim Helfer at a dinner organized by Thomas Hartmann at his home. Joachim visited me at my apartment on Monday. Between these meetings, I learned as much as I could about him and his relations with the friend he lived with. This information reached me from several sources, and all of it focused on the fact that he was gay and lived with a man who was more than seventy years old. The news would reach me sometimes discreetly, sometimes with affected naturalness, and other times with natural simplicity. All my sources were German, of course, since I didn't know anyone of any other nationality who knew him—either as a person or as a writer.

I myself started to refer to him as gay when asked about him. While I was waiting for him at the Wissenschaftskolleg, I met the exiled Egyptian intellectual Nasr Hamid Abu Zayd. This was the first time I had met him, so we sat down for a coffee together and I told him I was here at the invitation of the West-Eastern Divan program. He was aware of the program, and when he asked me about the writer with whom I would work, I informed him he was a "homo," using the foreign word and then following it with the Arabic word for gay. The thing is I didn't want to use the common word "queer" because it has negative connotations, so I used the neutral, recently coined word in Arabic, mithlī. This is a translation of the foreign word "homosexual," or "gay"—which in Arabic could mean "like me" (mithli) if you don't emphasize the last vowel. That's what Nasr Abu Zayd heard me say, so he asked, "Like you?" Mine was the haste of a man soiled by impurity as I disavowed any connection and clarified the matter. I wanted not a trace of doubt to linger in his mind.

Joachim was not long in telling me the "whole" story in such a way that my picture of him was no longer based simply on rumor, supposition, or unverified information. It was in the south of France when he was on holiday that Joachim met his partner, N., who is thirty-eight years his senior. Joachim was about nineteen and his partner was fifty-seven. For some twenty years they've never been apart. They live in the same house, sleep in the same bed, and share everything like man and wife, and no disagreement between them has ever led to divorce because their freely chosen bond is stronger than the bond of law or religion. Each found his fulfilling complement in the other, as they often say about a harmonious heterosexual couple.

N. is from a Berlin family that owned a building before the war in the region that became East Berlin after the city was split. He recovered it after reunification, sold a part of it, and repaired the top floor for himself and Joachim to live in. Joachim believes Providence sent him to live with N. and that this Providence itself wanted N. to have pleasure in him fully and profoundly as a man of this age can take pleasure in a young man in the prime of his youth. Joachim firmly believes in the existence of a Providence governing this world and overseeing our affairs in it.

From the moment he met N., Joachim never again approached a woman. In fact, he could no longer stand the female body as a source of delight and no longer paid attention to it even in its existence as a body. That was, in effect, the attitude I noticed during the days we spent together. In Munich, on the day we arrived to take part in several activities related to the program, we were having dinner when a young pregnant woman passed. She was proud of her pregnancy and wore clothing that hugged the roundness of her belly. It seemed as though she were naked, her clothing was so light and close fitting, as if she'd dyed her belly inky-black. This blackness revealed the beauty of her skin's uncovered portions. I looked at her in admiration, thinking she'd smile at me gratefully. Instead, she cast me an astonished, quizzical glare, as if she wanted to know why I was looking at her like that and what it was about her that called for this. And, by what right did I dare? I communicated my confusion and surprise to Joachim and told him nothing of the sort had ever happened to me in Lebanon or France—countries where I'd lived for years. I asked him whether the young woman's behavior was personal or part of the general culture. He said he hadn't noticed her.

Another time we encountered a woman whose clothing revealed a pair of very beautiful and elegant breasts, and this was remarkable given the cold November weather, five below zero Celsius. She attracted my gaze and I said to Joachim, joking, "Breasts should be outlawed." Surprised, he asked me what I meant. I asked him whether he'd seen the woman's breasts, how provocative they were, how extremely beautiful, how offensive. He said, "I hadn't noticed." His response surprised me even though I had begun to get used to him. A thing like this is a rare occurrence in Lebanon. A woman can't go about in such elegance and with such round breasts and in November (in Berlin!) without attracting attention. How could these breasts fail to turn heads? It was as if they were crying out against their confinement in that truss: "Get us out of here. Liberate us!" We Arabs are knights and it is in the nature of knights to be noble and not permit ourselves to refrain from coming to the rescue of innocence and beauty no matter how difficult the obstacle. Joachim didn't see the woman's body as I saw it or as men like me see it. He saw it as posing no problem whatsoever. What distanced him from the woman was not her body but her spirit. He had no need whatsoever for her softness and tenderness.

What did attract his attention from the first instant in the street and everywhere were the youths, and the young men in particular. He claimed he could spot a gay male in a group of young people. In the Pergamon Museum in Berlin, where the ruins of ancient Iraq are housed, I said to Joachim while we were standing in front of a bust of a magnificent woman: "A woman like that would make my days happy!" His response surprised me. "A man like that would make my days happy!" he said, indicating a young guard roaming in the room with us. I asked him whether he thought the young man was gay. He said, "Of course! I'll bet you everything I own!" I saw him sometimes contemplating young men in restaurants, on the street, in museums, or anywhere. He'd follow them with his eyes and blush.

One evening he invited me to attend *Aida* in the new Berlin Opera House. He told me over a drink afterwards he dreamed of a young man who would be for him what he was for N. He'd give him what he possessed of love and attention just as N. had given this to him. He said he was convinced the governing Providence of this world would help him find the young man of his dreams. He had no doubt whatsoever about it because he would love the young man and give of his heart and of himself. It was a rare moment of confidence for my colleague, and I listened to him with focused attention. It's in my nature to listen attentively to those who talk to me about themselves in the "right" way, without embellishment or exaggeration or presumption or anything of the like. I listen especially during moments of the "right" confidence. My colleague's words flowed, disclosing his dreams and making eloquent his preoccupations and plans.

Joachim dreamed of a young man.

I wanted to ask him here whether he was exposing himself to legal prosecution if he had relations with a minor, but I postponed the question for another time. It wasn't up to the level of the discussion. I wanted to ask him another question, too. If he craved a young man, it would be the son of another man. Joachim wanted to enjoy the fruits of the labor of others—I mean their children—without bothering to have a son himself to let another enjoy the fruits of his labor and his child. But I postponed that, too. I didn't want to break the flow of my friend's confidence. It wasn't appropriate to interrupt the conversation with a question that revealed other concerns. He said he had a great capacity for love and a desire to give, and the Providence in which he believed would ordain it. Because love guarantees.

Then one time I asked him if he'd like to have a child and he responded in the negative, but it wasn't a firm no because his problem was with women, not with a child. He didn't want to live with women and hadn't approached one for twenty years. If he ever wanted to have a child himself one day, he'd have to have it with a lesbian who would not want to live with a man. At any rate, he sometimes thinks he already has two children from two different women he'd slept with before meeting N. He had relations with the first one only once, and his relations with the second didn't last more than a week.

The first woman was an acquaintance who had been married a long time. He met her one evening, and they spent the entire night together in the same bed. She wanted a child and believed her husband wanted one, too, but he pretended he didn't because he was afraid of the responsibility and afraid that a child would change their relationship. He was afraid for her even when it came to his own child. This is what she thought about her husband. Then she added there was another possibility as well, that he was afflicted with a low sperm count and didn't want to admit it to himself, so he wouldn't go to the doctor in order not to face the plain fact of the problem. He was afraid of that possibility. The woman was somewhere in her thirties and he was seventeen. She knew Joachim was gay and that women were not the object of his desire. On the following morning, she mused while dressing: "If I get pregnant, it might be from you."

Slowly he asked, "Why didn't you ask me to use a condom? If I didn't mention anything myself, it was because I thought you were on the pill."

"That's a perfectly legitimate assumption, but I stopped taking the pill some time ago without telling my husband, and I haven't become pregnant by him yet. It's gotten to such a point I've started doubting myself and thinking I'm the problem and not him."

Some seven or eight months later, he met her by coincidence on the street. Her belly was swollen and she was manifestly proud of her pregnancy, but she blushed when she saw him. They traded perfunctory greetings without breaking stride, or perhaps pausing only briefly. This happened on the sidewalk near one of the cafés where they could have sat together for a coffee, but she didn't want to or couldn't.

I asked him whether he felt any desire for that child—for it to be his, for example—or whether he'd recognize his paternity, or talk to the mother about the child so things wouldn't remain vague and hidden. He replied, "No," but it wasn't a firm no. Then he added, "Maybe I was useful to them (he meant his friend and her husband) because I made them happy at little cost to myself."

"Did you ever see the child?"

"No!"

"You don't want to see it?"

"No!"

"Would you like to know some day whether you're the father?"

"No!" (He said this after some thought.)

The second woman he knew from his school days. She was about his age and soon to be married when they met one afternoon and slept together. She disclosed to him she'd slept with him because her fiancé was older than she and much more sexually experienced. In having sex with Joachim before her marriage, she wanted to acquire some experience in order to have some parity with her husband and keep the marriage from failing. They went on like that for a week or so, meeting several times, always during the afternoon. Several years later, he met her and she informed him that she had two children, and didn't hesitate to mention that her first child was perhaps his—I mean Joachim's. He never saw her after that, never contacted her, and doesn't know where she's staying now, or whether she's still in the same city—or even whether she's alive or dead.

Joachim didn't ask her what made her think her eldest was his! I conveyed my puzzlement at his total absence of curiosity, as if the matter had to do with another person and not him. He was surprised by my confusion and reflected for a moment like someone who is searching for a response but can't come up with anything. When I asked him whether the child was male or female, he said he didn't know. I asked him if it was important for him to know, but he raised his hand and his head in a gesture I couldn't understand. I didn't know if it was a gesture unique to him or one of the gestures Germans use to accompany their speech—or to take the place of speech—as a slight nod for us means "no" and a brief shake of the head left and right means "what?"

"She slept with me to acquire some experience! Women in Germany today decide, as I've mentioned to you on numerous occasions. She determines what she wants from a man. We are nothing to them." That's what Joachim said.

"Okay," I said, "but you're the natural father of the child. You're a parent!" He was silent. Then he mentioned without any prompt that his brother and sister had six children, three each. He said he loved them very much and always liked seeing them and spending time with them. He said his relationship with them was good even though they live in another city. I wondered whether he meant by this that his siblings' children were like his own and that his love for them perhaps exempted him from loving his own children, and, consequently, he could not be accused of lacking full humanity for not having direct offspring. He said his brother's middle daughter was very beautiful. She was twelve but looked like a fully developed woman, which preoccupied her father. It occurred to me here to ask him an embarrassing question, which was especially so after the neutrality he showed previously toward paternity. Suppose your niece, after attaining the age of consent, decided to become a porn film actress. What would your position be? Naturally, as I'd expected, he was surprised by the question.

What permitted me to ask it was a long conversation we'd had on a previous occasion about porn film actresses and their relations with their fathers and brothers. He'd personally helped me to interview a porn film actress whom I met in his presence at a literary café, the Literaturhaus Fasanenstrasse, and he served as interpreter. During the discussion (I mean before meeting the actress), he seemed completely liberated from dominant moral values. He didn't seem to me to cling to anything but the value of personal freedoms. He favored these values unreservedly, without hesitation, as if he'd never doubted them and as if they were a cause that steeled his nerves and invigorated him in speech and debate.

So I asked him what his stance would be if his niece chose to work as an actress in a porn film. Quickly mastering his sense of surprise, he responded that it would certainly sadden him if she chose this occupation and his brother would consider it a catastrophe. Then he added that if such were her decision, he'd respect it. "Why not?" he said after a moment's distraction.

His answer was that of somebody directly involved with the issue, not a neutral response or that of a sociologist who observes and analyzes. Nor was it the libertarian response he'd given during our discussion on this topic a few days previously. He said that, in any case, he didn't approach the matter from a moral angle, and if this occupation made her happy, he'd be happy for her. Then he caught himself and added that he'd talk with her before she made the choice, but if it was clear this would make her happy, then why not?

As for his brother, he'd surely feel hurt from a moral standpoint, but in the end, he wouldn't be able to do anything about it. What his daughter decides to do she'll do because once she attains legal age he has no right to compel her to do anything she doesn't want to do, or to forbid her from doing anything she wants to do. I pointed out he hadn't shown such enthusiasm during previous conversations on the subject, and he acknowledged he was speaking this time as somebody directly concerned and not as a person who gives his opinion on a general topic.

I visited his house for the first time on a Monday. He introduced me to his friend and we had lunch together. I had been prepared for, and even to a certain extent apprehensive about, this visit. But that's

14 not the important thing. The important thing was what I had in my mind unbeknownst to myself. Somewhere in my consciousness, the relationship between two men meant quite simply sexual relations. Asswork. This relation is reflected on things, leaving its traces everywhere: on household wares, door handles, plates, spoons, and in the bathroom . . . especially in the bathroom, where sin hides and grows. And in the kitchen sink where the food of two "bachelors" remains on spoons and plates and where traces of their lips remain on coffee and tea cups, on wine and whiskey glasses, and on other kinds of liquor glasses. Two men living together equal dirt, negligence, and the absence of women!

Women are concern, cleanliness, and purity. They care for household goods and fixtures. Women are by nature opposed to filth and decay, body odors, and forgotten corners. My mother used to wash my three older brothers' clothes every evening after they worked repairing cars all day. When they returned from work, their clothing was soaked in dirty grease and oil. She'd force them to wash and would scrub their clothes by hand (she didn't have a washing machine) every evening.

Before I got a maid, my intimate friend didn't enter my house without first transforming the kitchen into a place of splendor, gleaming with cleanliness, as if cleanliness were light itself. Quite charming, this association between cleanliness and light. After we broke up, I missed the incandescence of her cleanliness.

My friend and his partner's house was very clean and well lighted. Its wide glass façade loomed in the sky above the roofs of East Berlin. It was a surprise, and a good one. His furniture was spare, simple, and beautiful—every piece selected for its suitability, as if it had been made for the place. The whole formed a beautiful harmony: a roomy, wide space without voids, easy and pleasant to move through. On the three walls of the living room (except the glass façade) hung paintings by the artist Adami, who was N.'s friend. The surface area of each measured several meters square and perfectly suited the space. I'd never before seen anything like this house, save to a limited extent among the delicate and highly cultured wealthy.

Without a doubt, fear of dirt and filth within ourselves is deeper than we think. When Joachim washes his hands after urinating, he seems to be punishing them. He sets about scrubbing them with soap and water time after time as if trying to rescue them from a dangerous illness communicated via contact with the male organ, the source of urine. I saw many Germans doing this, as if the penis were a devil lurking in a dark sewer.

Their home was a great surprise to me in terms of taste, cleanliness, and culture, but visiting it roused my curiosity more than I'd expected. In truth, I'd never visited a gay "couple's" home before ("couple" meaning a married couple), so this was a first. I lingered in every room and corner of the house with Joachim, who took care to show me everything once he sensed my desire to see the house. This wasn't the only reason for my curiosity; there was something else. The sight of this "couple" composed of two men in this wide and spacious home transported me to the subject of humankind's procreation, its continuity, and the issue of increasing or decreasing numbers of inhabitants in diverse societies.

The subject of demographic development has always stimulated my curiosity and evoked in me deep and contradictory feelings. I feel blissful at the sight of people in the street rushing about in every direction to their various occupations. The sight of young men and their health gives me strength; I feel melancholy for, and fearful of, societies that grow old. I expressed this feeling once in an interview and said the incomplete and unaccomplished forms we see generalized in "developing" countries have their own poetry, which needs to be articulated. I mean this poetry needs to be displayed and defended until it is no longer suppressed or exposed to scorn in dominant discourse among the public in general and intellectuals in particular. They criticize the mentality that allows entire cities and buildings to remain unfinished, unlike "developed" countries where the city is complete and accomplished and everything is finished. Here in Lebanon, for example, they disapprove of the bare concrete posts spiked with steel reinforcement rods that thrust out of rooftops, which in their view is an affront to good taste and beauty. I am completely opposed to this discourse. Where they see ugliness, I see a scene of life bursting forth, like water flowing exuberantly down from mountaintops, delighting the heart and bubbling with promise. First, the father erects two posts on the rooftop of his house and then stretches between them a clothesline his wife drapes with clothes to dry in the sun and rushing wind. Then the father sets up other posts, builds a grape arbor over them, and eventually builds a roof over all of the posts for his recently married son to live under. Then he sets up two more posts with steel reinforcement rods ready for a new roof. In developed countries where houses are finished, you won't see many children. If you do, it seems like a pleasant and unexpected surprise.

Yet at the same time, I'm afraid for the world of this proliferation that some say will exhaust the fruits of the earth. I'm not among those who believe people reproduce according to a greater purpose. Without a doubt, there are reasons for reproduction but not goals of which we are conscious. I mean the birthrates of European and North American and Japanese societies are not dropping according to a well-drawn plan defined in their national missions. Likewise, Asian, African, and South American societies are not proliferating in order to achieve a particular aim either.

This subject interests me and stimulates my imagination. Joachim and I talked about it a lot. I asked him once, "Don't you see that the society that legalizes gay marriage is one that suffers from an internal malaise?" Germans are not reproducing but they are enacting laws for gay marriage as if they were convinced of their desire not to renew their society. He said, "Listen. In any society between two and four percent of the population is made up of gay men and lesbians, so what are we going to do with them?" I told him legalizing gay marriage was something different from legalizing gay rights to self-realization. He didn't respond to my concern; he responded to his concern. I mean, quite apart from the question of morality, all societies that genuinely legalize homosexual relations make them equal to those of man and wife. These are societies that somehow accept annihilation and disappearance, which is particularly applicable to German society.

I was told fifty percent of the apartments in Berlin are one-person households, and a friend informed me that he and his wife had great difficulty finding an apartment in the late 1970s because they had three children. A German woman poet of about fifty said during a discussion, "Thank God I don't have children by anybody else since I am my own child." Then there are those who bear the cares of the world on their shoulders, pointing out that since the world is choked with people, they don't want to add to the problem by bearing children. Joachim himself said to me once when I'd asked him if he didn't want to have a child, "There are eighty million people in Germany! Do you want more?"

Of course, I'm not saying the decline in Germany's birthrate is due to homosexuality; rather that the legalization of homosexuality goes hand in hand with this situation. It goes along with the decline in the birthrate, with the rise in living standards and cultural levels, with the priority on the individual and on individual freedoms, with the respect for women's rights, with their presence in society, and especially with their right to work and their right to promotion and other such things. It's a reason, a cause, and a part of everything.

My colleague is not overly interested in debate on the subject from this point of view. He is interested in defending his rights, especially since he suffered in boyhood from his situation—suffered from shame at the disclosure of his real desire, from his gender identity, and from other things gay men commonly experience. He clings with all his strength to the gains he has acquired.

Having always felt a strong attraction to males, he doesn't remember a beginning or even when he first slept with a man, but he clearly remembers the first time he slept with a woman. He'd always been attracted to males, whereas his attraction to females was new and discontinuous. Joachim believes he began to be conscious of his homosexuality from about the age of five and has been definitively gay since this early age. The whole problem came in having the courage to say it. Where could the courage come from when he was a small child who found it difficult to anger his parents and put them in an embarrassing position?

Shame. That's what's difficult to get over. Joachim had a friend who committed suicide. It was a friend from school who was gay. They'd spoken together a lot about this subject—Joachim's mother took part in the discussion and tried to help him—but the friend decided to put an end to his life because he couldn't overcome the forces arrayed against him, crushing him mercilessly.

When I asked him about his mother's position on his own homosexuality, Joachim responded with vigor that he hated emotional blackmail, hated it when his mother told him, "I'll love you if . . ." Whoever loves him must love him as he is without conditions. It isn't love if it's given only as a reward for pleasing others . . . "If you do this I'll be happy, and if you do that I'll weep out of misery and sadness." He stated frankly, "I think the strategy of emotional blackmail is a woman's specialty." His mother was a Catholic and a sociologist who worked in an institute of the Ministry for Social Affairs. She was cold, but his relationship with her was good. She was very understanding once the truth about him began to emerge and during the stages he passed through. She was even able to maintain good relations with his companion, N., after he introduced her to him.

Joachim's father was a prisoner of war during World War II for a period of a year and a half. A socialist activist, he was arrested in East Germany and sentenced to death, but the death sentence was never carried out and he remained in prison for more than eight years until he was released in a prisoner exchange with West Germany in 1957. He was cold, sarcastic and mocking, always wore a trench coat, and was never without a pipe in hand. Women liked him and fell in love with him. He left his wife, Joachim's mother, and went to live in Ghana where he worked as director of a German organization (Friedrich Ebert) and married a Ghanaian woman who is still living and provided for in Botswana. He was a Protestant. Regarding Joachim's homosexuality, the father was out of the picture.

His grandfather, who was very old when Joachim met N., apparently showed no animosity. This grandfather was a conservative bourgeois and a bit of a fanatical nationalist without being a Nazi. He worked as a judge in the 1920s and 30s presiding over the District Court of Saxony and served as an officer in the German Army during the Second World War. After the war, the Americans appointed him director of the Bank der Deutschen Luftfahrt, and he retained this position until the end of his life. This grandfather was not hostile but rather sympathetic toward the idea of Joachim forming a couple with a man—even mentioning in a letter that he was sorry not to have had a chance to meet N.

Joachim, "despite this," complains about what he endured. He speaks with grief on the pains of homosexuals in general and on the injustices inflicted upon them throughout history. The

Nazis persecuted them as they did the Jews, and gays continue to be persecuted today in many places around the globe. They hide like mice to avoid being exposed to the public; they are victims of humiliation and are often denied the right to work. Sometimes they are prosecuted and thrown in prison for no reason other than being who they are.

Joachim wasn't really preoccupied by the demographic future of Germany and the world but by his own personal future. For him, the future of Germany was akin to a natural matter in which he had no say, like clouds, rain, sun, evening, or daylight. I believe he was just humoring me in discussing these issues. It seemed to me he focused on and enjoyed speaking about two things: women, and his deep desire to find a man much younger than he who would be for him what he was—and continuing to be—for N. These seemed to me to be his main preoccupations at the time.

As for women, his opinion on the matter was fixed and final. The German woman today is the one who chooses you. You don't choose her, and if it happens that you want to choose her, she'll get angry, accuse you of being impolite, and maybe even of harassment. You are not entitled to "come on" to a German woman, no matter how politely and gently you do it. She is the one who comes on to you. It's up to you to be of good upbringing and scrupulous conduct: reserved, polite, and bashful. You reveal only gentle suggestions, and she is the one who takes the initiative if she wishes.

I remembered, while we were discussing this subject, how a polite girl from home must be moderate in eating when invited to others' homes. Among her qualities is moderation in eating even if she's plump and her moderation wouldn't fool anyone. I often heard the saying: "The amount a girl eats is inversely proportional to her good education." This was a truism in the past and remains so to this day, even if to different degrees and depending on social milieu.

There has been a role reversal between men and women in Germany, or at least there's been a move in that direction. We live this transformation and its effects, especially in young males. Young men today are in some ways the girls of yesterday. The percentage of women committing crimes has reached one third today, so for every three crimes in Germany, one is committed by a woman, which doesn't include infractions and misdemeanors such as pickpocketing in streets, crowded places, department stores, buses, and subways. The average number of German men who seek psychiatric counseling and other professional help in order to extend the duration of their erections and delay ejaculation as long as possible has increased because women are slower to reach orgasm than men and prefer men who are in accord with their nature and in step with their rhythm.

I thought about what my colleague had told me and examined it from every angle, but my experience with "German womanhood" was very limited. It didn't permit me to subscribe to or contradict what he'd said. I have only a memory of an incident that occurred when I was a child. I remember seeing a young woman passing in front of our house. Our front door opened directly onto the road, without a sidewalk. She wasn't alone but was accompanied by perhaps another woman friend and a man—or maybe two. I no longer remember because this was a long time ago, and I'm sure I was not yet ten. The young woman carried a camera in her hand and took a photograph of my little sister who was standing barefoot in the road, wiping her nose with her hand. I was dumbfounded. In my mind, photos were for special occasions and were taken of those who were wearing neat clothing. I said to myself this behavior was out of place and this young woman must be eccentric to allow herself to take a picture of my sister in such a state. I took my sister by the hand, pulled her in, and asked my mother to dress her in clean clothes because a blond foreign woman had taken her picture in this condition. My mother ran outside to see what was going on, but the woman had moved away. This moment is stuck in my mind (Would that I had that photo!). I heard the grown-ups say this young woman was German.

The memory of this woman began to grow in my mind—this woman who photographed my barefoot sister in dirty clothes, wiping her snotty nose. A deep affection grew in me toward her because she dared to make a gesture far beyond what was customary.

One time a German woman visited us on behalf of my brother who was working in Germany in the late 1960s. We treated her with incomparable deference, surely as much as Kaiser Wilhelm II enjoyed when he visited Baalbek at the beginning of the last century (in proportion to our means, of course). We served her the food

of weddings and feasts and showed her the places in our region we
loved and of which we were most proud. We loved her very much,
and she loved us too and kissed us warmly when she took final leave
of us. I remember when she leaned over to kiss my little brother,
he offered her his round, puckered lips as if he were clearly
pronouncing "noon" and my eldest brother scolded him, but she
burst into laughter and hugged him to her breast. Then, after my
brother's final return from Germany, news from her stopped and
news of us to her probably also stopped.

The only other contact I've had with German women since
then was in Paris when I was a student. It was a one-night stand with
a coed who was visiting a French friend of hers, and in the morning
she went her way, I went mine, and we never met again. That's all.

The events I'm narrating are very old, the most recent being from
more than thirty years ago when I was a student. Today things have
changed from what they were back then. My "experience" from that
time can no longer serve as a base upon which to build an opinion.
Today, what I know about German women doesn't go beyond what
everybody knows in our region, that they are emancipated and
they work. So I have no negative preconceptions about German
women—quite the contrary. For this reason, I cannot agree with my
colleague's depiction of them, but at the same time I can't contradict
him. I tended to believe him because he was speaking frankly with the
sincerity of one who was confiding. I believed his feelings even though
my experience in life generally led me to say there are different kinds
of women, not a typical woman. This certainly doesn't negate the
fact that some traits may predominate over others.

The second issue that preoccupies Joachim is his desire for
a young man; one could almost say a boy. Naturally, he clearly
distinguishes between pederasty (loving boys who have attained
sexual maturity) and pedophilia (loving children who have not
attained sexual maturity) and needs no reminder about these
elementary matters. Pedophilia is of course an illness, but all
peoples, especially the great civilizations, knew passion for youths
and acknowledged it. The ancient Greeks were famous for it. They
formed couples between married men who had children and young
men. The man would request a youth from a father who might then

grant permission for his son to go with him. The man would receive the youth a number of times a week and take his pleasure in him, teaching him at the same time such things as literature, philosophy, and other intellectual pursuits of the age. In this sense Joachim and N. are not an ordinary gay couple but rather a Greek couple, or closer to the Greek couple than to anything else.

True, N. wasn't married, had no children, and didn't receive permission from Joachim's father for his son as Greek couples did. True also, Joachim didn't marry when he got older as Greek youths did. Joachim, who was nineteen when he became acquainted with his friend, was in a sense raised at his hand in an affectionate, caring, and serene atmosphere. He helped Joachim to realize his dreams and, in short, gave him much, and it was all motivated by love. This is exactly what Joachim now wants. He feels deep within himself a strong capacity for love and an irresistible desire to give. He dreams of a boy—I mean a young man—on whom he can bestow his capacity for giving. He dreams of teaching him everything he knows: poetry since Joachim loves poetry, the novel since he is a novelist who has become well known (he is still a young writer with a future in front of him), and the lore of life now that he is within sight of forty. But Joachim is not satisfied with dreaming about a youth. He is striving with patience and forbearance to find one, especially since the need is becoming urgent. He hoped something would work out with one young man with whom he'd had a relationship. Together, they read Rainer Maria Rilke's *Duino Elegies*, a book Joachim loves very much, having learned many poems by heart since he was thirteen—when his mother had asked him at that age what gift he wanted for his birthday, he responded without hesitation: "The complete works of Rilke!"

When he read Rilke with the young man, Joachim concentrated on a few poems in particular—the first, second, ninth, and tenth elegies—which he'd expatiate on and delve into. The youth was very fond of these meetings, especially since he loved poetry himself. The relationship between them developed to the point that their bodies met at last. It was a beautiful moment that was repeated, and always with success. The beautiful thing about this sexual relationship was that the youth didn't cling to a role, be it feminine or masculine. He was capable of assuming both roles in a marvelously natural way.

Joachim began to fall in love with the boy and to hope the feeling was reciprocated. But the youth had not at that point decided the matter or determined his sexual orientation, so he asked for time to come to terms with his own nature—especially since at about that time, he met a girl his own age for whom he had strong feelings. He enjoyed going with her to the movies, to the theater, and very much enjoyed simply talking with her. He felt she understood something fundamental about him, but the relationship between them remained at this level, which was closer to friendship than to anything else. Even though she frankly wished to have sex, he didn't go along with it because he wasn't in the right state of mind, but he began to ponder the question after she revealed her desire more than once. He simply didn't feel sexual desire toward her when she surprised him by revealing hers.

Joachim was aware of this situation because the youth kept him informed. He was truthful with himself, with Joachim, and with his girlfriend, and this only increased his charm and attractiveness. Relations with this kind of person are very comfortable because you're not in the dark; you know where you stand, and if he forms an opinion or takes a stand, he does so from a clear base, unlike others, whose appearances belie their feelings.

Joachim was also truthful and consistent with himself and with the boy. It was the stance of one who wants the relationship to succeed, to be rich and open to the future, not an opportunity to be seized. So the relationship between the longed-for boy and a female didn't anger him, and he didn't make any attempt to convince the youth he was gay by nature rather than bisexual. Nor did he try to coax or push him into making his decision quickly. What happened was that Joachim was set to travel to Lebanon for a period of three weeks for the West-Eastern Divan program we had begun during my stay in Berlin from the beginning of November to the middle of December 2003. Joachim was to travel at the end of April and return to Germany in mid-May 2004, which would make a three-week absence. This was fortuitous because it gave the young man an opportunity to test his attachment to the girlfriend and to verify the nature of his feelings, his desire, and his sexual identity.

In Lebanon Joachim was at ease and I saw he was happy, no doubt about it. Apparently, nothing prevented him from enjoying

24   himself in Beirut and in other Lebanese regions we visited together
or that he visited with others. The weather was beautiful. The period
between the months of April and May is usually among the best
of the year in Lebanon, with daytime temperatures ranging from
twenty to twenty-four degrees Celsius and five or six degrees cooler
at night. During Joachim's visit, the days were always sunny, the sky
blue, and Beirut chock-full of young men. Males in the street were
more visible than females and most were brown of skin or verging
on it. What could be more attractive for a gay man on the lookout
for the boy of his dreams?

As for myself, I frankly enjoy meeting the opposite sex
during occasions such as lunches and dinners with friends and
acquaintances or at similar functions. I say in all candor that the
presence of women delights me, especially if they are free and
unattached, and I believe all men, married or bachelor, generally
share this feeling. Joachim is blond and he turned girls' heads,
which doubtless did something for his pride, but this wasn't what
interested him. In considering how to make his stay pleasant and
restful, my intuition was to introduce Joachim to some of the rare
gay men I knew, but I changed my mind, figuring it wasn't up to me
to make things happen, that I couldn't manage something like this
and that I didn't like this sort of thing anyway.

Yet many, if not all, of my friends were aware of Joachim's
visit to Beirut (newspapers covered our activities), and among these
friends were a man and his wife. G. is an engineer and L. a well-
known director and university professor whom I had informed about
the details of my trip to Berlin. I told them also about Joachim's
homosexuality as well as about his friend who lives with him. Their
interest and curiosity in this matter whetted my appetite to discuss it,
so they ended up being the most well informed about it. I remember
talking to L. about Joachim's upcoming visit and the issue of whether
it was appropriate to introduce him to gay men in Beirut while we
were strolling on the seawall. One of L.'s closest friends is gay, and I
remember we were leaning toward introducing them.

The next day, when Joachim arrived, I invited him with L.,
G., and some friends to dinner at City Café, near the lower gate
of Lebanese American University, where we had held a lecture-

discussion on our experiences in the West-Eastern Divan program. We sat at a table outside and stayed in the beautiful spring air until late in the evening. When we decided to leave, L. asked me to wait for a minute until Sader, her gay friend, arrived. She'd called him while we were having dinner and asked him to come after work. When he arrived, we had hardly introduced them to each other before they fell into discussion alone together as if they'd known each other for ages. Afterwards, we all got up to say our good-byes to each other before leaving, each to his or her home. I was surprised when I saw Joachim and Sader kiss each other good-bye almost on the lips, their bodies close together. While I was taking him back to his hotel, Joachim confided to me he'd immediately guessed Sader was gay.

Some time later, Joachim related he'd seen Sader on numerous occasions and that Sader had introduced him to gay nightclubs. He filled me in on how much homosexuals suffer in Lebanon and how they encounter insurmountable difficulties in affirming themselves. He told me what I already knew but without having been upset by it before. He was indignant while speaking. He'd already learned Lebanese law permits homosexuals to be imprisoned, that they are whistled at in the streets, and that some fathers who cannot bear their children's homosexuality threaten to kill them if they don't distance themselves from this "habit." Some rich fathers send their gay children to London to have specialists treat them. He learned that among these are some who despair to the point of suicide. When one gay youth told his family about his sexual orientation, a pall of unbearable sadness fell over the home. The mother isolated herself, the father isolated himself, and they were no longer able to speak to each other or to their son. A deep depression afflicted the youth, forcing him into the hospital where, after several days of treatment and during a guard's moment of inattention, he jumped from the window onto the street below and died. Tragedy!

Without a doubt, my colleague gained a good deal of experience during his Beirut trip and collected much information about this subject, but he is not by nature a Romantic revolutionary in the way many intellectuals are, especially Arabs. They nag and complain about "issues" and proclaim their dissent every chance they get.

26   Joachim, from what I could fathom, rebels only about matters that
concern him. This doesn't mean he's selfish; rather that he is a very
realistic person who dreams about what he can achieve. No matter
how distant his dreams may be from realization, they are of a kind
he can achieve. Among these dreams is that of finding a boy. In my
thoughts about Joachim, this was a constant and a key among keys
to his personality. I noticed how his eyes would follow certain boys.
They shine. His vision is ravished.

I introduced him to a friend of mine, and this friend liked him
and wanted to know him better and to introduce him to his wife and
children. The friend invited us to dinner at his home the next day. We
were six at dinner: the friend, who was about fifty; his wife, who was
about forty-two; their son, M., who was seventeen; their daughter,
who was about fourteen; and a friend of their son's, who was the same
age as him. I don't know if it was an illusion, but I thought Joachim
was charmed by M. His eyes never strayed far from the youth.

The mother sat at the table in front of Joachim, and her son, M.,
sat on her right. The father sat to the right of Joachim, and I was in
front of the son. Nobody noticed anything, certainly not M. Only I saw
Joachim's eyes move from the wife to her son, with or without a reason
for doing so. Nobody present was aware of Joachim's homosexuality.
"That's lucky!" I was saying in secret to myself at the time, but not out
of prejudice. As a matter of principle, I am completely on the side
of those who suffer on earth and of oppressed minorities, including
gay men and lesbians, but if anyone present knew about Joachim's
sexual orientation the atmosphere would've switched from friendly
and welcoming to one of unbearable embarrassment. My friend, the
host, once told me, "By God, Rashid, I don't know what I'd do if I
found out one day, God forbid, my son was, for example, gay." He
didn't say "gay" but rather "buggered" and said "for example" to delay
the instant of pronouncing it, as if that would delay a reality behind
the words. Then, after a sigh, he added, "I'd kill him!" Naturally, I
didn't respond to his statement because I was sure that if his son were
gay he'd never kill him. Nevertheless, I was sure it would transform
his and his wife's life into a living hell. It would crush both of them.

I remembered the phone call from Thomas Hartmann when
he informed me the writer he found for the program was gay. I

said to myself that Thomas must have had the right feeling about this and a knowledge about our country from his work in the field of Third World relations. Maybe this knowledge came from his experience in the leftist struggle during his youth, especially in the 1968 period. As I learned later, he was among the student leaders in Frankfurt back then and an activist in Spontis, a group of leftists who believed in spontaneous demonstrations. He worked in the Opel factory organizing workers, and was a founder of the leftist daily *Taz*, published in Berlin. The left at that time was generally supportive of Third World issues.

Nobody at the dinner was at all aware of what was secretly going on, and maybe Joachim himself didn't know his eyes never left the youth. The boy was very brown of skin, a deep and pure brown, and his eyes were penetrating such that you could hardly imagine bearing their gaze. He was riveted by Joachim's conversation, paying attention without being distracted by anything else, not even the ministrations of his mother as she hectored him to finish his plate. It was a habit she'd formed when he was young and would refuse to eat for hours on end, and she'd worry he was dying of malnutrition.

I don't think I'm mistaken about what I saw that evening, and I don't think I saw only what I feared to see. I know when misunderstandings arise with foreigners in Lebanon and Arab countries. I know it from experience since I've lived it for years. My ex-wife, the mother of my son, is French, and she lived with me a number of years in Lebanon and Syria, and we visited other Arab countries together. For example, I believe that building work relations between a foreign woman and a Lebanese or Arab man is much more difficult than between two Westerners. Sex is always an issue between a Lebanese man and a foreign woman and this is soon evident. It is very difficult for the Lebanese Arab man not to misread the free conduct of a foreign woman in dress, speech, going out at night, and interacting publicly. It's difficult for him not to read all this as her sexual availability. Joachim once said to me sex is not the fundamental thing in the lives of German women or men, and from what I have experienced with Europeans and especially with the French, I believe this is to a large extent true.

I always thought we knew more about Westerners than they knew about us, but I have to amend this to say it is not altogether true because our knowledge of them is often superficial and misses the essential. The Western woman is not as cautious in her dealings with men as an Arab woman is, and the Arab man reads this as availability. My wife would go out from time to time to shop, taking our son with her in his stroller. Some workers in the supermarket showed a special interest in our son, and when my wife returned and told me how kind and attentive they were, I listened without offering an opinion or remark of any kind. I knew at the time that two wives of friends lived in the neighborhood and did their shopping at the same supermarket. No workers were "interested" in their children or showed any special kindness toward them. The wives were Lebanese. Then my wife came along one day and said to me the supermarket workers' interest in the boy went a little too far. I narrate this to say there was, without a doubt, a misunderstanding.

That's why I was on the alert during that evening at my friend's house. Many things passed over Joachim's head by virtue of his being German. I saw him notice the woman stretch her arm in front of him to get a bottle of oil on his left. This would never happen in Germany or in France, where polite conduct calls for you to ask your neighbor to pass the salt, the bread, or the oil—if they have oil at the table—not to reach across to serve yourself. As for us, we serve ourselves in order to avoid disturbing our neighbor at the table. It's against etiquette to ask your neighbor to pass you something, especially if that neighbor is a guest. In that case, we are the ones who put ourselves out to get him everything he needs.

I saw Joachim was always confused when he was invited to lunch or dinner. How to begin? With what? We put all courses out on the table at the same time and there is no starter or main course; instead, we put everything out and everybody serves himself. You begin with whatever you wish and reach out to take seconds as much as you want without having to ask permission. A person at the table with us doesn't have to wait for others in order to finish his plate, or to wait for the lady of the house to ask if anyone wants seconds or to pass to the next course. In France, I found it burdensome when I was invited to lunch or dinner to be prevented the pleasure of finishing my meal without waiting for others. It took me some time to get used to this, and I still wait, when I have to, out of politeness.

The issue is not one of intentions but of culture. I remember, as a doctoral student, meeting a French girl at the beginning of my stay in Paris. This girl invited me to spend the weekend at her home in a suburb of the city. Her parents were out of the country on holiday and nobody was home except her older brother. I had not been more than a couple of months in France at the time. In the evening, after the three of us had dinner together and spent some time chatting in the living room, the time came to go to sleep. My friend rose and went to her bedroom; her brother went to work at his desk and I stayed alone sitting, confused, and not knowing what I should do. After about an hour, my friend returned and asked reproachfully what I was doing there. Why hadn't I followed her? I said, "Follow you where?" She responded in amazement, "How's that? 'Where?' To our bedroom!"

"Our bedroom?" I asked, but to myself.

While we were in bed cuddling (on her initiative), I asked, "Won't your brother be upset?" The question surprised her; she didn't understand what I meant, so I continued caressing her just to show her the question was but a passing thought of no importance whatsoever. We did continue making out but I with one eye open.

Joachim cannot imagine what my friend, our host, would have done if he'd known his guest was eyeing his son with such pleasure, such distress, and such insistence. If my friend had known, his mood would have taken a turn for the worse. In the first place, if he'd known Joachim was gay, he would not have invited him to dinner or to lunch.

On one occasion, Thomas Hartmann invited me in the company of my son to dinner at a restaurant in Berlin. The tables were long, relatively narrow, and numerous diners were seated as in a university restaurant. We were speaking French and among us was a certain complicity. The three of us sat at the end of one table and four others sat next to us, two on each side of the table. On one side were a young man in his early twenties and another in his late thirties. From time to time, they would kiss each other as if they couldn't swallow a bite without kissing. Facing them were a man and his wife. Thomas, who heard them easily, mentioned to us that the younger man called them Mom and Dad. I began observing; the scene preoccupied me to such an extent I couldn't tear my eyes away. I can safely say the parents were not delighted, especially when their son kissed his partner. Theirs was not the situation of parents in the presence of their son and his beloved girlfriend. If he were to kiss her, they'd be glad for him and happy for the love that joined them. The three of us agreed on that point but also on the fact that respect for the rights of others means you have to accept what you don't like and don't wish for.

That scene would be impossible in any Arab country.

Then again, everybody at the dinner liked Joachim and found him cultured and amiable, and their daughter found him handsome. As for M., he said nothing, nor did his friend offer an opinion. In the car after dinner, Joachim asked me about M.: his age, his plans for the future, and whether he really wished to travel to Germany to continue his university studies there. M. had asked Joachim during dinner about the conditions of university study for foreigners in Germany, student housing, and what have you. After this flood of questions, I asked Joachim about his friend, the German youth. He responded briefly that the youth was still in a state of self-examination and stopped at that, not wishing to dwell on the subject. I didn't divulge to Joachim what I alone had noticed about him at dinner. I was afraid he'd take it as a reproach and told myself we would doubtless return to the subject in the future.

The next day, I showed him the cedars, the famous cedars of Lebanon in the north of the country, above Bsharri, the town of Gibran Khalil Gibran. We talked about diverse things while roaming around this forest, pausing for a long while on Joachim's attachment to his favorite poet, Rainer Maria Rilke. He recited for me some passages of his poems and commented on them. Then he moved on in a rather surprising way to the subject of his German friend with whom he read Rilke and whose answer he was awaiting. He informed me the young man had decided to stay with his girlfriend because he could at last have sex with her, and he was very happy in this relationship, which had deepened and had convinced him beyond doubt that he was not gay. He told me all this with pain and mentioned they had agreed to meet on Joachim's return to Berlin in order to discuss the matter face-to-face. When I asked him if there remained any hope, he raised his hand to the sky!

Here I remembered the day he'd invited me to visit "The Lady of Berlin." He told me, "Today I'm going to show you the Lady of Berlin." I asked him who she was and he said, "I'll show you!" so I submitted without too many questions and let him lead me wherever he willed. I eventually found myself in a museum of ancient Egyptian art in Charlottenburg, Berlin, face-to-face with Nefertiti. He announced that this was "The Lady of Berlin" as if to say, "You always go on about your desire for women, so take this one! Look at her. Doesn't she make you feel you don't need any of the others?"

I was indeed taken aback. This was a beautiful woman for all time. It was as if her lips, her eyes, her eyelashes and eyebrows were the work of the greatest makeup artists of today and her clothing revealed her entire perfect neck. Everything about her was magnificent today, just as it was certainly magnificent in the past, maybe more so. She really is a lady, not only a work of art. She is a woman who shows you her face and knows of your existence in front of her or next to her as you contemplate her with pleasure. She is truly a woman, the quintessential woman. What is the secret of her beauty that makes it persist throughout time? Intelligence radiates from her; her arresting presence imposes itself. Blessed is he for whom she cares.

After the shock, I said to Joachim, "This is a woman," and he responded, as I expected him to, that this was woman in art. It seemed to me in the context of the discussion that if Nefertiti in the flesh had offered herself to him, she could not have displaced a young man in his feelings and interests. "This is a work of nature," I said to myself, "and you can't do anything about a work of nature."

He told me about the young man's decision in the cedar forest at an elevation of two thousand meters above sea level. It was springtime and the weather was misty, which made the already majestic place even more so. The mountain cedars have been a part of our education through many sources, among them the literature of Gibran Khalil Gibran, author of *The Prophet* and son of these valleys and hills that have sheltered monks devoted to God and are free of all filth and unseemliness. The cedars are a small forest consisting of a few hundred trees, among them some great, astonishing ones they say are thousands of years old. They have a history and many Lebanese think of them as mediators with God.

32   The image of the cedar at the center of the Lebanese flag was taken from one of these cedars we were wandering under.

It was in this holy place he told me the bad news. I asked myself if I felt a sort of contradiction between the sacredness of the place and the worldliness of the subject. In the holy atmosphere replete with "Gibranic" charm, romanticism, and mysticism, I felt sympathy with Joachim. I was sad for his failure to build the relationship he'd hoped for from the depths of his heart and of which he dreamed perhaps every day. This was in spite of the strangeness of thinking about such a relationship in that place. We had gotten used to hearing about such things in cities and especially in "grindstone" cities that sharpen their inhabitants' desires to such a point that no barrier can block their realization. The sincerity that emerged from Joachim's conversation put him in harmony with this place in spite of the peculiarity I mentioned or maybe (why not?) because of it. Joachim displayed his desire for a man twenty years his junior as if it were of a mystical nature because he deeply and fervently believed in a kind of providence, which believers would call God, that shepherds this world and would not forsake one who dreams of giving all. It had not forsaken his roommate, N., who also had a great desire to give. He gave and was given.

It's strange on my part, this feeling of sympathy I have for Joachim. It even occurred to me, for instance, to ask him about his friend N., whether he knew about Joachim's desire, his attempts to fulfill it, and whether this would hurt N. in any way. It would've put me at ease, but I decided against it. It crossed my mind to help him, but then I asked myself, "How? How can you help anyone in a personal, intimate matter like this?" If it was a question of a relationship with a woman, it would've been easier, but it was a question of a man—a male. How can I ignore this when in our culture, if we want to describe a liar with no conscience who is capable of weaving conspiracies and planting chaos, we would say he's "sticking male plugs together"? Nevertheless, I tried. I tried without saying anything about it and without alluding to anything.

I tried following the example of Zubayda, the wife of the great Arab Caliph Harun al-Rashid and mother of his son, the Caliph al-Amin, who was replaced in the caliphate by his half-brother al-Ma'mun after a war between them destroyed Baghdad, the capital of the empire, and left some tens of thousands dead. When Zubayda saw her son, the Caliph al-Amin, preferring young boys, she wanted to steer him in another direction, so she bought for him some early-adolescent slave girls and dressed them as boys, cutting their hair like that of boys. She offered them to him as a gift for his sexual needs, so he'd take his pleasure in them and give up young boys.

I invited Joachim to dinner at my house with a number of friends and acquaintances who I thought would be good for him to know. I invited, at the same time, a girl of twenty-six who was beautiful despite a clearly masculine aspect no one could miss. She was short of stature and anybody would say she resembled a young boy. She arrived before Joachim and sat on a love seat. When he arrived, Joachim spontaneously sat down next to her and stayed there next to her the entire evening, talking with her and she with him. I noticed her once rise to go to the kitchen and bring him back a glass of water, which he accepted while looking into her eyes, surprised. He mentioned later she'd sensed he was thirsty without letting on, so she rose spontaneously and brought him a glass of water without him having asked her anything and without her asking him if he wanted anything. Then she sat down and continued the conversation with him as naturally as could be, as if she hadn't paid attention to what she'd done. At the end of the evening, when everybody was saying their good-byes, he kissed her near the lips, and she blushed from shyness or from nervousness or from both at once.

I wanted to know if he'd set a date to see her again or if she'd left an impression on him or moved him in any way. I asked him at the end of the evening when only he and I were left in the house. I asked him clearly and precisely, mentioning I had noticed this girl's interest in him. He responded immediately with the honesty I had come to expect from him and that I quickly discovered was one of his distinguishing features, "You're right! I noticed, too. I found myself taken by conversation with her. The truth is she caught my attention. It's impossible to find a woman in Germany who'd bring you a glass of water! We all (he meant Germans, of course), men and women, learn to serve ourselves. She surprised me, this girl, by her initiative. She was very nice. It was a good thing you invited her.

A beautiful surprise." I hesitated but had to ask him whether he'd made a date to meet again. He said, "No," but it seemed to me he said this with some pain and regret.

He mentioned he'd become used to girls finding him handsome. He always heard this from them—he is confident of his beauty—but there was something different about this girl who found him handsome that evening and doubtless loved his beauty. Before asking him, "Why didn't you ask her for a date?" the thought of his friend, N., occurred to me, and I said to myself I was stabbing him in the back without there being any enmity between us. I remembered something I'd never really forgotten when I was in Berlin: I sometimes felt I was preventing N. from spending as much time with Joachim as he'd have liked.

I remember in particular an afternoon when we visited the Jewish Museum in Berlin and planned to go to the Literaturhaus to have dinner. Joachim hesitated before agreeing to my suggestion to have dinner there. He said to me first that he couldn't because he had to return, then fell silent. I considered the matter closed and was planning to have dinner alone and wait for a reading from a recently published novel in German, translated from French. Joachim returned and when we reached the Literaturhaus, he said, "Let's have dinner here." I noticed at that moment he'd been on the phone longer than usual, but I didn't take the thought any further or try to explain it. Right after dinner, we had to go up to the room where the reading would be held. Suddenly, he said, "I have to return home. N. likes me to be with him in the evening." I realized then the meaning of the unusual telephone conversation. It also dawned on me that I was dealing with a person in a relationship and that this was something I hadn't before fathomed. I noticed the relationship between two men had its obligations. The man had to return in the evening to the other man in this relationship just as a man in a marriage has to return to his wife. I noticed I didn't ask him about his partner as I would ask any other married man about his wife. I noticed I behaved with him as if his conjugal commitment had no existence, as if he were a bachelor and not attached. Such concerns didn't exist in my culture. The intimate relationship between two men in my "spontaneous" culture was secret, not public. I realized

I now had to take into consideration this relationship, not to forget to ask about N. from time to time and to suggest he accompany us when I invited Joachim someplace, or when we decided to do an activity, just as I would with a married man. I'm not used to such behavior. I say in all frankness, in our countries this behavior would immediately cause laughter and make one feel embarrassed. It's something almost impossible, except perhaps in extremely limited and isolated circles that resemble an underground.

Joachim seemed somewhat sad and embarrassed when he withdrew from the reading to return home or, as we would say when talking about a man and wife, "to return to the arms" of his partner. I asked myself at the same time whether I projected this into his behavior and his face or if he really was like this. In other words, was I reading according to the alphabet I knew how to read—or was I reading according to the right alphabet?

When Joachim left the room a few minutes before the reading began, I wanted to ask him to send my apologies to N. for delaying him that evening from his appointed return, but I didn't because this had simply not yet become a part of me. In addition to other questions, I asked myself after Joachim's departure whether N. felt jealous about Joachim spending all that time with me, working for the most part. I imagined what might happen between them by way of reproaches, give-and-take, and accounts to make—all because of me. I was embarrassed. Yes, in a way, I was embarrassed such a thing could happen. Then I blamed myself for being inattentive to the matter of their being a "married" couple and completely like man and wife or maybe even much more so. The link that bound them was more profound than the link between a man and a woman because society had made them suffer for it until it finally accepted them for who they are. Maybe they paid a very high price for their established situation, so what they had between them was no joke but rather serious—to the point of tragedy, perhaps. Maybe to this day they continue to suffer from numerous obvious and subtle discriminations and exclusions.

I remembered here that we would read anecdotes about homosexuals as curiosities in books of Arab literary history. It's not at all a curiosity, as anyone who consults the account of Ibn Munadhir in *al-Aghani* (*The Songs*) by Isfahani can see. The matter is certainly deeper than that. Ibn Munadhir was one of the most eloquent poets, knowledgeable and well versed in the Arabic language and an inspiration for its finest practitioners. He was enamored of Abd al-Majid Ibn Abd al-Wahhab al-Thaqafi, a brilliant expert in the Hadith, who was cited by the greatest Hadith scholars. It is said of them that one evening after prayer Ibn Munadhir left the mosque in Basra and Abd al-Majid followed him, and they conversed all night until dawn. If Abd al-Majid left to go home, Ibn Munadhir accompanied him until they reached Abd al-Majid's home, then Abd al-Majid would accompany Ibn Munadhir back to his home. Neither could bear to leave the other until morning!

It was also told about them that Abd al-Majid "was very gravely ill in Basra and Ibn Munadhir took care of him, nursing him and serving him himself, scorning to delegate tasks to anyone. A visitor who saw him with his own eyes reported: 'I went one day to visit Abd al-Majid. Ibn Munadhir was there and had heated water for his friend to drink, but his condition only worsened and he moaned, "Ah!" in a weak voice. At that, Ibn Munadhir plunged his own hand in the hot water to share Abd al-Majid's pain, scalding his hand almost to the point of it falling off before we managed to pull it out and cry, "Are you crazy? What are you doing? Does this do any good?" Ibn Munadhir only replied, "I'm helping him! This is the least I can do!"'"

It worried me to think I might come between a married couple, untying a strong and precious knot between them, but I said to myself that I shouldn't get mixed up in these concerns. I came to do a job that must be accomplished to the best of my abilities and that's it. I didn't have time or energy to manage sentimental issues and especially an issue of this nature, about which I am totally ignorant. Therefore, I felt something akin to guilt after the dinner during which Joachim harmonized so well with this girl. I vowed to stop my interest in this business and leave him alone. It was up to me to stop feeling the responsibility (I almost say paternity) I acquired as a result of the confidence and friendship that was quickly established between us as a result of his openness and natural goodness. Moreover, I was certain he would refuse the expression of such feelings.

I couldn't keep myself from asking, "Does N. know about everything you're doing?" He said, "No," which surprised me and

I didn't attempt to hide it. Joachim doesn't tell N. everything, but one way or another N. knows everything. He knows the broad brushstrokes if not the fine lines. The relationship between them, as it appeared to me and according to what I understood from Joachim, was more complicated than it seemed at first blush. The appearance gave the impression of considerable simplicity; the truth is—and this was a surprise for me—that they have been sleeping together in the same bed for twenty years but as far as I could tell, and I don't think I misunderstood, they have not had sexual relations for ten. It seems that the elder partner is no longer aroused except by youths and that outside this sphere he remains neutral. It also seems that the pleasure of the younger partner has changed, as pleasures of all sexes and persuasions will change. Pleasure decays with time.

The truth is that every time I decided to get out of this sphere of interests and to limit my attention and conversations to politics, society, culture, literature, and the novel, I saw myself drawn more and more deeply into it. You can't forget your colleague is gay. This is a matter that keeps cropping up in your mind in a most vivid way, refusing to sink below the surface of consciousness quickly or easily. That's what I discovered about myself, and I don't think it's a personal quirk peculiar to me alone. Indeed, I'm almost sure it's a cultural matter characterizing people generally in our countries. If I can't be sure about the situation in Germany, I am sure I never spoke with anyone who knew Joachim without his homosexuality featuring prominently in the discussion in one way or another.

In addition to that, Joachim, by nature, will help you to stay within this train of thought and not to forget it. I'm little acquainted with persons like him who have no secrets of any kind and who take the position (with me?) that personal and intimate relations are not secret; rather, they can be discussed as if they were a public matter. Joachim is a person who has conquered his shyness, and this is why, in this situation, he conceals nothing and talks about himself as if he were talking about a character in one of his novels. To a large extent, he's capable of speaking about himself from a distance as if he "himself" were independent from the speaking "I."

I, too, am the kind of person who enjoys distancing himself from what is close to him in order to discuss it as neutrally as possible and who enjoys also even distancing the "self" in order to narrate it. That's my nature. This of course doesn't mean I don't like anything close or that I don't like myself. On the contrary, I'm one of those who always say human beings can love someone, a group, or a religion to the point of martyrdom while remaining at the same time critical and neutral toward it. To keep from going blind.

In any case, I return to Joachim's relationship with the girl I invited to dinner for him. He didn't ask her for a date, but I understood from him that it was possible to ask her out and that it was maybe even incumbent upon him to get to know her, be it out of mere curiosity.

Joachim's sentimental "preoccupations" were certainly not the only subject of our conversations. We discussed various topics, and the program's list of prescheduled activities was full. In addition, outside the parameters of the program we decided on the spur of the moment to undertake various cultural, social, sightseeing and entertainment activities. Everything whetted our appetite for conversation. We talked about driving in the streets of Beirut, the weather, the mountains, the coast, and countless other things. We gave talks at Lebanese American University, the American University of Beirut, and St. Joseph University, as well as at the Antelias Cultural Union and the University Students' Club in Tripoli. We had meetings with writers, poets, and journalists. We visited places I assumed would help Joachim to form as complete an idea as possible of the situation in Lebanon and in the region, from Khiyam Prison in the south where resistance fighters were tortured to the cedars in the north by way of the Sabra and Shatila refugee camps—famous, unfortunately, for the slaughter that took place there. Among other activities, we ate home cooking and in restaurants throughout the country and sat in the famous cafés of Beirut.

Amidst all these activities came a phone call from a woman who worked in the Beirut Goethe Institute. She said a journalist from an English-language Beirut daily wanted to interview us. I told her that I couldn't hold a conversation in English, but she said the journalist spoke French and had a bit of colloquial Arabic and that she had German origins and German was virtually her maternal tongue. With Joachim next to me as I spoke with the woman, we settled on four o'clock in the afternoon of that same day to meet at the Goethe Institute.

At the main entrance to the Institute we met a woman whom Joachim approached, thinking she was the journalist who was waiting for us. She soon made it clear that she was a German journalist living for some time in Beirut as a correspondent for a Berlin daily, but she wasn't waiting for us. This journalist was shorter than Joachim, which was obvious to me when I saw them shake hands. She smoked. She wore a long dress that reached down to the middle of her shins and athletic sneakers that didn't go all that well with her dress. The strange thing about this is I found myself trying to see this woman through Joachim's eyes. This was impossible. How could I do that? What attracted my attention to her was her backside; it continued straight down from her back and the cheeks were not round or protuberant. Her hair was also cut à la garçonne. It was very short.

Her body was straight, like that of a conquering general who had won historically decisive battles. She stood proudly—why? I couldn't understand what motivated her pride—and with something haughty and maybe challenging about her also. Her head was lifted slightly back, as one who is trying to see the tip of her nose. Maybe because of this, she had an influential presence. It was a strong presence. After a short time, an employee of the Institute arrived and informed us that the journalist who wanted to meet us was waiting on the second floor, so we went directly up, but I noticed that Joachim lagged behind me a little, talking with the woman who was with us.

The journalist who worked at the English-language Beirut daily asked us many questions and we responded, Joachim in German and I in French, with Joachim or her translating for me what the other was saying in German. She asked us about our writing styles and subject matter and our points of view on the things we saw together. After she asked all her questions and it seemed to me the interview had ended and our conversation had morphed into a trading of comments on various topics, I indicated my desire to leave. Joachim did likewise, but (Coincidence! Coincidence!) at that very moment the director of the Goethe Institute entered and suggested to all three of us that we attend the vernissage of a Lebanese artist's work. I declined because I was really feeling tired and needed to get home to rest, but Joachim accepted the director's invitation and so did the journalist. I excused myself, said good-bye to everyone, and asked Joachim to call me after the vernissage, mentioning I was prepared to accompany him that evening if he wished.

Joachim didn't call that night. I wondered to myself whether he hadn't seen Sader, the gay Lebanese whom he'd met the day after his arrival in Lebanon. I always thought he was with Sader or on that track when he didn't show up without giving any sign.

On the morning of the following day, we had a date to go to my house in the mountains in Ehden, at fourteen hundred fifty meters above sea level and a hundred kilometers from Beirut. He arrived at the appointed time and everything seemed normal, but this normality was mixed with something else. He tended toward silence in the car, my car that I drove myself. When we arrived in Junieh, some thirty kilometers from Beirut, I asked him, "What's bothering you? Tell me."

So he told me.

I could never have guessed what he was about to tell me. He said: "As of last night, I'm a father!" and went on, "During the vernissage yesterday evening, I saw the German journalist we'd met at the entrance of the building and who I thought had been waiting for us. Afterwards, I remained at the Institute talking with her, and then she suggested we go somewhere to have a beer. I accepted. She took me to a nice place in Monot Street well known for its nightlife. She knows Beirut and its nightspots well. We drank beer like two Germans and at the end of the evening continued on to her place nearby, and we ended up in bed together."

"Naked?" I asked in naïve surprise.

"Naked."

He said, "When we reached the critical moment, she got up and left the room, to come back shortly afterwards and state: 'I don't have a condom.' I replied without thinking for an instant about what I would say, 'I'll be a father,' and that's how I became a father."

I said, "Wait a bit to see if it's so," but he replied, "Waiting won't change a thing."

"Oh my God," I said to myself. "What's happening? Has Germany been restored overnight? So has the German come back to his senses?"

He said, "This was the first time in twenty years or maybe more. This was the first time I slept with a woman!"

A wave of questions swept over me, and I couldn't decide which one to ask first. The event stirred an irrepressible curiosity in me. I was before a "literary" truth, as it were, one of those truths that seem tailor-made for writing. I asked him first if he'd enjoyed being with her as he enjoyed being with a man, and he responded in the affirmative. The point of my question was clear to him; I wanted to know whether the pleasure with her was superficial and ephemeral or authentic, genuine, and capable of lasting, so he added, "I had much and deep pleasure with her." I said to him, joking, "Germany has returned to its senses, then?" He smiled and said nothing.

"What attracted you to her and changed the course of your life?" I asked. He replied, "I don't know."

They talked a lot together, and she was attracted to him in particular after a few experiences with Lebanese men who didn't treat her as she liked to be treated or according to required conduct. There was, according to her as a German, something boorish in their behavior. It was as if they were simply emptying the contents of their scrotums and then leaving. Joachim remarked, "She saw something different in the way I treated her, an interest, a tenderness, and the like." Did he say "tenderness"? I didn't comment on what he'd said, but his remarks reminded me of a comment a Lebanese friend always made when he talked about relations he'd had with married women, "Her husband is inadequate," although he'd say it in the colloquial, "Hubby's not up to scratch!"

He said the probability of pregnancy was very high because she was in her fertile period, and she was in agreement with him that they would continue their encounter without a condom. She smiled when he told her, "I'm a father," and stretched out next to him on the bed, clinging to him, free of all constraints, free of all embarrassment, free of all calculation. A transformation had occurred over the course of a few moments. What had happened between them became more serious and acquired continuity. Together they initiated a continuity. The moment embraced the present and the future together.

Joachim was agitated as he related all this, and the thought crossed my mind that he was on the verge of tears as he asked with a wistfulness he could not conceal what his mother's feelings about this would've been if she were alive and he could tell her. He wished she were still alive; she'd have been delighted. It surprised me he remembered his mother. I'd have expected anything but for him to remember his mother at that particular time. "How ugly clichés are!" I thought. How is it Germans are said to be cold? I remembered when my wife was pregnant, I didn't think about my mother at all—or my father, who had died more than twenty years before.

Joachim spoke as if the pregnancy had occurred and giving birth was a sure thing after the required interval. On the road to Ehden, he chose a name for his son: Sebastian. I told him in jest, "Call him by my name, Rashid, then you'll become Abu Rashid. That will be your nickname in our countries." He wasn't convinced, so I said, "Then call him Lebanon, the name of the place that changed your life," but this suggestion didn't meet with favor either. I corrected myself, "Unless maybe this event didn't change the course of your life." He didn't respond. He liked the name Sebastian, so I started to call him from that time on "Abu Sebastian," according to the Arab custom I explained to him of calling the parents by the name of their eldest male child.

He said he'd tell his son early on of his father's homosexuality. He said he was confident that human beings could accept anything when they're young. "And what if your son grows up to be like you, gay?" I asked. "I can't do anything about that," he said. "That will be his lot and destiny, and it's not up to us to try to oppose it."

Joachim was agitated but there was no crisis. No psychological crisis. No financial crisis. No procedural crisis even. The matter seemed simple to him and this surprised me. Once again, I asked myself, "Am I reading this according to the right alphabet or according to the alphabet I know?"

What made matters easier for him was that his partner accepted the idea even though she hadn't expected it. Doubtless, she felt a need for a child but not a pressing need, and the notion hadn't crossed her mind that this would happen to her now at this particular instant. I translated for Joachim on that occasion the Arabic saying that coincidence is better than an appointment. What also made this risky matter easy for Joachim was his partner's apartment in Berlin and that she could count on her parents' support since she was an only child and they were well off. They could support their daughter and her child even if their daughter was forced to remain out of work for a long time. This put Joachim considerably at ease—the apartment and the support (or at least partial support).

The concern for the apartment was very understandable because he'd lived with his partner for a long time and didn't imagine himself one day outside this partnership, this home, or this couple. The apartment permitted him to have perhaps two houses. More precisely, the woman's apartment represented for him something of a temporary escape in order to catch his breath and make decisions without hurrying and without the pressure of having to find a quick solution. Joachim didn't yet have time to think about these things and wasn't yet used to looking at them from all angles. He was still under the influence of the initial shock and had spent only a few hours in this stage of the metamorphosis. Pregnancy, parenthood, the child's home, responsibility for its existence, and everything resulting from a person's saying yes to having a child, he consciously accepted—even if he was quick and impetuous about it. He'd have to face all these issues in the near future. That's what I said to myself and what I tried to get across to him as much as our conversation permitted. He didn't yet know what he was going to do about all of this.

I remembered on that occasion an autobiography, *The Secret Life of Salvador Dalí*. I was astonished when I read things in it that applied to me directly. Dalí writes that a person cannot know in advance where his feelings will lead, as if he were riding them and they were leading him wherever they pleased, sometimes independently of his will. He relates events that happened to him as illustrations, such as how, when he was a boy, he once pushed a visiting friend his own age from a bridge a couple of meters high and without railings. The boy, whom Dalí loved, fell, broke bones, and almost died. This is something I have a personal knowledge about. I mean I've lived it, I live it now, and I know that I'll live it in the future—according to my nature, not according to Salvador Dalí's, of course. I think this is what was happening to Joachim.

He mentioned many things and revealed many feelings to me on the way to Ehden that day. We talked about everything the event evoked in us without limits and however the thoughts came to us. We had plenty of time because of a traffic jam choking the northern exit from Beirut and because the automobile is an intimate place conducive to conversation. We didn't talk about whether Joachim would tell his friend, N., which surprised me a great deal because I had expected that to be the first point we'd discuss. I waited in vain for the appropriate moment until I finally asked him, "What about N.? When are you going to tell him?" He didn't say, but he did say, "I'm trying to imagine what his reaction will be." He was wondering whether he should tell him by phone from Beirut or wait until he returned to tell him face-to-face. He was leaning toward telling him in person.

Events were rushing ahead and he'd not yet had time to catch his breath. He couldn't escape, and in any case he didn't want to. He feared leaving N., who had become elderly, to old age and loneliness. Or maybe he didn't fear so much as reject it. I don't know. When I see something, I always ask myself which alphabet I'm reading it by.

I recall a French friend married to a man twenty-five years older than she. She was around fifty when he reached seventy-five. As he grew old, she became free to have sexual relations with others. She didn't tell him about these relations, but she insisted on being with him to give him his medicine and on being in the house at his bedtime, around ten o'clock. She told me he'd been her professor and had taught her a lot. She fell in love with him, married him, and gave him two children, but he'd become another person "to a certain extent," she added, and said she was committed to him and could not stray from her commitment.

It seemed to me that Joachim's imagination couldn't admit the possibility of living outside the home of his partner N. Would N. accept Joachim's friend and a newborn to live with them? I don't think Joachim knew in advance whether N. would accept this. He might not even have asked himself the question yet.

When we were on the road to Ehden, Joachim mentioned several times a desire to contact his female friend when we arrived.

As soon as we entered the house, he asked permission to use the mobile phone and went out on the balcony for privacy while he spoke with her, even though they spoke in German and I wouldn't have understood a thing if he'd stayed with me. Actually, I would have. I'd have understood a lot—in fact, everything. Even if he was speaking with her in German, his proximity to me would've meant that he wasn't alone with her. "That's love," I said to myself.

Is it possible? Did Joachim fall in love with this journalist whom he'd met only yesterday? Was it love at first sight, *un coup de foudre*, as the French would say? After the first call, it wasn't more than two hours before he called her again. Each time he had to ask my permission because he'd left his own mobile in Germany. I grew annoyed with myself because I'd become like a warden to him, so I placed the phone on the table we were sitting at and told him to make himself at home and use the phone without asking permission whenever he wanted.

We'd agreed to stay in Ehden as long as we felt like it, but he indicated a desire to return to Beirut the following day, so we returned the next day in the afternoon. I dropped him off at the hotel, leaving him free to contact me for dinner and an evening out if he wished—or not if that were his pleasure. He didn't call until the following morning, when he informed me of some bad news, the gist of which was that N. had skin cancer, was very anxious, and wished that Joachim were by his side because he'd had medical tests and was awaiting the results that would show if it was malignant.

This bad news pained Joachim greatly and he felt somewhat guilty for being far from N., but he did not decide to cut short his trip and return immediately to Berlin in order to be at his friend's side, as N. had wished and as Joachim would've wished if he'd not been committed for two more weeks. Since his arrival in Beirut, Joachim wouldn't leave his hotel room without first speaking with N. It was N. who called every morning, but Joachim began to call him sometimes during the day to check on him. He spent the next few days worrying until the test results came back. Finally, the tests showed no call for alarm. The matter was serious, requiring treatment and follow-up, but it wasn't the dire fate it had seemed at the beginning.

Once Joachim was reassured about N., I proposed that we spend the following weekend in Ehden and that he invite his journalist friend. He welcomed the invitation but said he'd have to consult with her before he could say yes or no. I told him it was natural for a man and woman to consult with each other, especially at the beginning of their relationship. His friend declined the invitation because her work required her to stay in Beirut for the municipal elections that were taking place at that time. "And you?" I asked. "Would you like to go without her?" He said, "No, I'd prefer to stay."

I don't remember a day that passed since his friend's pregnancy without our talking about it or something related to it, if only in passing. He anticipated the time of her period with worry and impatience. He didn't want to announce the news before being completely sure she was pregnant, so he asked me several times to keep the news of their liaison secret. He said this was her will; he didn't tell her I knew about the relationship and its details. Even so, she wasn't so simple as to not suspect I knew.

Matters stayed so during the time remaining in Joachim's trip, and we continued our activities and performing our duties for the program that united us. We also discussed this unusual event as the time approached for his return to Berlin. With some Lebanese and German friends, I decided to give him a farewell dinner on the evening of his departure. We invited him and his friend. Before the appointed time, I passed by the hotel where he was staying to pick him up and take him to the restaurant. She was with him and came down from his room with him. Naturally, I wasn't surprised by this; on the contrary, it was to be expected (by me anyway). What surprised me was something else—the presence of Sader at the dinner.

I didn't expect Sader to be among those attending the dinner. In fact, I surprised myself by feeling as if I were disturbed by this presence. I didn't ask Joachim who had invited him. That question, as I said to myself, would seem as though I were sticking my nose into his business, and maybe he'd take it as an implicit reproach and be embarrassed by it. It would look as though I were saying to him that since he was now awaiting a baby, he should adopt a more critical posture and not permit himself such transgressions. That's not what I wanted to do at all. It was not my intention. Of course, I wasn't naïve to the point of claiming I expected him to change his behavior after his friend's pregnancy. But I surprised myself that I behaved as if I aimed for this, or as if I were driven by this desire without being conscious of it.

I didn't ask him then who invited Sader to the evening's dinner, but I guessed that it must have been him since who else could it have been? I observed his friend, who seemed as if she was alone most of the time even though she was among us and with us. She carried a glass in her hand as a princess would, observing, not waiting for anybody and not expecting anything from anybody. She observed as if she were in the party and above it because she was several days pregnant and self-contained. As for Joachim, it was clear that he wanted to be with her but Sader occupied him much. Finally, he returned to her and remained by her side, and they began talking between themselves or with others, and to Sader, of course. I asked myself whether he'd told her anything about Sader, and in truth I know nothing about his relationship with Sader—I don't even know if there ever was a "relationship" in the first place. Joachim didn't tell me anything about it, and I didn't want to ask.

Of course, Joachim told his friend about his relationship with N. It was inescapable and impossible to hide even if he'd wanted to. Yet he could have hidden his new "relationship" with Sader. It was clear to me that Joachim sought to consolidate his relationship with Sader and it was clear that he wanted this relationship to continue. At the same time, next to him was a woman, pregnant by him, who no doubt knew about the relationship. He told me himself that he'd told her just about everything, so she was doubtless in agreement with all these relationships and had no problem with him seeking out men while she was pregnant by him. She wanted from him only that drop of semen and nothing else. This phenomenon is becoming well known in Europe and the West, generally, where women have relations with men in order to become pregnant on purpose, telling the men only after becoming pregnant, or telling them after the baby is born, or not telling them at all. They want the men to stay out of their lives, informing them only because they should know. A French woman and friend who works as a psychoanalyst in Paris told me that she knows of many such cases.

Between two environments, the German and the Arab, much discussion must take place in order to clarify things. That's what I kept repeating to myself. At the end of the evening, Joachim remained with his friend and Sader and told me not to worry about taking him back to the hotel, that he'd manage a ride back. I said good-bye and left.

Joachim doesn't like calling on the phone, and I don't like writing letters, so after his return to Berlin we exchanged only a few emails—not more than eight—and fewer phone calls. The first email I received from him was on the day of his return. He informed me of his safe return, thanked me for the hospitality, and said that he was reassured regarding the state of N.'s illness, which in spite of its seriousness was not as dramatic as it had first seemed, and this put him considerably at ease.

Joachim left in the middle of May. In mid-June, he wrote informing me that he'd visit Beirut in the second week of July and that he'd stay with his friend. In the same email, he wrote in parentheses that his friend "was not pregnant . . . not yet!" It wasn't difficult for me to grasp that the first attempt had failed, that he was coming back for a second try, and that he insisted on having a child.

Did he come upon just the right woman to achieve his desire for a child under the conditions that he wished? I don't know for sure what these conditions are, and I don't know, for that matter, whether he has a clear notion of them himself; but from our conversations, I was able to glean the essentials: a woman of independent means and housing who is content with the child and demands of him nothing else, materially or emotionally. Did Joachim insist on this return to Lebanon simply to impregnate his friend or to be a parent or both together? Did this woman touch a hidden nerve in him and is this what made him return?

Joachim decided then to return to Lebanon and to stay a week in order to give it another try with her. I reveal in all frankness this surprising news made me very happy—it "stirred" me. As they say on such occasions in the English language, *It was exciting!* I think this is a suitable expression. The news stirred me for several reasons, no doubt. I tried to resolve the matter within myself: did I want his visit to Lebanon to form a turning point in his personal history?—"in the history of a German writer!" Look closely at this expression, as if it were taken from a book. Did I want the discussions we had between us to leave a trace in him and to help push him to choose a "normal" life that I can understand? Am I traditional to such a degree? This was a way of life very far from us and not only outside all the usual but outside all acceptable possibilities in our environment. It wasn't in reality a matter entirely foreign to me personally.

I don't know for sure what pleased me or stirred my interest to this extent. It could be simply that I was before a narratable event and a truth that interested me in a literary way. This was largely because it was an unusual truth that broadened horizons and pushed back borders, and this is in the nature of literature as I see it.

Joachim decided then to return to Lebanon within two months of his departure, and I decided to welcome him as I would a close friend. A few days before his arrival, I visited a dear friend of mine who was recovering from lung cancer. We talked about everything, and I told him about the visit of a German friend the following month. He wasn't aware of the program that had brought us together or of the activities we had undertaken in Berlin and Beirut, because he'd been undergoing difficult treatment. I told him my colleague was gay and that he had met a woman here in Beirut, and began a relationship with her that was the first he'd had with a woman in twenty years. He said in the tone of a princely commander: "Then throw him a party! Give him a wedding! Make a feast!"

This friend is a theater director who studied direction in Moscow during the time of the Soviet Union and whose works were marked with distinction in the Lebanese and Arab theaters from the late 1960s through the late 1990s. He was married to a woman of a different religious community and permitted his children to adopt whatever creed or religion they desired—or not to adopt a creed or religion. He was open to the furthest limits in all political, social, and moral matters. In addition to being an avant-garde director, he was also an avant-garde human being. So he told me: "Throw him a party! Give him a wedding! Make a feast!"

I thought a lot about what he said, turning it over and looking at it from all the angles, and I thought about his motives for saying it. Many scenes in my friend's plays feature epic moments: diverse celebrations and, in particular, weddings, funerals, and fateful moments. I thought about what he'd said and asked myself whether it was a result of an overwhelming desire for joy and for life because this rude illness had depleted his energy and he was now at the stage of recovery.

So I threw him a wedding party. I invited Joachim and his friend to Ehden in July—a beautiful period of mild temperatures and deep, close skies that yield the best fruits of the summer. Ehden increases in beauty and brilliance at this time of year, especially if you compare it to Beirut in the summer months where the heat and the humidity are lethal. I invited him then to Ehden but didn't tell him what I had planned for him.

In the evening, we headed for a small outdoor restaurant near the source of a spring. I had previously agreed with the owner that he would prepare for us a wedding table and had requested that he find us a singer adept at playing the oud and singing classical Arabic and regional songs—anything that delights the heart and makes the earth shake under listeners' feet. I invited a number of friends among those who like this kind of evening entertainment, including one friend who lives to dance and to lose herself in dance. I began to organize this whole evening from the time my friend, the director, advised me to throw him a wedding party. I say throw "him" and not "them" because in truth, I didn't know her or her likes and dislikes. This is why the initiative was intended for him, not her.

Our dinner began around nine in the evening. It was a beautiful evening—a person could not hope for one more beautiful. The sky was so pure you could pluck the stars from it, and the wind was but a mild springlike breeze. Flowing water from the spring nearby was audible, and from within this wild calm, humans and jinn are altogether awestruck. The restaurant was deep in a forest classified by UNESCO as a protected natural area for its rare plants and trees. In addition to all this, the security situation in Lebanon was calm and would not worsen for a few months yet.

We drank, sang, and danced. The singer the restaurant owner had hired sang with all his heart as if he wanted to convince the "foreigners" among us of the genius of Arabic song and of his ability to entrance the mind. In this task, he succeeded brilliantly. The "bride" danced in rhythm to his songs, imitating the friend who really did lose herself in raptures of dancing, cutting loose as never before. The "bride" began shaking her belly, hips, and chest—she didn't really have a chest for the occasion, it being almost flat—and the shy and cautious "groom" also danced. I, too, danced and that is a rare event. My God, how the success of that evening made me happy! The party lasted to the wee hours, until the couple tired of dancing and had quenched their thirst for drink.

In the house everything was ready for them: the bed and the snow-white sheets just as in bygone days. At fourteen hundred fifty meters above sea level, near a window giving onto the holy Qadisha Valley and from there to the Mediterranean Sea and the world, I lit for them incense from the holy trees of Lebanon: cedar, pine, and larch. Before they entered the bedchamber, I prepared for each a cup of herbal tea made from July wildflowers, herbs, wild thyme, mint, and a drop of orange petal essence in each cup. They savored the delicious infusion.

I feared at first that Joachim might be one of those boisterous city dwellers who soon feel bored and cramped in these natural settings, but he was quite the opposite. He resembled me and yearned for a home in the mountains or in the countryside, far from the city, where he could work or take refuge when he needed solitude.

The next day, I rose before they did and prepared a special breakfast for them. I knew that Joachim didn't eat in the morning, but I was sure that this time breakfast would please him. I prepared them a breakfast, not for two but for many more: yogurt, local cheese, green olives, black olives, eggs fried in local olive oil, fresh breads topped with meat or dried thyme in olive oil, a pot of tea, and wild honey. I placed all this on the balcony table that opens to the whole world, and took leave of them, so they could have the house to themselves. I knew that Joachim always desired conversation with his friend. He made an effort to speak in French with her in my presence, which was very polite but I wanted to free them of my presence.

After a few days, Joachim returned to Berlin, leaving his seed to grow within his friend in the beautiful land of Lebanon. The probability of his friend's getting pregnant this time was very high since they'd no doubt chosen the right time. On the eighth of August, less than a month after the "wedding" party, I received one of Joachim's rare emails. It was signed "Abu Sebastian," from the name he'd chosen for the child if it were a boy. So Joachim was now sure that his friend was pregnant.

In the same letter, he apologized to me for something that stirred many questions within me. He apologized because he'd delayed in writing owing to tension in the relationship with his friend and therefore with "all of Lebanon," as he put it. He added that the matter had been resolved and signed "Abu Sebastian." At the end, he asked me to keep the matter between us and let it go no further. I wasn't fully aware of the reason for this tension between them that necessitated he refrain from writing me, but I was confident we would discuss the issue at length when we met in Frankfurt the following October. I was invited there with a number of other Arab writers on the occasion of the "Arab World" being chosen as the principal theme of that year's annual Frankfurt Book Fair.

On the thirty-first of August, Joachim wrote me a letter devoted to a subject I'd asked him about in a previous letter, and he ended it with four words he put in parentheses—"(Ingrid lost the baby)"—and signed the letter, "Joachim Aggrieved." The news shocked and saddened me. This was the last letter Joachim wrote me before our meeting in Frankfurt some two months later in October at the Book Fair.

When I met Joachim in Frankfurt, his friend Ingrid was with him. I asked him about N., who had stayed in Berlin. He said his health was fine and that he sent me his greetings. I asked him about his friend, the young man, and whether he saw him. He replied there had been some new, unimportant developments, but there was no time to talk about them just then.

Time was short in Frankfurt. We were not able to talk together as we'd have liked, and his friend Ingrid accompanied him most of the time, which of course kept us from speaking freely in man-to-man "collusion." We did meet alone one time for lunch in one of the restaurants at the Fair, where we talked at length about our experiences in the West-Eastern Divan program that had brought us together. The main idea that emerged during the discussion was that I would write about his experiences in Lebanon as I saw them from my point of view. In particular, I would write about his experience of meeting a woman (Ingrid) and of his desire to impregnate her or to see her through the birth of a child, or both, after life as a homosexual for twenty years. We also agreed he would write about this same experience but from his own point of view.

It wasn't strange to his nature or habits—or to mine for that matter—to agree to this plan; nevertheless, our agreement was a surprise to me. I felt somewhat embarrassed because what had happened with him was a very personal and intimate affair. It embarrassed and annoyed me a bit to write and publish what I saw, and what I saw might have been different from what had really happened because I had to read it through the alphabet I knew, and see it through my eyes, and hear it through my ears. However, I conquered these feelings and decided to implement our agreement regardless of any potential problems. Joachim's only admonition was not to hurt his friend Ingrid's feelings, not to touch her personal dignity, and to refrain as much as possible from publishing things about her with a frankness and clarity that might be damaging.

The last time I saw him before my return to Beirut, Ingrid was present. I wished to speak with her about just that subject. I wanted to ask her about her view of this relationship and whether she was in agreement. Many other questions crowded my mind as well, but it was almost impossible for me. How to begin, and from where? Would she accept such a discussion? Did she have a specific desire, like mine, to talk and respond to my questions and preoccupations? I wanted to talk to her and to listen to her in order to know what she was thinking about, what she felt, and how she saw the present and the future. I wanted to hear how she decided to become pregnant by a gay man in a long-term relationship, a man who was trying to establish a lasting and fated relationship with a young man, a man who at the same time pursued men like Sader—or let himself be pursued by men like Sader? Was she really in agreement with all of this? Or did she want from him only that drop of semen?

While bidding them farewell, I said to myself that much discussion must take place in order to achieve a clear understanding between Arabs and Germans. Much discussion—and a fervent desire for discussion.

EPILOGUE

It was in November of 2005 and this book was in publication when I met Thomas Hartmann, who gave me news that Ingrid had given birth to a baby girl. I was aware that Ingrid would have a girl because I'd met Joachim the previous September during an invitation to Berlin to participate in the activities of the International Literature Festival. Joachim officially introduced me with great kindness and invited me, on the evening of my arrival, to dine at the Einstein Restaurant near the hotel where I was staying (the Esplanade Grand Hotel Berlin) next to the former Berlin Wall. With him was Ingrid, in the middle of her ninth month of pregnancy. They told me they had chosen an Arab name for their daughter. I didn't ask them why, but perhaps they wanted the name to carry the history of her origin and a reminder that this coincidence happened in Lebanon. Thomas Hartmann mentioned that the baby was given the family name of her mother and not that of her father, and also that Joachim remained with his partner but spent his time between both his partner and Ingrid—and his daughter, of course—in something of a ménage à trois, as the French would say.

Thomas advised me to publish this epilogue to complete the account, and he informed me Joachim had no objection to it.

THE QUEERING OF THE WORLD

RASHID AL-DAIF & JOACHIM HELFER

TRANSLATED BY KEN SEIGNEURIE & GARY SCHMIDT

RASHID AL-DAIF: I met the German writer Joachim Helfer as part of the West-Eastern Divan program sponsored by the German government and administered by the Goethe Institute and other German foundations. This program provided for a writer from an Arab or Islamic country to visit a German writer in Berlin for a period of six weeks. During this time, the writers participated in various cultural activities, and afterwards the German writer returned the visit to the other writer's country for three weeks of similar activities. All these occasions provided ample opportunity for the writers to become well acquainted with each other and served the purpose of the program, which was to promote cultural dialogue, especially among writers.

JOACHIM HELFER: Participants are also expected to describe the impressions and experiences gained from the encounter in a concluding essay or in another literary form. My Lebanese colleague and friend Rashid al-Daif has completed this task in the account you find before you, the subject of which is me. Not the author, whose work he hardly knows, since it has not been translated at length into a language in which he is proficient, but the private individual whose personal life has noticeably been of greater interest, if not fascination, to him; a life into which he was able to gain insight partly by asking pointed questions that I answered candidly and partly through what coincidence allowed him to witness.

It quickly became clear to me that Rashid's acute but rarely indiscreet interest in my way of life, although indeed very one-sided, was purely intellectual and serious, not least of all because I—in contrast to him—was able to read Rashid's novels before we met. Although unfortunately until now only one has appeared in German, the greater part of his oeuvre is available in French or

56 English. Its subject is almost always sexuality, sexual mores, gender roles, and the intimate connection between the personal and the political—which is precisely what my books are about, although they are set in my part of the world: the West. It may ultimately have been this common topic that swayed the jury of the Divan project to choose me as the appropriate exchange partner for Rashid.

While I did not expect to become an intercultural specimen as a person rather than as an author, this is acceptable to me as long as it serves the advancement of knowledge. After all, I do not handle my biography overscrupulously in my own texts; when I put its portrayal in the hands of another I place my trust in the responsible adult reader who knows that every observation reveals more about the observer than about the person who is observed.

Rashid's portrayal of my personal life in the following text has been carried out with my fundamental approval, granted on condition that consideration be shown for third parties and that I also be given the opportunity to tell the story "with my alphabet," as Rashid would say. In the spirit of our open conversation, I have made use of this opportunity by adding commentaries such as this one to Rashid's text, which in turn inevitably allow more conclusions to be drawn about me, my existing knowledge, my prejudices, and my typical Western perspective, than about Rashid. At the same time, I have attempted to portray in this fashion how I experienced our encounter and what I learned from it.

Naturally, we did not exclusively discuss gender and sexuality and did not make observations only in regard to these topics when visiting the other's country;[1] yet I gladly accept the fact that Rashid has, for the most part, limited his essay to these questions, for this seems to me to be very fruitful for the mutual understanding of our cultural spheres.

---

1. German does not distinguish between "sex" and "gender" in the way that English does (although in common usage, the latter has almost completely supplanted the former, hence obviating the distinction between biological sex and culturally and socially constructed gender that the separation of the two terms originally advanced). Throughout most of the text, I translate *Geschlecht*, which Helfer also uses to refer to the male sexual organ, as sex, because it clearly refers to biological sex; here I have translated it as gender, because as an object of discussion coupled with *Geschlechtlichkeit* (sexuality) its cultural variability is foregrounded.

It should be clear to both of us that even—and especially—in such a dialogue, our statements are directed first and foremost at our own societies. Neither of us is, after all, a typical representative of his respective society, and we can only represent our societies to the extent that what we live and advocate can be lived and advocated in our respective societies without scandal, while in the other's it would mean the violation of a taboo.

RASHID AL-DAIF: Thomas Hartmann, the director of the program, called me from Germany to inform me he'd chosen the writer I would work with during my six-week stay in Berlin. Naturally, he told me his name, Joachim Helfer, his age, thirty-nine, and summarized his works, activities, and other such things—but the remarkable thing was that he insisted on informing me Joachim was gay. When I saw he was insisting, I told him this was something personal that didn't concern me. He responded, "Okay, but I saw it as my duty to inform you in order to complete the profile." His voice was uneasy as he addressed me on this one point whereas it leveled off with satisfaction when he affirmed that at last he'd found a suitable writer for me.

I was of course thinking about the reason for his insistence on telling me the writer, my future colleague, was gay. I wondered whether this might have something to do with my being an Arab, or that Arabs refuse to accept homosexuality as a human right whereas Germany has accepted it for quite some time now. Maybe he wanted to know whether I'd be opposed to this choice and request that the program find another writer. After all, it was among the conditions of the program that this writer would come to Lebanon to participate in cultural activities with me, and his homosexuality might be an obstacle to our working together. Or maybe he quite simply wanted to inform me about this writer's orientation because he felt it must be known and indicated, neither more nor less, especially if the person concerned was a man.

JOACHIM HELFER: If it had been a similar exchange with, for example, a French author, Thomas Hartmann would undoubtedly have broached the topic less explicitly if at all. One of his concerns may have been my personal safety, another a possible strain on the intercultural dialogue, but not Rashid's personal views regarding homosexuality and homosexuals. His own contemporary European conditioning demands (as was earlier the case for one's own sexual identity) that one keep private one's own opinion about the private lives of others, which no doubt accounts for the apprehensiveness in his voice when he believed it necessary to address something that nowadays in Europe, when addressing it, places one quickly under suspicion of discrimination—regardless of intent.

He did not waste a single syllable on the topic with me, and I myself thought very little about it ahead of time. I knew some gay Lebanese men from France who had informed me that in Beirut— in their portrayal a kind of San Francisco of the Arab world—gay men can live quite freely and unmolested in spite of the fact that laws criminalizing homosexuality continue to remain on the books. In contrast to the invitation to Iran that I had received some time earlier, I never had any doubts about whether or not I could or should accept the one to Lebanon.

RASHID AL-DAIF: But to be quite honest, despite my response to Thomas Hartmann that the whole matter was the writer's business and not mine, I was pleased he'd told me. I said to myself, "It's a good thing he did!" because, frankly, the whole thing preoccupied me somewhat. I thought about it a lot and then said to myself, "Why not? Let him be gay!" This experience might be very instructive, especially since I'm interested in moral issues and sexual morality in particular. I've written about it and consider morality a battleground between Western modernity and our current situation in the Arab world. When my novel *Who's Afraid of Meryl Streep?*, which is related to the subject, was translated into French, I'd mention every chance I got in television, newspaper, and radio interviews that the bed was the site of the real battle between East and West. The bed is a frontline between Arab "tradition" and Western modernity. Something in this expression is not fully precise, but it does approximate a factual truth, that women have antennae that can pick up anything new faster than men can, and that women feel novelty more than men do. They smell it from afar and feel it as soon as it arrives, especially if it has anything to do with moral habits and practices—and sexual morality in particular. This is what creates tension in their relations with men. Women see, feel, and understand, and men don't realize they are like this. Sex is the "moment" that defines and exposes controversies.

The bond between a man and a woman, marriage and divorce, having children, celibacy, cohabitation, free love, the split between sex and sentiment, the connection between sex and sentiment, and so on and so forth—all these topics interest me a great deal. I observe their development in the world and stay informed as much as I can.

JOACHIM HELFER: I admit to experiencing sexuality, regardless of with whom, as tenderness and, in any case, as a moment of extreme spontaneousness rather than as violence; therefore I cannot, from my own experience, comprehend the metaphor of the bed as theater of war. Or rather that is precisely what I take it to be: a metaphor used in sexual role-play. In a real war, at least, I certainly couldn't get it up.

Although I know that even up to the present day the rape of women and girls (but not infrequently also of young men) has been deployed regularly as a war tactic and the phallus as a weapon of war, I also know that my personal preference for embraces in which the reality of top and bottom is exchangeable rather than symbolically fixed is certainly not typically homosexual.

But it is certainly the case—I am in full agreement with Rashid on this—that much can be learned about our respective societies, as well as about their differences and conflicts, whether these are real, imagined, or deliberately fabricated, from the way we make love, the manner in which we socially sanction and organize it, and perhaps even more importantly, the manner in which we speak of it. It seems to me (and I told this to Rashid in response to his statement) that, regardless of one's sex, it is always the oppressed and powerless who can best smell change, for change is what they are hoping for! Hope opens up one's nose, and those for whom night is nothing but a prison catch the scent of morning air. The powerful, on the other hand, to the extent that their power is based on force rather than law and respect, must fear all change. Consequently, they attempt to ignore signs and symptoms of it until one day they are too late and are punished by life.

When Rashid perceives women—which can only mean the women in his society—as those who sense change earlier, I understand him to mean nothing more than that he experiences them in general as the oppressed. From my perspective I can only say that the few people among Rashid's acquaintances in Lebanon with whom I was able to speak freely were either themselves gay or were women: for example, a sociologist from Cairo and a film director from Beirut— neither of whom were from the Christian segment of the population to which Rashid belongs, but were Sunni Muslims.

RASHID AL-DAIF: As for homosexuality, I follow the news on it in general but as one who is not directly concerned. I'm from an environment that honors and celebrates procreative masculinity; one that revels in it every chance it gets. The father in our culture is called "Abu" followed by the name of his eldest son, and the eldest son is named after his grandfather. The ancient Arab critics described the greatest and most creative poets as stallions. For us, the homosexual act is disgraceful, shameful, and must be suppressed. It's a crime punishable by law. Homosexuals are called perverts and their practices are considered sex acts against nature.

As a rule, I exercise constant vigilance to keep at a distance from the behavior and ideology of the society I belong to and count myself among those who reexamine at every turn society's convictions— and indeed my own personal convictions—yet many of my society's ideas have penetrated me and do their work in me without my realizing it.

JOACHIM HELFER: Oh, if Rashid had only told me that he likes to be called a "stallion," even by men, as long as they are just critics, then I could have introduced him to a Berlin that is neither uncritical nor unacademic, where the celebration of masculinity, of the phallic, the muscular, and the aggressive knows no curfew . . . In all seriousness: from the elite Spartan troops, formed from couples of male lovers, to the macho cult of the contemporary gay leather and uniform subculture, homosexual models of living have in all times provided examples of every imaginable interpretation of a "masculinity" that is more than a mere synonym for heterosexuality.

Rashid was amazed when I told him about the proud rider who was depicted in the monument on Berlin's Unter den Linden—Fredrick, Prussia's great king and most awesome warrior—and due to the one-sided progression of our conversation I could not refrain from adding the mischievous postscript, "And by the way, he was just as gay as Alexander the Great." From the way he looked he simply must not have believed the historical fact, which is hardly questioned any more, and considered my mentioning of it to be an example of that "typically gay" eagerness to diagnose one's own sickness in others. For he persists in the equation of homosexuality with unmanliness and femininity, which may be typical for the views of his society, but is refuted by abundant manifestations in societies in which gender roles can develop without restriction.

When he characterizes his society as one that celebrates and proudly exhibits masculinity, he gives us only half of a generalization, for Beirut—the most European, colorful, and liberal of Arab cities—contains all possible subcultures, from political feminism to a lesbian and gay scene. Even if these structures and their foundations are not as noticeable in the cityscape as they are in Berlin, they are nevertheless by no means only present behind closed doors. They are also politically and culturally active—which, to my surprise, I was able to ascertain on site.

The question to ask is whether Rashid, a sociologist interested in gender issues, does not himself perceive them or whether he did not wish to point them out to me. In any case, they obviously do not fit into his image of the city or his view of the mainstream in gender issues. What Rashid describes is a traditional Arab city, for example Cairo or perhaps the Beirut of his youth, probably his home village, and certainly the bizarre reality of the Gulf States, where the Middle Ages are alive and well among postmodern glass palaces.

The streets of Beirut, resurrected from the ruins and traumas of civil war, turbulently renewing themselves more strongly than ever before along the lines of Western models, are only semidominated by the "celebration and proud exhibition of masculinity." For it is not the case that modern Beirut women are chained to their houses

62   and wear burkas if they venture into the street; indeed, in the inner-city districts, including those inhabited by a Muslim majority, fewer veiled women can be seen than in Berlin.

In the stylish new business districts of present-day Beirut, the so-called Paris of the Middle East, the celebration and proud demonstration of femininity is evident in almost the same degree as the proud images of masculinity. But how should one imagine this newly constructed Lebanese masculinity and femininity? Cutting across all religions and denominations, the men are disinclined to physical exertion and, in a nation always fond of a good meal, tend to put on baby fat and develop bellies, drive their cars every step whenever possible, like to grab their sex organs demonstratively when they get out in front of a restaurant, and display a lot of gold chain on their black-haired brown chests.

In contrast, the corresponding feminine caricature (yes, exaggerations are illustrative and without the courage to make abstract images one cannot obtain an abstract concept), the stereotypical female in the new Beirut, is conspicuously delicate, often downright thin, dresses on average even at the office more provocatively and daringly than women of her age in Berlin, and exhibits no less proudly what is more of a girlishness than a womanliness. I will never forget the sight of a Middle Eastern beauty who was made-up like a Pharaoh's wife strutting across Hamra Street, the main shopping avenue of the Muslim western quarter of the city, in a miniskirt and pink frill top with bare midriff, and therefore, for form's sake no doubt, had revealed rather than concealed her hair under a transparent green silk scarf, through which one could also see the bronze skin of her shoulders glistening just as charmingly . . .

The often quite grotesque exaggeration of the differences between men and women in the streets of Beirut is striking: a human being is either a pasha or the little woman. The no-doubt intended effect of this artificial intensification of the differences between the sexes is the increase of tension between them.

In traditional Beirut, where, as in the rest of the Arab world, the display of naked skin is unthinkable, the same eroticizing—not to say sexualizing—effect that seems ultimately to be the point is achieved through opposite means: among Muslims via the veil, which clearly emphasizes what is being veiled just as it also stresses the play of gazes that are all the less veiled, such that I have no doubt that it is intended to have the very effect of an aphrodisiac.

In addition, in all confessions one sees the traditional exclusion of women from public spaces, or rather from certain public spaces reserved for men. In contrast to the student pubs or the restaurants of the gilded youth, the clientele of Rashid's favorite bar, the venerable, intellectual Café de Paris, consists almost exclusively of men: old boys who are always properly dressed and, of course, emphasize their sex without the simian gestures of the gold-chained upstarts; after all, men are among themselves here to a degree that would most likely only be possible in Germany nowadays in a gay bar.

For the people of Beirut, Berlin must seem to be in contrast downright androgynous. Upon seeing the clothing and behavior of a school class on the street, Rashid once commented that one can hardly recognize the sex of Berlin's young people at first glance; the observation was correct, except for the fact that a Berlin school class would normally be dominated by the gender roles of the Middle Eastern immigrants, whereas these young people had come to Berlin on a field trip from the provinces.

In principle he had observed correctly: due to the rougher climate that conditioned the lives of our ancestors in Northern Europe, women have on average a more robust build than Arab women and also act, dress, and move in a more angular and aggressive fashion. In Rashid's alphabet they are therefore more "masculine," whereas the young men—at least those from the educated classes, and especially when they set great store in pleasing women—are more reserved in their behavior toward them, avoid gestures of dominance in particular, and in their haircut, clothing, and behavior often emphasize precisely those soft (for Rashid, feminine) characteristics that their counterparts in Beirut would conceal at all costs. From Rashid's point of view these men appear more homosexual than heterosexual precisely when they are attempting to please women!

I explained to Rashid, who was unfamiliar with the term "metrosexual," that the transitional spaces between superficial manifestations of gender, but also between actual patterns of sexual

64   behavior (i.e., what have perhaps wrongly been called identities), have become increasingly fluid in our society during the past few decades, and that whoever wishes to find images of pure femininity and pure masculinity in the sense of the Arab role-play would have the greatest chance of success at the Gay Pride Parade on Christopher Street Day, where both extremes are embodied by gay men.

He laughed, as if I had been joking. In reality I was talking about the realization that culture is alive and, hence, is never "being" but always "becoming." Attempts to base something like identity, which by definition is never static, on a culture that is always in flux must of necessity fail and result in violence—this can be studied in the historic example of the Third Reich as well as in the current Islamic Republic of Iran.

When the avant-garde of the Gay Pride Parade points the way to the future with a wink of the eye, it is also pointing back to the past at the same time: here, too, homosexuality was considered a scandal and was illegal until just a few decades ago. This difference, like many of the other ones alleged to be rooted deep in our cultural background, proves on closer examination to be simply an example of noncontemporaneity (*Ungleichzeitigkeit*).[2]

At our readings in Germany, Rashid liked to mention one of his novel chapters as an example of an Arab author's difficulty in obtaining success with a European audience. The chapter portrays how a young Christian Arab man who wants to go out with a young Christian Arab woman on the weekend for the first time spends days thinking about which café is correct and irreproachably respectable, and how the girl, for her part, ponders whether she should drink tea, as is proper, or whether instead she might order a beer as she really wants to. "Nobody in the West understands these conflicts or their connotations!"

He simply did not believe my response that, although he was not portraying the German present, he was certainly describing the world in which my mother grew up: the Catholic Lower Rhine in the years after World War II.

---

2. In using "noncontemporaneity" for *Ungleichzeitigkeit*, I follow Neville Plaice and Stephen Plaice's translation of Ernst Bloch's *Heritage of Our Times* (Berkeley and Los Angeles: University of California Press, 1990).

Specifically regarding homosexuality, the most striking difference between Orient and Occident consists in the fact that the ancient topoi of pederasty disappeared from the literature of Christian countries, while they continued to be cultivated in classical Arabic.

I asked Rashid, who teaches classical Arabic literature at the Lebanese University of Beirut, how, for example, he introduces his students to the work of Abu Nuwas, the court poet of his namesake Harun al-Rashid, who even today is considered without equal and sings almost exclusively—and sometimes quite drastically—of the joys of pederasty. Rashid's answer was vague, evasive, and placating; it relegated the explosive content to the ivory-towered, ineffectual realm of classical art.

RASHID AL-DAIF: I remember feeling an overwhelming joy the first time my son and a girlfriend withdrew into his room. "Ahh!" I said to myself when I heard him lock the door. His masculinity was assured. Fulfilled. I myself was fulfilled and my fear vanished for good, unregretted.

He was fourteen years old at the time and staying with me in Beirut after having lived with his French mother in the city of Lyon and studying in one of its schools. I had been terrified for him about two things while he was in France: that he'd get mixed up in drugs and that he'd become gay. I'd keep a worried eye out for news about him and ask around in order to reassure myself he was free of anything to do with either of these calamities. From the age of three, my son lived in France with his mother, who returned to her country after our divorce. We agreed he'd live with her there because Beirut was witnessing a particularly dark period of the civil war. Later, when he was fourteen, he returned to Beirut in order to complete his secondary school studies. I was relieved by his return because it was easy for a young man to become gay in France, whereas it was very difficult in Beirut. That was my understanding and those were my feelings.

From the depths of my heart, I wanted my son to resemble me, but a much better version of me—a million times better. And maybe, at the same time, I wanted him to resemble us (and by "us" I mean we Lebanese Arab Middle Easterners) but without, of course, any of our inveterate faults.

I truly liked that girl, my son's girlfriend, and wished them to love each other and stay together for eternity. Without the slightest doubt, I still prefer—even as I write these words and without the slightest hesitation—that my son not be gay, but that doesn't mean I'd have let him down if he had been. I'd have stood by him, of course.

JOACHIM HELFER: This touching story of his concern about his son's becoming a man reveals, of course, first of all—and with admirable frankness—Rashid's own insecurity about the sexual identity of the homosexual and the "normal" man, which he explicitly conceptualizes not as a product of nature (e.g., a genetically determined trait) but as acquired, and therefore constructed.

Yet his concern is directed only toward his son, for whom he wishes happiness, not toward his own reputation or the so-called family honor, for the sake of which gay sons of less enlightened parents in the Islamic world (but also in India or in the Christian countries of South America) are still today often driven to suicide or killed.

Uncovering the latent homosexuality in Rashid and in every man on earth is not the concern of our intercultural project; instead we must ask to what extent his behavior toward his son is "typically Arab"? What strikes me first of all is how freely his adolescent son was allowed to discover and experiment with (hetero)sexuality with a girl who was presumably of the same age.

I was allowed, or in any case able, to do that in a similar fashion at the age of fifteen, albeit with adult women—but that was at a time when birth control pills were considered by young women almost without exception to be a positive means toward, and sign of, their sexual equality and self-determination. This was before the AIDS crisis and the neoconservative shift in values; it was also in Europe.

Even in today's Europe there are no doubt many fourteen-year-olds with less generous, easygoing, or, as the case may be, irresponsible parents; the same holds true more than ever in America—and what of the Arab world, of all places? For example, a girl in the Shiite south of Beirut, in Egypt, Algeria, even Saudi Arabia? According to everything you can read, certainly not!

Premarital sex may by now be the rule among the urban middle classes of Beirut, which is not called the Paris of the Middle East for no reason and has a reputation in the Arab world of relaxed mores conducive to tourism;[3] it is tolerated, although not welcomed, by society (as long as it remains invisible).

Yet, even among the educated classes of Cairo it continues to be a genuine scandal; among the urban lower classes and everywhere in the Arab countryside it is simply life threatening. Honor killings in response to violation of virginity are still the order of the day in all Lebanese religions and denominations.

And the girlfriend of Rashid's son? Did this girl he liked not have a father? Was he perhaps French, which would explain a lot? But if Rashid had been her father, would he also have shouted "Hurrah" if she had spent the night with her boyfriend at the tender age of fourteen? The whole story is not only anything but typical; it is downright improbable.

Perhaps it only happened in Rashid's imagination, which was tormented by the demon of homosexual menace. Perhaps it really did happen, in an unusual setting and time: in the chaos shortly after the end of the civil war, in the house of a Christian who was holding out in the Muslim quarter of the city because he was a communist.

The sexist and/or racist double moral standard possibly evident in this would by no means be typically Arab: the contradiction between the injunction to chastity for girls and the expectation that boys "sow their wild oats" was typical for nineteenth-century Europe; the commonly practiced solution to the contradiction was found in girls from foreign cultures who were made available under European colonialism. In contrast, even today it is true that the majority of Arab men experience their first sexual intercourse with a woman at forty rather than fourteen: on the night of their

---

3. I have translated "der Orient," "der Orientale," and "orientalisch" as "Middle East," "Middle Easterner," and "Middle Eastern," respectively, which correspond more accurately to the geographical parameters of the German term than do the English "Orient" and "Oriental," which in their common usage can refer to both the Near East and the Far East.

wedding, which they can perhaps only afford at that time and in any case, not as teenagers or young adults. Modern Arab literature, including Rashid's own books, describes how difficult it is to fulfill this norm rather than to circumvent it.

The initiation of Rashid's son, who he hoped would become an ideal Middle Easterner, seems to me to be readable—however it really happened—not so much as a description of conservative cultural practices but as Rashid's utopia, which he constructed in reaction to a Western freedom while overlooking freedom's twin brother, responsibility, because it is less visible when observed from the outside; freedom is thus reduced to the sexual availability of the girl.

Yet first and foremost the story of Rashid's son is the poetic reflection of the youthful yearning and sexual frustration of the father. Is he, as a writer, perhaps even playing upon the fact that "Hurrah" is the Latin transcription of the Arab word for freedom? I owe my knowledge of the beautiful word "brushstroke" to my reading of his novel *Dear Mr. Kawabata* (that is to say, I owe the German word *Pinselstrich* to Hartmut Fähndrich's congenial translation), used to describe a method of playing with a girlfriend's virginity, which must be maintained at all costs; a practice dubbed "outercourse" in the slang of American teenagers.

In the isolated mountains of the sternly Christian region where he grew up in the north of Lebanon, Rashid showed me the lonely spring where he kissed a girl for the first time and then later, further down in the valley, the creek in which he—one of eight sons—bathed with his brothers and friends and masturbated to fantasies about a pretty young widow in the village.

The image of the clear mountain stream in its flat gravel bed reminded me immediately of the bucolic Friuli region of Italy described in the autobiographical novels of the young Pasolini, which even in Italy could only be published long after his death. Is it conceivable that homosexuality, not only its practice but also the very thought or fear of it, truly did not play any role whatsoever in Rashid's youth, as he had already claimed in Berlin?

I asked him again on the banks of that brook and once again received a clear no in response. I dug deeper: "And your insults and curse words? Can it be true that you never called each other faggots?" "Of course we did," he responded. "*Pédé!*" (We were speaking French, and he used the French word instead of an Arabic one.) "*Sale pédé!*" was the most frequently used curse word, but why?

He found it to be "very psychoanalytic" when I suggested logically that one can hardly revile someone as a "dirty faggot" without having some kind of concept of homosexuality, and apparently a negative one. With that he dismissed the matter as if "psychoanalytic" were a synonym for absurd, erroneous, or irrelevant.

On the other hand, however, he recognizes and writes candidly that his fear that his son might be a homosexual has more to do with himself than with his son. Yet the fear of homosexuality, or more precisely the fear that one might be seduced into homosexuality, seems to me in no way unique to Rashid but rather a widespread phenomenon in his society. In any case, without recourse to this fear I would not know how to explain what I was able to observe not at one but several of the relatively small number of places catering to physical fitness in Beirut.

In the habit of swimming for an hour two or three times a week, I had been looking forward to doing this in the sea, but upon my arrival was urgently dissuaded from doing so: I was told that the sewage treatment plants of the metropolis had not been repaired since their destruction in the civil war. If I did not wish to avoid the filth by traveling at least fifty kilometers to the north or south to the popular beaches of Tyre or Byblos, my only options were a few expensive but clean and modern health clubs with swimming pools.

The information—at least in regard to fees and decor—proved to be correct, although my attempt at swimming my usual two thousand meters in the posh pools brought me to the verge of a heart attack since the water was almost at body temperature, comparable to the temperature of a hot tub in Germany: going swimming in Lebanon means splashing around a bit in warm water.

But the point of my story is another difference between these swimming pools and the refreshing mountain stream of Rashid's youth in the valleys of the glaciated Mount Lebanon: even I, a Teutonic child of nature, had not expected to be able to swim naked in a city pool, as I prefer to do in the sea. But I was indeed surprised that I was not allowed to simply change from my underpants into my swimsuit in front of my locker in the men's dressing room but instead had to carry out this switch behind a curtain.

I found it even stranger when I saw the showers: individual, tightly sealed cabins with walls of frosted glass, just opaque enough to be able to recognize from the outside that only one and not two shadows were inside. I burst out laughing when I saw the multilingual sign next to the mirror as I blow-dried my hair: "Esteemed patrons are urgently requested to dry their hair fully clothed and not in their underpants"!

But afterwards, when on my way out I discovered that next to the men's locker room there was also another one that boys between the ages of twelve and eighteen were required to use, I felt a shiver go down my spine. Could it be that these people, who, as Rashid claimed, considered homosexuality to be a phenomenon of the decadent West, were actually completely obsessed with it, that they lived in constant panic toward a demon that could overwhelm them beyond all defense every time they saw just a half-naked man or even a teenage boy?

RASHID AL-DAIF: When Thomas Hartmann informed me about my colleague's homosexuality, I said, "Why not?" This would be an opportunity to become closely acquainted with openly lived homosexuality—and in Berlin to boot, the city where the largest gay pride demonstration takes place every year. Nor, to say the least, was this an exhaustively treated topic in our countries. When people hear about homosexuality in Europe or America, they laugh or smile ironically and look at the matter from a distance, considering it no concern of theirs. But I warned myself—and without the slightest compunction: I must be cautious from the beginning, clear from the beginning, dissuasive from the beginning, in such a way that boundaries are drawn from our very first meeting and that each of us stays within them! Because some gay men don't remain within their limits and don't hesitate to disturb others, especially when you consider I'm a hairy man—even if I don't have a mustache to show for it. I say this in all candor and without a qualm.

I'm afraid I'm locked into the cliché, the rigid stereotype of homosexuality, but what happened with me and with several of my friends permits me to say that hairy chests, arms, and mustaches are tempting for our rare gay friends. My friend M. told me his mustache aroused our mutual French friend, the Arabist J.B., who died of AIDS in the 1980s. J.B. was sharp-witted, deeply erudite, and at the same time he had an acute sexual desire that knew no limits when he felt the need for a man. Night and day, he ventured out into a West Beirut blackened out by the prevailing chaos and the law of the jungle, searching for prey or more precisely a wolf that would prey on him. I was astonished when I'd meet him afterwards and he'd tell me where he'd been the night before or over the past couple of days, which security checkpoints he'd crossed, and what dangers he'd faced. I couldn't believe it. If he spent two days without satisfying his desire, he'd explode! My thick chest hair aroused J.B. himself, but he had the wisdom to restrain himself.

F.Q., also French, worked with me on the translation of one of my texts into French. He was aroused by the hair on my hands and once pulled on it while blushing. I asked him firmly not to try that again. Another time he reproached me because I had scraped my wrist and left it exposed; he asked me to conceal the hair. Something similar happened with a Lebanese man, A.B., who told me hairy hands and chests excited him. When the matter between us settled down and he knew his limits, he confided to me that the sight of a mustache excited him the most, and he told me facial hair for him was an indicator of a man's body hair, his virility, and his animality.

Undoubtedly, these were special cases. I would not call them widespread tendencies that permit us to sketch an image of gay men based on them alone. I admit my understanding of homosexuality is not deep and my reading very limited. I also admit that much of the information I've gathered is marked more by the negative than the positive. For example, during the AIDS panic in the late 1980s, it was commonly said that homosexual practices increased the danger of the virus spreading. The virus spread among gay men in a frightening way, but, of the many reasons cited to explain this, what sticks in my mind is that the percentage of sexual encounters was much higher in the gay community than in others and that gay men changed partners much more often than heterosexuals did. Somewhere in my mind is also the idea that they hate men who don't return their affections. They also hate women although I don't know why. A thousand reasons.

JOACHIM HELFER: Yes, of course; that must be the reason why every year thousands of heterosexuals worldwide are driven to suicide or murdered by hate-filled gays, as well as tens of thousands of women, not to mention the millions of women who are mistreated and abused by gays annually . . .

In all seriousness: in reality I should refuse to comment on these remarks, less out of respect for myself than for Rashid. But when examined closely, "in reality" means "on the basis of the norms, understandings, and, above all, knowledge of one's own society" (i.e., on the basis of knowledge that Rashid himself admits to possess only in fragments and that was the prerequisite to understandings that are in part still quite new in the West).

As the citizen of a republic that has recognized homosexual partnerships for a few years and of a capital city whose current mayor was elected by the citizens after he publicly announced, "I am gay—and that's okay!," one might dismiss these passages as an utterly comical amalgamation of prejudices, false judgments, ignorance, projection, fear, and vanity, which only insults Rashid's intelligence. This reaction would, however, hardly do justice to a text that is not addressed primarily to European, but rather to Arab readers.

This passage is, however, also highly illuminating for European readers, for it would be naïve to take its unabashed naïveté, which is typical for Rashid's entire oeuvre, to be authentic. In fact, I believe it to be an attempt, through the creation of ironic distance from the self using a literary mask called "Rashid," to speak of things about which one usually remains silent in his society.

As a researcher, Rashid is describing his previous state of knowledge at the beginning of a study; the fact that he is a sociologist trained in France, and on top of that a leftist and atheist from the Christian population of the traditionally most Western Arab country, is a portent of how things stand more generally in the Arab world, at least in his world: that of the middle generation.

At the same time, and it is important to acknowledge this, he is describing people whom he has actually encountered—both foreign and domestic homosexuals—as effeminate nymphomaniacs (i.e., in the way that they typically appear in his perception, which, although certainly not representative, definitely strives for objectivity).

What is enlightening about this observation, the accuracy of which I do not doubt, is not the fact that there are effeminate nymphomaniacs among French and Lebanese men—for they exist everywhere in the world—but rather the fact that homosexuals routinely must be effeminate men who obtrusively and intrusively desire masculine men in order to be perceived by Rashid and his friends as homosexuals.

That, of course, does not mean that in both East and West there are not other inconspicuous men, even considerably more of them, who are indistinguishable from married men (in Lebanon more often than in the West they are actually married), that desire others like themselves or prefer effeminate men or youths; but Rashid's generation in Lebanon would not perceive them to be homosexual or label them as such.

The concept of homosexuality is apparently different for Rashid than it is for us, but not just for him personally. We take the word quite literally, which as a scholarly term is only one hundred years old; that is, we translate it as meaning same-sexed: homosexual refers to matters of love between people of the same sex regardless of their sex, age, or sexual role.

In Lebanon, however, at least to the extent that Rashid's selective perception is typical, these are precisely the things that matter: neither a man who desires a homosexual or a youth nor the youth himself is perceived or labeled as homosexual, but solely the adult man who desires another adult man for his potency, symbolized for Rashid in his beard and body hair, and allows himself to be penetrated—or at least would allow it if his insistent advances were successful.

It is only possible to find a logical correspondence between the various characteristics of homosexuality enumerated by Rashid when one presupposes this restriction of the term; if, on the one hand, homosexuals desire neither beardless boys nor their own kind but instead hairy, ergo manly, ergo heterosexual men, and if, on the other hand, homosexuals have an above-average amount of sex with an above-average number of partners, then this only fits

74   together if the men with whom they have sex are neither homosexual
nor become so through the act, however often it is repeated. Ergo:
he who penetrates, regardless of whom, is not homosexual.

In that case, however, homosexuality is nothing but a synonym for
penetrability and therefore femininity, while masculinity is in turn
merely a synonym for the ability to penetrate—and heterosexuality!
This system of equations implicitly contained in Rashid's concept
of homosexuality is once again anything but an idiosyncratic private
affair to be exposed using psychoanalysis. It corresponds rather to the
normative distinctions of Greek antiquity, which found their longest
historical resonance in the culture of classical Arabia, without which
we Europeans of today could never have come into an inheritance
that was scorned by Christianity.

The Arab development of this system lies solely in the fact that
pederasty, which the system does not call into question but instead
supports, is no longer practiced openly; instead it is overlooked and
violently repressed. In light of the sexual frustration of Arab teenagers
it must even today be more frequently practiced than in Europe, just
as the sexual tourism of Western pederasts in Morocco originating in
the nineteenth century continues to this day (think of authors like
André Gide, Oscar Wilde, or Paul Bowles), or just as in Berlin and
all of Western Europe, in spite of all the competition from Eastern
Europe, the hustler scene is dominated by Arab and Turkish boys.

The fatal consequences of the taboo surrounding this pressure
valve is the totalization of the fundamental contempt for women,
for penetrable beings, that is obviously at work in Arab societies
and contained already in the equation masculine = penetrating
= heterosexual = superior; feminine = penetrable = homosexual
= inferior. Arab culture appears to sense this problem itself, for
poets attempt to veil the position of women in the system of values
by extolling them with beautiful words, but to no avail: if it is
mainly the tension between women striving for freedom and men
persisting in their dominance that is discharged in the sexual act,
if penetration is thus not merely occasionally felt as a gesture of
subjugation but is fundamentally meant that way, then what Arab
or Turkish boys in Berlin consider to be the worst possible threat
imaginable when they quarrel becomes understandable.

Whoever fantasizes an absolute triumph over his humiliated opponent as "I'll fuck you!" expresses with these words not only his own rage at a society that "fucks" him on a daily basis but also what he thinks of fuckable human beings: nothing.

RASHID AL-DAIF: In any case, I'm hairy even if I don't have a mustache. I was conscious of this when I met Joachim alone, face-to-face, for the first time. It was in Berlin in the apartment the Wissenschaftskolleg gave me for my six-week stay. At one point he rose from the sofa and sat next to me as I explained to him an Arabic expression written on a gift I had given him. I was somewhat surprised when he sat next to me. I got up to examine the gift and reflect on the inscription. I made a point of sitting on another sofa and told him my girlfriend in Beirut had chosen this gift for him, but the truth was I had chosen it, not my girlfriend. I claimed this to create a pretext that permitted me to talk about my girlfriend, and from there I proceeded to talk about my relations with women in general. The conversation between us began smoothly on these personal topics because, first of all, my colleague had an open disposition and also because each of us desired openness toward the other. It was in a way one of the "conditions" the program imposed on us.

I was in Germany to work, not to deal with such matters, so I was determined to fill him in from the beginning. I took advantage of every chance to make him understand how much I loved women, how life for me without a woman was unbearable, and how I smelled the odor of putrefaction and armpits when in the company of men without any women. I didn't want to be crude but was resolved to avoid any trouble. So let matters be clear from the outset. He was free to be himself and I was free in my desire to avoid finding myself in unpleasant circumstances that could jeopardize our work while it was still in its infancy.

In this atmosphere, I realized the meaning of being a girl or a woman, of being a source of arousal and a center of sexual interest. It had never before crossed my mind. Strange how a woman feels compelled to bring her legs together when she's seated in order to avoid revealing "more than she should" and how she must be careful about how she bends forward so as not to expose her breasts, which "should remain hidden." And that's in "liberated" countries, let alone others where women veil themselves in order to conceal anything that might arouse men's desires.

I didn't have to cover the hair on my chest because the weather in Berlin was cold, and I was wearing a woolen sweater that covered me to the neck. I surprised myself though by automatically pulling my shirtsleeves down from time to time to cover the hair on my hands as a seated woman pulls down her skirt to cover what she can of her thighs. It came to me as something of an epiphany that women are completely different from men. Men and women really lead two different daily lives. At one point I exclaimed to myself, "Oh my God! This can't continue." We were sitting together on the bus when he stretched his hand over the seat back where I was sitting without touching me, as if he simply wanted to relax while sitting and nothing more. I rose and stood in the aisle. He supposed that I thought we had arrived and that I was getting ready to get off, so he said, "We're not there yet."

I arrived in Berlin on a Friday in late October of 2003, and on the evening of that day, I met Joachim Helfer at a dinner organized by Thomas Hartmann at his home. Joachim visited me at my apartment on Monday. Between these meetings, I learned as much as I could about him and his relations with the friend he lived with. This information reached me from several sources, and all of it focused on the fact that he was gay and lived with a man who was more than seventy years old. The news would reach me sometimes discreetly, sometimes with affected naturalness, and other times with natural simplicity. All my sources were German, of course, since I didn't know anyone of any other nationality who knew him—either as a person or as a writer.

JOACHIM HELFER: I too still remember well our first encounters and also that from the beginning there was an atmospheric disturbance. Characteristic of my own relationship to the topic, I did not imagine for one second that Rashid's oddly stiff and reserved behavior toward me—not exactly impolite, but also not relaxed and collegial—could have anything to do with who I share my life with.

I believed it had to do with the difference in age and status and that he, an author fairly well known in his home country and already translated into other great languages of the world, would have wished to have a partner whose national and international prestige more closely corresponded to his own.

This asymmetry, which is evident in all of the pairs in the West-Eastern Divan, illustrates the different degrees of development of our literature markets and, consequently, of our societies: contrary to the complaints of Arab colleagues, there are more contemporary Arab authors translated into German than German authors into Arabic, not to mention English and French; conversely, a well-known German author comparable to Rashid would hardly be able or want to dedicate so much time in return for the honorarium that we are given.

I understood that these structural differences between rich and poor countries might be considered offensive; I did not think, however, that it might be held against me personally, which caused me to be somewhat offended by Rashid's apparently noticeable difficulty in accepting me as an adequate exchange partner; after all, at that time I was the author of three novels. Nevertheless, I was determined to the best of my ability to make Rashid's stay fruitful for both of us, which, of course, also meant that a pleasant personal atmosphere between us had to be created.

I had met enough Middle Easterners and read enough about the Arab world to know that symbols and rituals still play a greater role there than in our present-day society, which tends more and more toward informality and formlessness: this too, mind you, is just a noncontemporaneity and not a difference originating deep in cultural tradition, for it is not the case that, for example, we have never been familiar with or have completely forgotten the symbol of the host gift and the ritual of presenting it.

If I needed to sit down somewhere when I was presented with the host gift in Rashid's guest apartment in the Wissenschaftskolleg (a multicolored pane of glass, apparently typical of the country, with a word written in calligraphy in the middle and a band of writing around it), it was because of the translation that Rashid recited for me with a certain degree of pathos when I exclaimed, "Lovely, and what does it mean?" "Allah, of course!" was his answer, and for the band of writing: "There is no God but God!" Was he trying to pull my leg? Test me? Provoke me? After all, I had read his novels and knew that as a youth he had fled the Christianity of the Maronite backwoodsmen for the atheism of the Beirut communists, but, after his traumatic and sobering experiences in the civil war, in which he fought on the side of the predominantly Muslim Left and was gravely injured, had developed a profound skepticism, even antipathy, for all religions and ideologies—and now this?

He must have noticed my uncomprehending look, and explained to me what many Europeans in fact do not know or do not want to admit: that Allah is simply the Arab word for God also used by Arab Christians, and that Muslims, in spite of all their differences, expressly recognize in the words of their prophet that Jews and Christians pray to the same God as they do.

When, in spite of this explanation, which explained nothing, I still looked uncertain and he stood up with a jolt from the sofa and said that his girlfriend had selected it, I believed that I finally understood: he had simply forgotten the antiquated ritual of the host gift and at the last minute his girlfriend had purchased something that corresponded more to her taste than his—this is how I made sense of it in a way that was comfortable for me.

I found the little man with the sharp birdlike eyes in his scoffing face who enjoyed frequent laughter to be quite lovable, even with and precisely because of his idiosyncrasies: for example, from the beginning of his stay in Berlin he took the November cold, by no means more bitter than the cold at the house he owns fifteen hundred meters above sea level, as an occasion to wrap himself up like a polar explorer even in closed rooms.

Or that, although in Beirut he would get in a taxi to travel a mere stone's throw, he was reluctant to use the public transportation system in Berlin for which he held a month's pass—probably because he felt lost in the giant network—and how cleverly he used this aversion to attempt to mask another one, his aversion to museums, indeed to everything that one can call the memory of a society, by fending off my suggestion that we visit the Gemäldegalerie with the argument that it was not on "his" bus line from the Grunewald.

Or that in the bus at the end of the school day (i.e., surrounded entirely by schoolchildren) he could express such unhappiness about the extinction of the blond, blue-eyed Germans, so that I felt almost as if I had to protect him from the Turkish occupation force—whereupon he placed himself right in the midst of the little black-haired children just to inform me that we did not have to get off the bus yet.

I believed that I had come across a foreigner for whom Germany was the epitome of a metaphorical rather than climactic coldness and who found my attempt to show him a different Germany, my spiritual homeland, to be an excessive demand: "I already saw old pictures in Florence!"; "Music exhausts me!"

Of course, he knew more than the average Beirut inhabitant, who interprets the colors black, red, and gold as the logo for a used car dealer who sells those Mercedes models that dominate the cityscape much more strongly than in Berlin. His utterly two-dimensional image of Germany consisted, on the one hand, of Mercedes and, on the other hand, of the genealogy Hegel-Marx-Brecht.

He knew amazingly little about the profound rupture in Germany since the Reformation, about the history of Europe between the Thirty Years' War and the Second World War, in comparison to which all the strife in Lebanon and the Arab world seems like a historical footnote; he did not wish to know anything about things of yesterday like Bach or Romanticism, and he dismissed as sentimentality my attempt to convince him of the connection between the art of the fugue and the art of building a Mercedes, between Caspar David Friedrich and the law to promote renewable energy sources.

He was stiff; I believed this was because Berlin was too big and too cold for him, and I attempted to thaw him out. If I had possessed an inkling of the nature of the reservations that in reality lay concealed behind his behavior, then I would have been forced to believe that he had brought me the glass religious fetish in a manner approximating how one brings Count Dracula a bulb of garlic: I would have been offended and possibly have ended the exchange—as a result, I would have missed out on a great deal more than just a highly instructive intercultural encounter.

RASHID AL-DAIF: I myself started to refer to him as gay when asked about him. While I was waiting for him at the Wissenschaftskolleg, I met the exiled Egyptian intellectual Nasr Hamid Abu Zayd. This was the first time I had met him, so we sat down for a coffee together and I told him I was here at the invitation of the West-Eastern Divan program. He was aware of the program, and when he asked me about the writer with whom I would work, I informed him he was a "homo," using the foreign word and then following it with the Arabic word for gay. The thing is I didn't want to use the common word "queer" because it has negative connotations, so I used the neutral, recently coined word in Arabic, *mithlī*. This is a translation of the foreign word "homosexual," or "gay"—which in Arabic could mean "like me" (*mithli*) if you don't emphasize the last vowel. That's what Nasr Abu Zayd heard me say, so he asked, "Like you?" Mine was the haste of a man soiled by impurity as I disavowed any connection and clarified the matter. I wanted not a trace of doubt to linger in his mind.

Joachim was not long in telling me the "whole" story in such a way that my picture of him was no longer based simply on rumor, supposition, or unverified information. It was in the south of France when he was on holiday that Joachim met his partner, N., who is thirty-eight years his senior. Joachim was about nineteen and his partner was fifty-seven. For some twenty years they've never been apart. They live in the same house, sleep in the same bed, and share everything like man and wife, and no disagreement between them has ever led to divorce because their freely chosen bond is stronger than the bond of law or religion. Each found his fulfilling complement in the other, as they often say about a harmonious heterosexual couple.

N. is from a Berlin family that owned a building before the war in the region that became East Berlin after the city was split. He recovered it after reunification, sold a part of it, and repaired the top floor for himself and Joachim to live in. Joachim believes Providence sent him to live with N. and that this Providence itself wanted N. to have pleasure in him fully and profoundly as a man of this age can take pleasure in a young man in the prime of his youth. Joachim firmly believes in the existence of a Providence governing this world and overseeing our affairs in it.

From the moment he met N., Joachim never again approached a woman. In fact, he could no longer stand the female body as a source of delight and no longer paid attention to it even in its existence as a body. That was, in effect, the attitude I noticed during the days we spent together. In Munich, on the day we arrived to take part in several activities related to the program, we were having dinner when a young pregnant woman passed. She was proud of her pregnancy and wore clothing that hugged the roundness of her belly. It seemed as though she were naked, her clothing was so light and close fitting, as if she'd dyed her belly inky-black. This blackness revealed the beauty of her skin's uncovered portions. I looked at her in admiration, thinking she'd smile at me gratefully. Instead, she cast me an astonished, quizzical glare, as if she wanted to know why I was looking at her like that and what it was about her that called for this. And, by what right did I dare? I communicated my confusion and surprise to Joachim and told him nothing of the sort had ever happened to me in Lebanon or France—countries where I'd lived for years. I asked him whether the young woman's behavior was personal or part of the general culture. He said he hadn't noticed her.

Another time we encountered a woman whose clothing revealed a pair of very beautiful and elegant breasts, and this was remarkable given the cold November weather, five below zero Celsius. She attracted my gaze and I said to Joachim, joking, "Breasts should be outlawed." Surprised, he asked me what I meant. I asked him whether he'd seen the woman's breasts, how provocative they were, how extremely beautiful, how offensive. He said, "I hadn't noticed." His response surprised me even though I had begun to get used to him. A thing like this is a rare occurrence in Lebanon. A woman can't go about in such elegance and with such round breasts and in November (in Berlin!) without attracting attention. How could these breasts fail to turn heads? It was as if they were crying out against their confinement in that truss: "Get us out of here. Liberate us!" We Arabs are knights and it is in the nature of knights to be noble and not permit ourselves to refrain from coming to the rescue of innocence and beauty no matter how difficult the obstacle. Joachim didn't see the woman's body as I saw it or as men like me see it. He saw it as posing no problem whatsoever.

82   What distanced him from the woman was not her body but her spirit. He had no need whatsoever for her softness and tenderness.

What did attract his attention from the first instant in the street and everywhere were the youths, and the young men in particular. He claimed he could spot a gay male in a group of young people. In the Pergamon Museum in Berlin, where the ruins of ancient Iraq are housed, I said to Joachim while we were standing in front of a bust of a magnificent woman: "A woman like that would make my days happy!" His response surprised me. "A man like that would make my days happy!" he said, indicating a young guard roaming in the room with us. I asked him whether he thought the young man was gay. He said, "Of course! I'll bet you everything I own!" I saw him sometimes contemplating young men in restaurants, on the street, in museums, or anywhere. He'd follow them with his eyes and blush.

One evening he invited me to attend *Aida* in the new Berlin Opera House. He told me over a drink afterwards he dreamed of a young man who would be for him what he was for N. He'd give him what he possessed of love and attention just as N. had given this to him. He said he was convinced the governing Providence of this world would help him find the young man of his dreams. He had no doubt whatsoever about it because he would love the young man and give of his heart and of himself.

JOACHIM HELFER: First of all, I would have liked to allow Rashid to share in those things that nourish my soul and gladden my heart. Pleasure, as Rashid calls it in the French tradition, the sensual joie de vivre that is always also erotically charged, need not exhaust itself in physicality but, for such old-fashioned Europeans like myself and my partner, might also have an intellectual dimension—and this cannot be found on the street.

Hence, toward the end of his stay I decided, instead of making suggestions that he could evade, to set up an obligatory program of cultural events. If he did not wish to be seduced by the spirit of my country, then he might at least perhaps be interested in the traditional image of the Middle East in Germany; if he could not be enticed by the *Weihnachtsoratorium* or the Alte Nationalgalerie, then at least by the Pergamon Museum, Nefertiti, and *Aida*.

Although he was neither lonely nor lacking in occupation in the framework of the program or in the Wissenschaftskolleg, Rashid would have liked to have met more Germans and engaged in discussion with my friends, the writers in the artists' café (as he imagined it), because he does this almost daily with his friends in Beirut. The problem was, first of all, that in Berlin, in contrast to Vienna, there is no single café where the intelligentsia meets without appointment, and, secondly, he was just learning English but could not really understand it or speak it. Since the circle of people I could introduce him to was therefore limited to the unfortunately quite small Francophone minority of today's Berlin, it was mainly I who conversed with him for six weeks about various things: politics sometimes, but also poetry and poetics, and above all personal matters—more specifically my private life, to which he steered the conversation again and again.

Soon after our first meeting I had narrated my life as if I was giving an outline of my first novels, which were autobiographically inspired; that was only fair, for I had already read his, and this way we both at least knew as much of the other as an attentive reader can possibly know about a novelist.

And Rashid was attentive! It was, of course, clear to me that openly practiced homosexuality represented something fascinating for him, and I had nothing against embodying this not insignificant achievement of Western Civilization, which, not least of all as a measure of the preparedness for EU membership of applicants such as Turkey, must be legalized and respected without persecution.

I would never have thought, however, that his reason for constantly emphasizing his erotic affinity for the female sex, the fact that he was excited by women, their bodies, their scent, and their hair, was my own erotic affinity for the male. I took his active interest in my homosexuality as a healthy curiosity, the natural consequence of his well-developed interest in sexuality in general, to which his novels are a testimony, and I still believe that today.

In any case, the idea never crossed my mind that his reason for repeatedly staring cavalierly at young women's breasts and behinds was just to keep me from ripping the clothes off his hairy body.

I certainly never would have supposed that already at our first meeting he had the experience, for him undoubtedly disturbing, of imagining himself as an object rather than the subject of a desiring gaze, of feeling the compulsion and the desire to hide his own body in order not to send erotic encouragement to the wrong address. Imagining himself as an object, mind you, not experiencing himself as such: as much as a small affair with an esteemed older colleague would have been an honor for me, and as much as I fear hurting him with this unchivalrous statement, it is indispensable for the understanding of our dialogue to state clearly that our encounter was free of erotic undertones, on my part in any case.

It wasn't my behavior, however, but what he knew about me—or rather what he believed to know about what he knew about me—that brought him to an experience that was not only disturbing but also instructive: "What it means for a human being to be a girl or a woman and what it means to be the object of arousal and sexual interest."

Through me, without my having actively contributed to it, he was able to experience in his own body how women feel in the presence of such cavaliers who, out of pure animalistic gallantry, cannot see a breast without immediately liberating it, at least visually, from the prison of its clothing.

But why did he draw no conclusion from this epiphany? Or rather such an illogical one: having just observed himself tugging at his own shirtsleeve *exactly* like a woman does at her skirt, he concludes that men and women are *different* and constantly behave *differently*. For Rashid seemed to become more and more "chivalrous" the more it became clear to him that not all German women appreciate his manner (which, by the way, is more cutely clumsy and entirely self-deprecating than truly intrusive) as a refreshing violation of political correctness in the relations of the sexes.

In part because I wanted to spare him the culture shock from experiencing that young Berlin women, more precisely the women of Berlin's relatively progressive Kreuzberg district, can get rough when they feel harassed or even just irritated and because I had every sympathy for the awkward situation of spending six long weeks away from one's native hearth or familiar "battleground," but above all, because the culture of flirting belongs to the core assets of every culture and needed to be an object of our intercultural dialogue, I explained to him how he—who was lacking neither charm nor wit—could immediately improve his chances with the opposite sex: if, when he saw a woman he liked, he did not look at her face first, he should at least look at it longer than her body, should indicate his basic interest with a smile, but then should not show off in front of her and impose himself like, in any case, the Turkish boys did in the Frankfurt discos of my youth, chronically bungling their own chances. He must leave it to her to decide how far and how quickly she would respond to him.

Chivalry, which has only disappeared as a word but not as a thing from everyday life in Germany, is for us above all a matter of self-control—i.e., it demands that you leave a distant princess whom you like in peace instead of forcing her attention, in the (at least theoretically conceivable) case that, conversely, she is able to curb her own enthusiasm for you. "So men here are supposed to behave like women!" he summed up—correctly, I assume. Later, on various occasions he pointed out to me that I too only look young men in the eye with a smile when I believe they are not fundamentally disinclined but that I survey others for their purely visual qualities out of the corner of my eye. True, I admitted (and indeed without blushing like a maiden), that is precisely the difference: under conditions of equality and freedom homosexuality is undoubtedly less complicated; it has and causes fewer problems than heterosexuality!

If I had thought about it longer, it would have occurred to me that this is, of course, all the more true under the conditions of traditional Arab society, in spite of all dangers and difficulties.

RASHID AL-DAIF: It was a rare moment of confidence for my colleague, and I listened to him with focused attention. It's in my nature to listen attentively to those who talk to me about themselves in the "right" way, without embellishment or exaggeration or presumption or anything of the like. I listen especially during moments of the "right" confidence. My colleague's words flowed, disclosing his dreams and making eloquent his preoccupations and plans.

Joachim dreamed of a young man.

I wanted to ask him here whether he was exposing himself to legal prosecution if he had relations with a minor, but I postponed the question for another time. It wasn't up to the level of the discussion. I wanted to ask him another question, too. If he craved a young man, it would be the son of another man. Joachim wanted to enjoy the fruits of the labor of others—I mean their children— without bothering to have a son himself to let another enjoy the fruits of his labor and his child. But I postponed that, too. I didn't want to break the flow of my friend's confidence. It wasn't appropriate to interrupt the conversation with a question that revealed other concerns. He said he had a great capacity for love and a desire to give, and the Providence in which he believed would ordain it. Because love guarantees.

Then one time I asked him if he'd like to have a child and he responded in the negative, but it wasn't a firm no because his problem was with women, not with a child. He didn't want to live with women and hadn't approached one for twenty years. If he ever wanted to have a child himself one day, he'd have to have it with a lesbian who would not want to live with a man. At any rate, he sometimes thinks he already has two children from two different women he'd slept with before meeting N. He had relations with the first one only once, and his relations with the second didn't last more than a week.

The first woman was an acquaintance who had been married a long time. He met her one evening, and they spent the entire night together in the same bed. She wanted a child and believed her husband wanted one, too, but he pretended he didn't because he was afraid of the responsibility and afraid that a child would change their relationship. He was afraid for her even when it came to his own child. This is what she thought about her husband. Then she added there was another possibility as well, that he was afflicted with a low sperm count and didn't want to admit it to himself, so he wouldn't go to the doctor in order not to face the plain fact of the problem. He was afraid of that possibility. The woman was somewhere in her thirties and he was seventeen. She knew Joachim was gay and that women were not the object of his desire. On the following morning, she mused while dressing: "If I get pregnant, it might be from you."

Slowly he asked, "Why didn't you ask me to use a condom? If I didn't mention anything myself, it was because I thought you were on the pill."

"That's a perfectly legitimate assumption, but I stopped taking the pill some time ago without telling my husband, and I haven't become pregnant by him yet. It's gotten to such a point I've started doubting myself and thinking I'm the problem and not him."

Some seven or eight months later, he met her by coincidence on the street. Her belly was swollen and she was manifestly proud of her pregnancy, but she blushed when she saw him. They traded perfunctory greetings without breaking stride, or perhaps pausing only briefly. This happened on the sidewalk near one of the cafés where they could have sat together for a coffee, but she didn't want to or couldn't.

I asked him whether he felt any desire for that child—for it to be his, for example—or whether he'd recognize his paternity, or talk to the mother about the child so things wouldn't remain vague and hidden. He replied, "No," but it wasn't a firm no. Then he added, "Maybe I was useful to them (he meant his friend and her husband) because I made them happy at little cost to myself."

"Did you ever see the child?"

"No!"

"You don't want to see it?"

"No!"

"Would you like to know some day whether you're the father?"

"No!" (He said this after some thought.)

The second woman he knew from his school days. She was about his age and soon to be married when they met one afternoon and slept together. She disclosed to him she'd slept with him because her fiancé was older than she and much more sexually experienced. In having sex with Joachim before her marriage, she wanted to acquire some experience in order to have some parity with her husband and keep the marriage from failing. They went on like that for a week or so, meeting several times, always during the afternoon. Several years later, he met her and she informed him that she had two children, and didn't hesitate to mention that her first child was perhaps his—I mean Joachim's. He never saw her after that, never contacted her, and doesn't know where she's staying now, or whether she's still in the same city—or even whether she's alive or dead.

Joachim didn't ask her what made her think her eldest was his! I conveyed my puzzlement at his total absence of curiosity, as if the matter had to do with another person and not him. He was surprised by my confusion and reflected for a moment like someone who is searching for a response but can't come up with anything. When I asked him whether the child was male or female, he said he didn't know. I asked him if it was important for him to know, but he raised his hand and his head in a gesture I couldn't understand. I didn't know if it was a gesture unique to him or one of the gestures Germans use to accompany their speech—or to take the place of speech—as a slight nod for us means "no" and a brief shake of the head left and right means "what?"

"She slept with me to acquire some experience! Women in Germany today decide, as I've mentioned to you on numerous occasions. She determines what she wants from a man. We are nothing to them." That's what Joachim said.

"Okay," I said, "but you're the natural father of the child. You're a parent!" He was silent. Then he mentioned without any prompt that his brother and sister had six children, three each. He said he loved them very much and always liked seeing them and spending time with them. He said his relationship with them was good even though they live in another city. I wondered whether he meant by this that his siblings' children were like his own and that his love for them perhaps exempted him from loving his own children, and, consequently, he could not be accused of lacking full humanity for not having direct offspring.

JOACHIM HELFER: Mohammed, to whose commandments neither of us felt bound, prohibited the consumption of wine to believers, albeit not from fear of overly loose tongues but because parched obedience on earth should come first, and only afterwards the drunken reward of wine and eternal virgins in paradise . . .

Then again, the things you do, dream of doing, or have already done, even in bed, are the very things that do not belong to that realm that must be kept silent because you cannot speak of it—and this is certainly true of Arab culture as well: just think of the tales from *The Thousand and One Nights*. The scandalous aspect of Rashid's novels consists less in what they talk about than in the direct, unveiled expressions that he uses, which although shocking in literature are certainly not so when heard in the coffee house, as Rashid assures me.

Ultimately, everyone hears what he himself can imagine: hence, my story of an important and by no means ephemeral relationship in my youth with a married woman, which found its natural (and, as I believed, beautiful) conclusion in my giving her and her husband the child that they desired, becomes a half-hearted, one-time incident. Underlying this misunderstanding is a notion that precisely in Arab culture is not traditional: the idea that homosexual or heterosexual orientation can be unambiguously identified. In fact, the "third sex" is a construction of the modern West that continues to prevail there.

Mere beliefs cannot be spoken of in any language, and so I leave it to the discretion of the reader to divine that a word like "Providence" (Vorsehung), which carries historical baggage in German that Rashid cannot be expected to know, never passed my lips. Perhaps the gesture that he observed expresses it best: lifting my head as if I have caught scent of something and showing my empty hands, which is not to be misinterpreted as defense but means we know nothing, hope for many things, and are looking out for everything.

But one can speak of love; indeed, it is the most beautiful and the best, at the same time the most entertaining and edifying topic. In short: the topic most intrinsically agreeable to human beings. I allowed my tongue to be loosened by wine that evening because, as was so often the case during Rashid's visit, I once again felt more like crying; I was acutely lovesick that autumn, worse than ever before in my life. It is possible that I spoke to him, whose dauntless cultural-anthropological interest I had already grown to appreciate, about my dream boy as a theoretical ideal.

In truth, however, I was preoccupied with a very real young man, let him be called Daniel; a young man whom I had been allowed to observe and accompany as he grew into adulthood; a young man who displayed a distinct intellectual inclination and talent and who spoke with me about poets and thinkers, about God and the world, with as much noticeable pleasure as I experienced when I spoke with him; a young man who enjoyed my company—that of an openly homosexual man—just as much as I enjoyed his.

In his sixteenth year—how else could it have happened?—I fell in love with him, but only after his seventeenth birthday did I confess this love growing in me against all objections of reason, this unplanned child that did not fit into my life but had now been conceived. Half amused that I had held out for so long, half dismayed about what he had managed to stir in my heart, we became the couple that we had actually been for a long time.

Presumably it was easier for him to admit his own carnality, suspect to his intellectual nature, when at the same time he took pity on something else: my desire to let him feel also in a physical way the tenderness that I felt for him and was almost causing me to burst. Wise beyond the measure of his years as he was, he well understood that it is the failure to allow the sexual drive that makes harmless gunpowder into a destructive explosive.

He had ended our relationship completely out of the blue, shortly before Rashid had arrived. And indeed, in such a way that caused me to fear that I had disappointed and hurt him, and without any remaining chance for apology, clarification, or a friendly transition into a new phase of life. Enough said: I suffered like a teenager hardly could suffer who knows only the torments of disappointment and rejection but not the pangs of conscience.

This was the condition in which Rashid found me: too wounded by love to feel any shyness or shame in speaking about it. Whatever Rashid wanted to ask, I felt it to be a release—almost therapy—to answer him. No, the theory and practice of reproduction were not foreign to me, nor was the idea of its moral claim. It was also clear to me that equating physical/heterosexual with intellectual/homosexual reproduction, as Plato does in the *Symposium*, does not oppose death with new life.

(This, too, was one of many classics that I read with Daniel, arm in arm, alternating roles on a bench in the Tiergarten, while we were stared at not only by retired ladies taking their dogs for a walk but also gay men who were cruising. Like all lovers of the world, we were a couple that had fallen off the world but also, above all, fallen out of its time, a couple whose true home would be a classical Arab poem or a Persian miniature . . .)

But what more could I do in matters of reproduction? I had tried it often enough with a man whom I had chosen not simply because he was a man, and not because I had an insurmountable antipathy toward women, but because he was the first human being with whom I could imagine sharing my life: my partner—and how lovingly and gladly I would have conceived his children and have given him, of all people, the gift of continued life in the children we had together. Nature, however, did not wish it . . .

In no way did I feel myself to be an incomplete human being in and because of my childlessness, and even now I find this formulation to be distasteful. Morality and humanity are not so simple that their claims can be met with an act that rats, presumably the victors of evolution, no doubt master better than we do. Loving a fathered child without fathering one myself only makes me a good-for-nothing if I give nothing else back to the world.

A completely different question would be whether or not I, as the defender of my own happiness—like Rashid and every other human being—feel a deficiency in my life. I no longer remember if I translated the last sentences of my three novels to him at that time in Berlin. They are, in the following order: "I?" "I love you!" and "I want a child!" But what Rashid asked me was only if I wanted a *son*.

RASHID AL-DAIF: He said his brother's middle daughter was very beautiful. She was twelve but looked like a fully developed woman, which preoccupied her father. It occurred to me here to ask him an embarrassing question, which was especially so after the neutrality he showed previously toward paternity. Suppose your niece, after attaining the age of consent, decided to become a porn film actress. What would your position be? Naturally, as I'd expected, he was surprised by the question.

What permitted me to ask it was a long conversation we'd had on a previous occasion about porn film actresses and their relations with their fathers and brothers. He'd personally helped me to interview a porn film actress whom I met in his presence at a literary café, the Literaturhaus Fasanenstrasse, and he served as interpreter. During the discussion (I mean before meeting the actress), he seemed completely liberated from dominant moral values. He didn't seem to me to cling to anything but the value of personal freedoms. He favored these values unreservedly, without hesitation, as if he'd never doubted them and as if they were a cause that steeled his nerves and invigorated him in speech and debate.

So I asked him what his stance would be if his niece chose to work as an actress in a porn film. Quickly mastering his sense of surprise, he responded that it would certainly sadden him if she chose this occupation and his brother would consider it a catastrophe. Then he added that if such were her decision, he'd respect it. "Why not?" he said after a moment's distraction.

His answer was that of somebody directly involved with the issue, not a neutral response or that of a sociologist who observes and analyzes. Nor was it the libertarian response he'd given during our discussion on this topic a few days previously. He said that, in any case, he didn't approach the matter from a moral angle, and if this occupation made her happy, he'd be happy for her. Then he caught himself and added that he'd talk with her before she made the choice, but if it was clear this would make her happy, then why not?

As for his brother, he'd surely feel hurt from a moral standpoint, but in the end, he wouldn't be able to do anything about it. What his daughter decides to do she'll do because once she attains legal age he has no right to compel her to do anything she doesn't want to do, or to forbid her from doing anything she wants to do. I pointed out he hadn't shown such enthusiasm during previous conversations on the subject, and he acknowledged he was speaking this time as somebody directly concerned and not as a person who gives his opinion on a general topic.

JOACHIM HELFER: "Enthusiasm" must mean here something like personal concern or dismay; the idea of individual freedom and responsibility that I had previously defended with what I would describe "in my alphabet" as enthusiasm is, in contrast, impersonal and abstract.

Respect for individual freedom in the framework of boundaries drawn only in respect for the freedom of others is for me not only

a nonnegotiable cultural achievement of the West, but also nothing
other than its prevailing morality. Forced by fate to make a decision
such as that constructed by Rashid, the decision is easy: you can live
with a broken heart but not with broken morals.

Brutality arises from self-pity; the compulsion to dominate
others from weakness. Rashid's little research project illustrated that
for me yet again. For those who are familiar with gay pornography,
which has long since climbed out of the gutter into the lifestyle
and is a part of the everyday design of the subculture, heterosexual
pornography displays immediately the fear and feelings of
inferiority that "normal" men have toward women: almost never
does it portray joy or delight in one's body but almost always power;
not the maximizing of pleasure in equal, exchangeable roles but
almost always, whether blatantly or subtly, degradation—usually of
the woman by the man but sometimes reversed.

Regarded in this fashion, the bed is indeed a battle site for men
and women. It is a shame that Rashid did not also research the other
side: I could have introduced him to a few flicks that would have
been unusually relaxed for him and, perversely, not about power but
pleasure, and from which more could have been learned about gender
roles than from an interview with an actress who is doing her job.

The thing that strikes me upon reencountering Rashid's
question is that at that time I still thought it was innocent; an
extreme personal example of a philosophical problem. Today, after
the notorious case of a young Turkish woman living in Berlin who
was murdered by her brothers because she had lived "like a German
woman" (i.e., with a man of her own choice), I am more sensitive.
The countless women who are murdered every year in the Middle
East because they do not bow to the prevailing morals in matters
of love and partnership are routinely first labeled as whores, then
stigmatized and dehumanized.

Consequently, Rashid's question concerning the possibility of
accepting a career as a porn actress for one's own daughter, whether
he intends it or not, also implies the question of what boundaries
are to be set by the family around the sexual self-determination of
adult human beings: this question must be rejected based on the
principle of individual freedom and responsibility.

RASHID AL-DAIF: I visited his house for the first time on a Monday. He introduced me to his friend and we had lunch together. I had been prepared for, and even to a certain extent apprehensive about, this visit. But that's not the important thing. The important thing was what I had in my mind unbeknownst to myself. Somewhere in my consciousness, the relationship between two men meant quite simply sexual relations. Asswork. This relation is reflected on things, leaving its traces everywhere: on household wares, door handles, plates, spoons, and in the bathroom . . . especially in the bathroom, where sin hides and grows. And in the kitchen sink where the food of two "bachelors" remains on spoons and plates and where traces of their lips remain on coffee and tea cups, on wine and whiskey glasses, and on other kinds of liquor glasses. Two men living together equal dirt, negligence, and the absence of women!

Women are concern, cleanliness, and purity. They care for household goods and fixtures. Women are by nature opposed to filth and decay, body odors, and forgotten corners. My mother used to wash my three older brothers' clothes every evening after they worked repairing cars all day. When they returned from work, their clothing was soaked in dirty grease and oil. She'd force them to wash and would scrub their clothes by hand (she didn't have a washing machine) every evening.

Before I got a maid, my intimate friend didn't enter my house without first transforming the kitchen into a place of splendor, gleaming with cleanliness, as if cleanliness were light itself. Quite charming, this association between cleanliness and light. After we broke up, I missed the incandescence of her cleanliness.

My friend and his partner's house was very clean and well lighted. Its wide glass façade loomed in the sky above the roofs of East Berlin. It was a surprise, and a good one. His furniture was spare, simple, and beautiful—every piece selected for its suitability, as if it had been made for the place. The whole formed a beautiful harmony: a roomy, wide space without voids, easy and pleasant to move through. On the three walls of the living room (except the glass façade) hung paintings by the artist Adami, who was N.'s friend. The surface area of each measured several meters square and perfectly suited the space. I'd never before seen anything like this house, save to a limited extent among the delicate and highly cultured wealthy.

Without a doubt, fear of dirt and filth within ourselves is deeper than we think. When Joachim washes his hands after urinating, he seems to be punishing them. He sets about scrubbing them with soap and water time after time as if trying to rescue them from a dangerous illness communicated via contact with the male organ, the source of urine. I saw many Germans doing this, as if the penis were a devil lurking in a dark sewer.

JOACHIM HELFER: Rashid's text is more discreet here than he was himself in conversation: the dirtiness that he, but also in his account Arab men in general, associates with homosexuality has much less to do with the lack of a competent housewife than with the perception of anal intercourse—the image of the male organ living in a dark sewer could not be more obvious.

His statement that the Germans' hygiene strikes him as excessive seems to me to be a distraction from the issue. I, for one, found the culture of hygiene in Lebanon to be superior to that of the West—at least, in all places where poverty did not hinder its development.

Concretely stated: in Lebanon (as, according to my experience and knowledge, everywhere in the Arab world) one does not use toilet paper to clean oneself, but rather running water from a hose. Toilet paper is considered a luxury and is used for drying but not cleaning. Even in men's bathrooms there are only individual stalls; if, in addition to the bowl, there is a urinal present—most likely in consideration of the habits of Western guests—then there is also a roll of toilet paper hanging next to it! The etiology of this undeniably higher level of civilization is Islamic (in further development of both the Jewish tradition of ritual cleansing and the level of civilization attained by "heathen" late antiquity): the Qur'an, Hadith, and fatwas offer detailed instructions for purification. They exhibit characteristics of an exorcism in regard to the male organ, much more so than the often negligent practices of the average European: for example, an Indian fatwa demands that the urethra be completely emptied after urinating by slapping the penis against a wall or a rock!

Rashid's ironic position on German hand washing manifestly has less to do with a European/Arab antithesis than with one between Muslims and Christians in his own society. It belongs to a tradition of anti-Islamic polemics from the epoch of Arab/Turkish conquests and the Crusades. Such polemics were common everywhere in medieval Christendom and allowed it to fall into pious squalor for centuries, but unlike in the Middle East, have long since been forgotten in Europe for lack of Muslim neighbors.

The reduction of sexuality to penetration and, consequently, of male homosexuality to anal intercourse, appears, in contrast, to be Pan-Arab if not Pan-Middle Eastern; in any case, all Western travelers since Lawrence of Arabia unanimously report it to be this way. I, too, made use of this reliable penchant of the Turkish paterfamilias when I, who had grown up among women and become accustomed at an early age to giving them pleasure, felt the psychic and sexual need for the simple physical affection of a man to create a balance . . .

Yet, not only gay men told me about this conspicuous preference of Arab lovers but also Western women who live there. Rashid himself revealed this fixation to me when I succeeded in dragging him to a museum and interpreted Lehmbruck's statue *Der Gestürzte* (The Fallen Man), which had attracted him immediately, as a symbol of mourning for the millions and millions of senselessly slaughtered young men in the First World War. To my great astonishment he turned away with the disdainful statement, "*C'est très obscène*" (that is very obscene). The image of a naked young man in a position in which he could theoretically be penetrated meant for him, in spite of the utter lack of sensuality in the artist's fashioning of the body and bearing, nothing more than that: an invitation to penetration!

In his reaction I recognized again, on the one hand, that traditional Christian polemic against the prayer posture of Muslims—which can be seen in many radical works of visual art of the Christian Middle Ages—and, on the other hand, the anti-Hellenistic abhorrence of nakedness; its knee-jerk equation with sexuality that links Christians and Muslims.

Yet this anal fixation of the Arab lover cannot only be observed in the unaccustomed contact with visual art but also in the customary act of love, not only by gay men but also by Western women.

There are many conceivable explanations for this: an early development characterized by the traditional concern for preserving the hymen—or, on the contrary, the desire to act out among the more sexually permissive Europeans what would not be possible at home; also the influence of modern pornography, which precisely does not display sexuality in a naturalistic fashion but for the purposes of the power fantasies of our society, in a society that indeed imports such hard core films but is unfamiliar with a gentle sexual education that would throw light on the actual physical and psychic needs of both sexes. Or the desire to work off one's own feelings of inferiority toward Europeans through a sexual practice intended to be demeaning.

But in any case—and this is what counts—the disgust that Rashid had to overcome before visiting an incarnate male couple was most likely not directed toward a particular sexual practice but solely toward the idea that a man could behave like a woman. The contempt for homosexuals in the Arab world cannot be separated from contempt for women but is only intensified in respect to the latter by the hate for the traitor who joins the ranks of the contemptible although he was created as one who shows contempt. This analysis may seem to be excessively harsh for some people in my society who understand dialogue to be anticipatory self-denial. Perhaps they are even right. Nevertheless, it has the advantage that I am able to console my partner in regard to one other point: my dear "N." feared that Rashid had not wished to eat a single bite with us, not only at lunch but also later in the evening when we served roast goose, because he was not merely a Berliner but came from a *Jewish* Berlin family.

RASHID AL-DAIF: Their home was a great surprise to me in terms of taste, cleanliness, and culture, but visiting it roused my curiosity more than I'd expected. In truth, I'd never visited a gay "couple's" home before ("couple" meaning a married couple), so this was a first. I lingered in every room and corner of the house with Joachim, who took care to show me everything once he sensed my desire to see the house. This wasn't the only reason for my curiosity; there was something else. The sight of this "couple" composed of two men in this wide and spacious home transported me to the subject of humankind's procreation, its continuity, and the issue of increasing or decreasing numbers of inhabitants in diverse societies.

The subject of demographic development has always stimulated my curiosity and evoked in me deep and contradictory feelings. I feel blissful at the sight of people in the street rushing about in every direction to their various occupations. The sight of young men and their health gives me strength; I feel melancholy for, and fearful of, societies that grow old. I expressed this feeling once in an interview and said the incomplete and unaccomplished forms we see generalized in "developing" countries have their own poetry, which needs to be articulated. I mean this poetry needs to be displayed and defended until it is no longer suppressed or exposed to scorn in dominant discourse among the public in general and intellectuals in particular. They criticize the mentality that allows entire cities and buildings to remain unfinished, unlike "developed" countries where the city is complete and accomplished and everything is finished. Here in Lebanon, for example, they disapprove of the bare concrete posts spiked with steel reinforcement rods that thrust out of rooftops, which in their view is an affront to good taste and beauty. I am completely opposed to this discourse. Where they see ugliness, I see a scene of life bursting forth, like water flowing exuberantly down from mountaintops, delighting the heart and bubbling with promise. First, the father erects two posts on the rooftop of his house and then stretches between them a clothesline his wife drapes with clothes to dry in the sun and rushing wind. Then the father sets up other posts, builds a grape arbor over them, and eventually builds a roof over all of the posts for his recently married son to live under. Then he sets up two more posts with steel reinforcement rods ready for a new roof. In developed countries where houses are finished, you won't see many children. If you do, it seems like a pleasant and unexpected surprise.

Yet at the same time, I'm afraid for the world of this proliferation that some say will exhaust the fruits of the earth. I'm not among those who believe people reproduce according to a greater purpose. Without a doubt, there are reasons for reproduction but not goals of which we are conscious. I mean the birthrates of European and North American and Japanese societies are not dropping according to a well-drawn plan defined in their national missions. Likewise, Asian, African, and South American societies are not proliferating in order to achieve a particular aim either.

This subject interests me and stimulates my imagination. Joachim and I talked about it a lot. I asked him once, "Don't you see that the society that legalizes gay marriage is one that suffers from an internal malaise?" Germans are not reproducing but they are enacting laws for gay marriage as if they were convinced of their desire not to renew their society. He said, "Listen. In any society between two and four percent of the population is made up of gay men and lesbians, so what are we going to do with them?" I told him legalizing gay marriage was something different from legalizing gay rights to self-realization. He didn't respond to my concern; he responded to his concern. I mean, quite apart from the question of morality, all societies that genuinely legalize homosexual relations make them equal to those of man and wife. These are societies that somehow accept annihilation and disappearance, which is particularly applicable to German society.

I was told fifty percent of the apartments in Berlin are one-person households, and a friend informed me that he and his wife had great difficulty finding an apartment in the late 1970s because they had three children. A German woman poet of about fifty said during a discussion, "Thank God I don't have children by anybody else since I am my own child." Then there are those who bear the cares of the world on their shoulders, pointing out that since the world is choked with people, they don't want to add to the problem by bearing children. Joachim himself said to me once when I'd asked him if he didn't want to have a child, "There are eighty million people in Germany! Do you want more?"

Of course, I'm not saying the decline in Germany's birthrate is due to homosexuality; rather that the legalization of homosexuality goes hand in hand with this situation. It goes along with the decline in the birthrate, with the rise in living standards and cultural levels, with the priority on the individual and on individual freedoms, with the respect for women's rights, with their presence in society, and especially with their right to work and their right to promotion and other such things. It's a reason, a cause, and a part of everything.

My colleague is not overly interested in debate on the subject from this point of view. He is interested in defending his rights, especially since he suffered in boyhood from his situation—suffered from shame at the disclosure of his real desire, from his gender identity, and from other things gay men commonly experience. He clings with all his strength to the gains he has acquired.

Having always felt a strong attraction to males, he doesn't remember a beginning or even when he first slept with a man, but he clearly remembers the first time he slept with a woman. He'd always been attracted to males, whereas his attraction to females was new and discontinuous. Joachim believes he began to be conscious of his homosexuality from about the age of five and has been definitively gay since this early age. The whole problem came in having the courage to say it. Where could the courage come from when he was a small child who found it difficult to anger his parents and put them in an embarrassing position?

Shame. That's what's difficult to get over. Joachim had a friend who committed suicide. It was a friend from school who was gay. They'd spoken together a lot about this subject—Joachim's mother took part in the discussion and tried to help him—but the friend decided to put an end to his life because he couldn't overcome the forces arrayed against him, crushing him mercilessly.

When I asked him about his mother's position on his own homosexuality, Joachim responded with vigor that he hated emotional blackmail, hated it when his mother told him, "I'll love you if . . ." Whoever loves him must love him as he is without conditions. It isn't love if it's given only as a reward for pleasing others . . . "If you do this I'll be happy, and if you do that I'll weep out of misery and sadness." He stated frankly, "I think the strategy of emotional blackmail is a woman's specialty." His mother was a Catholic and a sociologist who worked in an institute of the Ministry for Social Affairs. She was cold, but his relationship with her was good. She was very understanding once the truth about him began to emerge and during the stages he passed through. She was even able to maintain good relations with his companion, N., after he introduced her to him.

Joachim's father was a prisoner of war during World War II for a period of a year and a half. A socialist activist, he was arrested in East

Germany and sentenced to death, but the death sentence was never carried out and he remained in prison for more than eight years until he was released in a prisoner exchange with West Germany in 1957. He was cold, sarcastic and mocking, always wore a trench coat, and was never without a pipe in hand. Women liked him and fell in love with him. He left his wife, Joachim's mother, and went to live in Ghana where he worked as director of a German organization (Friedrich Ebert) and married a Ghanaian woman who is still living and provided for in Botswana. He was a Protestant. Regarding Joachim's homosexuality, the father was out of the picture.

His grandfather, who was very old when Joachim met N., apparently showed no animosity. This grandfather was a conservative bourgeois and a bit of a fanatical nationalist without being a Nazi. He worked as a judge in the 1920s and 30s presiding over the District Court of Saxony and served as an officer in the German Army during the Second World War. After the war, the Americans appointed him director of the Bank der Deutschen Luftfahrt, and he retained this position until the end of his life. This grandfather was not hostile but rather sympathetic toward the idea of Joachim forming a couple with a man—even mentioning in a letter that he was sorry not to have had a chance to meet N.

Joachim, "despite this," complains about what he endured. He speaks with grief on the pains of homosexuals in general and on the injustices inflicted upon them throughout history. The Nazis persecuted them as they did the Jews, and gays continue to be persecuted today in many places around the globe. They hide like mice to avoid being exposed to the public; they are victims of humiliation and are often denied the right to work. Sometimes they are prosecuted and thrown in prison for no reason other than being who they are.

JOACHIM HELFER: Let us leave aside the fact that the formulation "persecuted like the Jews" is not mine, for I know too much about both: the persecution of the Jews and the witch hunt for homosexuals. Whereas Rashid, the burnt child of a religiously and ethnically dismembered society that tore itself to pieces for years under the pretext of differing traditions and memories, mistrusts all traditions—as he himself states—and would prefer only to know what he has personally observed, experienced, and suffered. I was indeed filled with pain and rage when I saw the video recording of the public execution of a pair of gay lovers in Iran that can be viewed on the Internet. My pain and rage were not, however, one bit greater or different than what I feel when I see the pictures of a woman being executed for adultery in the Afghanistan of the Taliban. The fact that I am glad to be living in Germany rather than Iran does not mean that I examine my life or my homeland exclusively in regard to the fact that I can live my life here in peace and freedom, whereas there I would have to hide, disguise myself, or allow myself to be hanged.

Thus, I am not, for example, a homosexual by profession but a writer: those who write would also like to pass on part of what makes them who they are; unlike painters or musicians perhaps, they want people who survive them not only to read "their" language but also to continue to speak it as part of their mother tongue—in my case German.

But even if I had become an architect or a lawyer, I would not have been indifferent to the noticeable graying and foreseeable extinction of my nation; it certainly would not fill me with relief like some of my compatriots who seem to see in it a way out of their own unbearable history. The truth is that not only do I love the country in which I was born and grew up—whose language I speak and whose cultural practices and traditions have left as deep a mark on me as its landscapes have—but also, in spite of everything, I can only imagine a world without the German contribution to the culture of humanity as very impoverished.

Openly vocalizing feelings like this—which are not solely negative and not even primarily negative toward one's own nation— is only now beginning to be possible again in Germany but still runs the risk of arousing incorrect suspicions, or even worse, of being applauded by the wrong side; it is particularly uncommon to express such feelings to foreigners such as Rashid, which is the reason why I refrained from doing so.

That does not mean, however, that I had not already witnessed with unease the current effects of the long-term tendency toward singlehood, on the one hand, and on the other hand, childlessness long before he had pointed them out to me—and by no means only or primarily their logical consequences: problems of the social welfare state that basically can be solved through its restructuring. Life among aging children, without its renewal in the new beginning that only real children can provide, does not become better and more beautiful.

Culture does not climb higher when an entire society always understands self-realization exclusively to mean solipsistic ego trips such as, not least of all, gay monks, artists, dandies, and adventurers once exhibited as an elitist countermodel to normal life—without in their worst nightmares ever imagining that Joe Consumer could make them into an off-the-rack fashion.

If I, in spite of my openness in all other matters, withheld from Rashid my unease about the cool barbarism of our society of fun-loving Babbitts, it was because I was never certain (and still am not today) if his criticism of the German zeitgeist was backward-looking or forward-looking, if he desired to overcome the evident aberrations or cite them as a reason to pine for social conditions that, after great sacrifice, we fortunately have left behind.

Thus, I, who grew up with two siblings in the years of strong birth rates in a suburb dominated by children, am no less saddened than he is about cityscapes in which, although there is a playground on every corner, there are hardly any children, as is typical of many Berlin districts, and I am glad to be living in Prenzlauer Berg, where there are noticeably more offspring. Above all I am saddened by how many friends and acquaintances—of both sexes and every sexual inclination mind you, but consistently talented, educated, and more or less successful in life—do not reproduce themselves in children to whom they in particular would have much to pass along.

I just cannot understand what these regrettable facts have to do with the state recognition of same-sex partnerships—which, by the way, Rashid told me he would support at any time *as a political demand.*

We seem, therefore, to have been in agreement after all that gay marriage seeks to enable that minority of individuals within the homosexual minority who live in couplings that are sometimes lifelong to lead a life in accordance with their inviolable dignity. In this respect, it is a logical consequence of our constitution and a living expression of our culture, which holds the highest value to be the dignity of the human being, and indeed of every individual human being, in whatever shape or form, not of human beings in the abstract.

Practically speaking, only a few thousand couples make use of this institution in Germany, and it would be absurd to suppose that the over fifty percent of young German men who, according to surveys, do not want to have children have been led to this attitude by gay marriage, or that they—except for a few percent themselves heterosexual—could have confused a few thousand homosexual couples with a societal norm that they have to fulfill.

If a signal can be sent at all by such an evanescent minority as couples in gay marriages, then it points in the other direction: even the commitment to a long-term same-sex partnership is a commitment to long-term partnerships, and the demand that has been raised but not yet fulfilled for adoption rights for such couples also cannot be interpreted as a vote against children!

I presented my argument in this fashion to Rashid, but he stuck to his position: for him, gay marriage, regardless of its actual causes and effects, is a symbol of a cultural development that ends in extinction but began with the emancipation of women—indeed with the discovery of the individual's inalienable freedom and dignity. Forced to put such a fine point on it and pressured into a chain of causality that even at that time I did not believe to be inevitable, I found the answer again came easily to me: if the price for the physical survival of the Germans and Europeans were really to consist of giving up their own cultural achievements of the last century and regressing from the unconditional respect for the dignity of the individual to a world in which the individual can only realize his dignity in the obedience to morals and tribes (whether this "we" is constructed patriarchally, matriarchally, or communistically . . .), then this price would be much too high; in a manner of speaking, paying it would be suicide out of fear of death.

RASHID AL-DAIF: Joachim wasn't really preoccupied by the demographic future of Germany and the world but by his own personal future. For him, the future of Germany was akin to a natural matter in which he had no say, like clouds, rain, sun, evening, or daylight. I believe he was just humoring me in discussing these issues. It seemed to me he focused on and enjoyed speaking about two things: women, and his deep desire to find a man much younger than he who would be for him what he was—and continues to be—for N. These seemed to me to be his main preoccupations at the time.

As for women, his opinion on the matter was fixed and final. The German woman today is the one who chooses you. You don't choose her, and if it happens that you want to choose her, she'll get angry, accuse you of being impolite, and maybe even of harassment. You are not entitled to "come on" to a German woman, no matter how politely and gently you do it. She is the one who comes on to you. It's up to you to be of good upbringing and scrupulous conduct: reserved, polite, and bashful. You reveal only gentle suggestions, and she is the one who takes the initiative if she wishes.

I remembered, while we were discussing this subject, how a polite girl from home must be moderate in eating when invited to others' homes. Among her qualities is moderation in eating even if she's plump and her moderation wouldn't fool anyone. I often heard the saying: "The amount a girl eats is inversely proportional to her good education." This was a truism in the past and remains so to this day, even if to different degrees and depending on social milieu.

There has been a role reversal between men and women in Germany, or at least there's been a move in that direction. We live this transformation and its effects, especially in young males. Young men today are in some ways the girls of yesterday. The percentage of women committing crimes has reached one third today, so for every three crimes in Germany, one is committed by a woman, which doesn't include infractions and misdemeanors such as pickpocketing in streets, crowded places, department stores, buses, and subways. The average number of German men who seek psychiatric counseling and other professional help in order to extend the duration of their erections and delay ejaculation as long as possible has increased because women are slower to reach orgasm than men and prefer men who are in accord with their nature and in step with their rhythm.

I thought about what my colleague had told me and examined it from every angle, but my experience with "German womanhood" was very limited. It didn't permit me to subscribe to or contradict what he'd said. I have only a memory of an incident that occurred when I was a child. I remember seeing a young woman passing in front of our house. Our front door opened directly onto the road, without a sidewalk. She wasn't alone but was accompanied by perhaps another woman friend and a man—or maybe two. I no longer remember because this was a long time ago, and I'm sure I was not yet ten. The young woman carried a camera in her hand and took a photograph of my little sister who was standing barefoot in the road, wiping her nose with her hand. I was dumbfounded. In my mind, photos were for special occasions and were taken of those who were wearing neat clothing. I said to myself this behavior was out of place and this young woman must be eccentric to allow herself to take a picture of my sister in such a state. I took my sister by the hand, pulled her in, and asked my mother to dress her in clean clothes because a blond foreign woman had taken her picture in this condition. My mother ran outside to see what was going on, but the woman had moved away. This moment is stuck in my mind (Would that I had that photo!). I heard the grown-ups say this young woman was German.

The memory of this woman began to grow in my mind—this woman who photographed my barefoot sister in dirty clothes, wiping her snotty nose. A deep affection grew in me toward her because she dared to make a gesture far beyond what was customary.

One time a German woman visited us on behalf of my brother who was working in Germany in the late 1960s. We treated her with incomparable deference, surely as much as Kaiser Wilhelm II enjoyed when he visited Baalbek at the beginning of the last century (in proportion to our means, of course). We served her the food of weddings and feasts and showed her the places in our region we loved and of which we were most proud. We loved her very much, and she loved us too and kissed us warmly when she took final leave of us. I remember when she leaned over to kiss my little brother, he offered her his round, puckered lips as if he were clearly pronouncing "noon" and my eldest brother scolded him, but she burst into laughter and hugged him to her breast. Then, after my brother's final return from Germany, news from her stopped and news of us to her probably also stopped.

The only other contact I've had with German women since then was in Paris when I was a student. It was a one-night stand with a coed who was visiting a French friend of hers, and in the morning she went her way, I went mine, and we never met again. That's all.

The events I'm narrating are very old, the most recent being from more than thirty years ago when I was a student. Today things have changed from what they were back then. My "experience" from that time can no longer serve as a base upon which to build an opinion. Today, what I know about German women doesn't go beyond what everybody knows in our region, that they are emancipated and they work. So I have no negative preconceptions about German women—quite the contrary. For this reason, I cannot agree with my colleague's depiction of them, but at the same time I can't contradict him. I tended to believe him because he was speaking frankly with the sincerity of one who was confiding. I believed his feelings even though my experience in life generally led me to say there are different kinds of women, not a typical woman. This certainly doesn't negate the fact that some traits may predominate over others.

JOACHIM HELFER: Strangely, it seemed to me that Rashid was the one who was constantly bringing up the topic of women—but he is certainly correct: what he was talking about was indeed neither women nor "Women" (i.e., female homo sapiens however abstract or concrete), but rather women's scent, women's hair, women's gait, women's breasts, women's behinds, once even the scent of women's sexual organs.

I was, admittedly, familiar with such lectures aimed below the belt ("The scent of female genitalia—clean, of course—is paradise for me, or, let us say, an anticipation of God!"), except for the conscious religious twist, from German heterosexual males, or better said, heterosexual boys of all ages. Not only Arabs are provoked by gay men to portray their own biochemical controllability, originating in the animal kingdom, as a moral accomplishment. Men who pride themselves on their animality perhaps believe that decadent gay men are disgusted by women, whereas in reality they are, if anything, disgusted by their unwashed, ranting fellow males.

The women to whom I introduced Rashid in Berlin, except for the porn actress, were all endowed with above-average intelligence, and he certainly also knows women with brains in Beirut. Was I deceiving myself, or was there in the way they sometimes looked at him both in Germany and Lebanon, in addition to slight amusement, also a maternal emotion toward his always noticeable oversensitivity for their physical charms—which he never denied, but in fact put on display, and sometimes made him appear as dependent as an infant?

He could not, however, introduce me to the concrete woman whom he had mentioned to me in Berlin as his girlfriend, for the relationship had ended during, and perhaps even because of, his absence in Berlin. "Take a look at that!" he called to me in his country house in the Lebanese mountains and pointed with an accusatory gesture to the curtain rods above the patio door, which, in contrast to the office, was unprotected by fabric from the midday sun. "She had started to sew such pretty curtains! Couldn't she have waited to leave me until after she was finished with them?"

It is not the case that my friend Rashid is incapable of self-deprecation: for example, he was indignant when we saw an author portrait at the Frankfurt Book Fair that I had to translate for him from a German newspaper. The portrait made the outrageous claim that his French wife had once left Lebanon because of the civil war, to which he responded: "Because of me, because of me she left the country!"

What I talked about occasionally was not "Women," and certainly not those in our company, but what can be ascertained about women and men in German society on the basis of relevant statistics and studies. What emerges there is, of course, not a reversal of gender roles but their equalization (i.e., interchangeability): women become aggressive more often than formerly, but not more aggressive than men; men suffer from depression more often than formerly, but not more often than women. The patterns of training, gainful employment, income, and assets are also tending more toward equality, like those of social and addictive behavior.

Of course, a man can still offer himself to a woman here; indeed, he has to do this even more so in a hierarchy that is not determined by gender than he did under patriarchy; he should not, however, force himself on someone. Yet, in general, in a society that ostracizes all appearances of sexual imposition, the decisions are made by women. The manner of young Turkish and Arab men in Germany had led me naïvely to assume that it was different in the Middle East, that the men there simply take what they desire sexually.

After my trip to Lebanon I believe the opposite: that individual men, particularly young men, are in regard to sexuality even bigger nobodies than they are here; there, sexuality is much more strongly subject to social control via the family than here. An Egyptian student who lived with his girlfriend in Beirut, unofficially but also unchallenged (which would be inconceivable in Cairo), was offended by the Western notion of the sexual aggressiveness of Arab men. He expressed himself in the following manner to me: rapes, incidentally like all violent crimes, are statistically less frequent in the Middle East than in the West; all this is monitored by the family, and by no means just by the father, but at least just as much by the mother.

In Lebanon, I actually became familiar with the ideal image of a worthy matriarch as the uncontested ruler in the circle of countless adult sons and grandchildren: Rashid's mother! The fact that Maronite churches are ordinarily adorned with statues of Mary, the queen of heaven, granting her protection and blessing, rather than with crosses, is fitting. In practice, men both here and there— especially young men—can hardly be in control of the procedure in matters of heterosexuality. Here it is women themselves who play the determining role in this regard, whereas there it is the family in whose lap both are living: a protection that leads to violence against only those women who wish to live in self-determination like Western women.

For young Middle Eastern men, even in the West, the determining difference consists not in practice but in appearance: the important thing is to appear in public as if one is wearing the pants at home! Thus, they focus their own frustration on the modern Western woman as a whore who no longer veils her real sexual power and the modern Western man who, although not yet typical by any means, is gradually becoming typical in educated classes and acts accordingly—no longer caring to mask his real sexual dependency through affectations of machismo.

And what of the modern Western gay man? On the one hand he is a reminder that in every man there lurks something as contemptible as a woman; on the other hand he is precisely an embodiment of independence from these beings who are hardly ever attainable: in the immortal words of a (white Anglo-Saxon Protestant) American drag queen to a (Hispanic Catholic) teenager who was harassing her: "Listen, my boy, I'm more man than you'll ever be and more woman than you'll ever get!" How could this provocation not draw the hate of frustrated young men!

RASHID AL-DAIF: The second issue that preoccupies Joachim is his desire for a young man; one could almost say a boy. Naturally, he clearly distinguishes between pederasty (loving boys who have attained sexual maturity) and pedophilia (loving children who have not attained sexual maturity) and needs no reminder about these elementary matters. Pedophilia is of course an illness, but all peoples, especially the great civilizations, knew passion for youths and acknowledged it. The ancient Greeks were famous for it. They formed couples between married men who had children and young men. The man would request a youth from a father who might then grant permission for his son to go with him. The man would receive the youth a number of times a week and take his pleasure in him, teaching him at the same time such things as literature, philosophy, and other intellectual pursuits of the age. In this sense Joachim and N. are not an ordinary gay couple but rather a Greek couple, or closer to the Greek couple than to anything else.

True, N. wasn't married, had no children, and didn't receive permission from Joachim's father for his son as Greek couples did. True also, Joachim didn't marry when he got older as Greek youths did. Joachim, who was nineteen when he became acquainted with his friend, was in a sense raised at his hand in an affectionate, caring, and serene atmosphere. He helped Joachim to realize his dreams and, in short, gave him much, and it was all motivated by love. This is exactly what Joachim now wants. He feels deep within himself a strong capacity for love and an irresistible desire to give. He dreams of a boy—I mean a young man—on whom he can bestow his capacity for giving. He dreams of teaching him everything he knows: poetry since Joachim loves poetry, the novel since he is a novelist who has become well known (he is still a young writer with a future in front of him), and the lore of life now that he is within sight of forty. But Joachim is not satisfied with dreaming about a youth. He is striving with patience and forbearance to find one, especially since the need is becoming urgent. He hoped something would work out with one young man with whom he'd had a relationship. Together, they read Rainer Maria Rilke's *Duino Elegies*, a book Joachim loves very much, having learned many poems by heart since he was thirteen—when his mother had asked him at that age what gift he wanted for his birthday, he responded without hesitation: "The complete works of Rilke!"

When he read Rilke with the young man, Joachim concentrated on a few poems in particular—the first, second, ninth, and tenth elegies—which he'd expatiate on and delve into. The youth was very fond of these meetings, especially since he loved poetry himself. The relationship between them developed to the point that their bodies met at last. It was a beautiful moment that was repeated, and always with success. The beautiful thing about this sexual relationship was that the youth didn't cling to a role, be it feminine or masculine. He was capable of assuming both roles in a marvelously natural way.

Joachim began to fall in love with the boy and to hope the feeling was reciprocated. But the youth had not at that point decided the matter or determined his sexual orientation, so he asked for time to come to terms with his own nature—especially since at about that time, he met a girl his own age for whom he had strong feelings. He enjoyed going with her to the movies, to the theater, and very much enjoyed simply talking with her. He felt she understood something fundamental about him, but the relationship between them remained at this level, which was closer to friendship than to anything else. Even though she frankly wished to have sex, he didn't go along with it because he wasn't in the right state of mind, but he began to ponder the question after she revealed her desire more than once. He simply didn't feel sexual desire toward her when she surprised him by revealing hers.

Joachim was aware of this situation because the youth kept him informed. He was truthful with himself, with Joachim, and with his girlfriend, and this only increased his charm and attractiveness.

Relations with this kind of person are very comfortable because you're not in the dark; you know where you stand, and if he forms an opinion or takes a stand, he does so from a clear base, unlike others, whose appearances belie their feelings.

Joachim was also truthful and consistent with himself and with the boy. It was the stance of one who wants the relationship to succeed, to be rich and open to the future, not an opportunity to be seized. So the relationship between the longed-for boy and a female didn't anger him, and he didn't make any attempt to convince the youth he was gay by nature rather than bisexual. Nor did he try to coax or push him into making his decision quickly. What happened was that Joachim was set to travel to Lebanon for a period of three weeks for the West-Eastern Divan program we had begun during my stay in Berlin from the beginning of November to the middle of December 2003. Joachim was to travel at the end of April and return to Germany in mid-May 2004, which would make a three-week absence. This was fortuitous because it gave the young man an opportunity to test his attachment to the girlfriend and to verify the nature of his feelings, his desire, and his sexual identity.

JOACHIM HELFER: Since it was only later, in Lebanon, that I told Rashid a little about Daniel, some things have gotten mixed up in this rough outline of our tender mutuality—which, however, is not relevant. I will say this much: after Rashid's departure we entered into dialogue again, and I understood that my young friend was not angry—as I had feared—but had only needed distance, time, and space for himself and for new experiences.

Like every young person he had to clarify the question of how he wanted to live as an adult; a child of the generation that, not unjustifiably, had struck Rashid in Berlin as androgynous—although an unusually mature and smart one. He was not, however, concerned with choosing between two mutually exclusive potential identities, and certainly not ones based on something that is as well nigh negligible as sexuality when the sexual drive is permitted and not repressed.

The freedom enjoyed by these fortunate ones thanks to the struggle of their predecessors consists precisely in loving whomever they wish, however they wish, publicly kissing whomever they like without pigeonholing themselves as one thing or the other. For Daniel it was a question of an open-ended departure for new horizons, not of the predefinition that Rashid refers to as sexual orientation. If in the process he behaved more drastically than necessary, it was because, on the one hand, he was afraid of hurting me with this wish and, on the other hand, feared losing his freedom through this very concern—which was as kind as it was unfounded.

I only gave Rashid a vague outline about Daniel and me, because I did not find Rashid's objectivizing, matter-of-fact grasp of what connects people to be appropriate and even found it unpleasant in this case, in contrast to when speaking about adults and myself: a secret that demands respect is part of the magic and freedom of youth. He had to rely all the more on his own interpretations and readings, which are correspondingly illuminating.

I recommended the shortcut through the *Duino Elegies* to Rashid, who was not familiar with my favorite poet. The readings with Daniel ranged from the Bible to Faust to Bertrand Russell, and it was by no means the case that only I spoke, as the elder, and Daniel, as the younger, only listened, as Rashid had assumed my statement that we had talked about such topics to mean. As a matter of fact, I learned from Daniel, who was no longer a child when I met him and already had a not-so-easy childhood behind him, at least as much as he did from me.

It is even more significant for Rashid's reading of my relationship with Daniel that he misunderstood my clarification in this regard: when I attached importance to the statement that, like every real relationship, it was a mutual give and take of different but equal partners, he promptly interpreted this description of communicating souls as a sexual metaphor in strict conformity to the classical pederastic model, in which the norm prescribes that the adult erastes, as man, teaches, gives, and penetrates and the youthful eromenos, as not-yet-man, hence virtually a woman, learns, takes, and is penetrated! It is a Greek legacy when, to this day, Arabs interpret any kind of penetration as an expression of masculine superiority! Interpreted in this fashion, my statement that I also learned from Daniel would have to describe our sexual practices—although I never uttered a word about it and, unlike Rashid, would never divulge the intimate details of a relationship with a third party.

Irrespective of the particular topic, the most general (and, admittedly generalized) misunderstanding is demonstrated here: Germans are accustomed to clearly stating what they want to say and concealing what they do not want to say; we mean no more than what we say. Middle Easterners, in contrast, never state clearly what they mean but instead always just insinuate it. Precisely this is what is admirable about Rashid's text: that he clearly and openly states what in the context of his culture could otherwise be said at best via circumlocution.

The communication problem that typically occurs is the false conclusion: he who has learned to speak as a Middle Easterner, instead of taking what others say at face value, consistently interprets it as a cautious intimation of a meaning that regularly exceeds the nominal value of what is said: a German means gnat and, for the sake of clarity, rounds up to sparrow; the Middle Easterner hears sparrow and interprets it to mean elephant.

When I, for example, responded evasively to the indiscreet question—which involved a third party and not me—of whether Daniel not only had a girlfriend but also slept with her, by saying that, as far as I knew, the two of them had slept in the same bed several times, Rashid interpreted it to mean that there must be a "problem," something that cannot be right. The idea that a boy and a girl who like each other could sleep in the same bed without having sex, in spite of being allowed and having the opportunity to do so, is, arguably, inconceivable to someone who never had this freedom and opportunity as a boy.

Rashid also writes that I had begun to fall in love with this boy *after* our relationship had become physical—whereas I had specifically told him about the shift from an intellectual-spiritual attraction to a physical desire. One might almost believe that he cannot imagine an affection that first engages the spirit and the mind—although he was the one who told me about the topos of classical Arab poems: the joys of secret lovers silently holding hands that cannot be surpassed by a sexual act!

I am not trying to conceal anything: if instead of being lovesick I had only enjoyed physical pleasure, I would not be afraid of admitting it. But it is illuminating for the dialogue with Rashid that, although he understood it was about love, he speaks in the end only about sex. By no means do I believe that Rashid perceives women only as bodies and not as mind and spirit or that he can only desire but not love them, even if he often expresses himself this way privately and literarily. This fixation on sexuality seems to me rather to illustrate our cultural conditioning.

The difference that comes to light here is, first of all, in the degree of frustration: the less we are able to fulfill our sexual desires, the more important sex becomes in our thinking; conversely, the more easily we can do this, the more secondary it becomes. The fact that the tension between the sexes in the Middle East is purposefully kept high does not also mean that it can be discharged more easily.

This conscious emphasis of the dualism of mutually exclusive alternative identities patterned after primal archetypes of man and woman apparently distinguishes Beirut from Berlin and the Middle East from the modern West—but I also take that to be a mere noncontemporaneity: for it is neither the case that the development from the *Bubikopf* (boy's head) hairstyle of the self-supporting stenotypist of the Weimar era to today's unisex fashion among youths and in business has already led to complete androgyny, nor that women in Lebanon, as in most Middle Eastern countries, are not allowed to vote or work outside of the home.

When Rashid takes it for granted that one must choose between a homosexual and a heterosexual identity in the basic way that parents (or, more often than one thinks, doctors!) have to decide if a daughter or a son has been born to them, he is illustrating less an Arab than a modern Western concept that confers on gays and lesbians the status of belonging to their own tribe, comparable to an ethnic minority. The erosion of this ghetto has just begun in the West.

Rashid, however, still lives completely within this either/ or logic: thus, a woman whose body he desires cannot also have a brain; a homosexual cannot, as a woman, be a father; a physical relationship, as a sin, cannot also be spiritual; and a boy who enjoys the love of a man cannot also love a girl. I, in contrast, have the good fortune of living in a logic of "this but also that," which in my society too has only just become possible and is by no means common: Daniel knows and likes my longtime companion, and I took to his girlfriend at once. Because I can distinguish between the feelings of a lover and those of a father but do not consider it to be necessary in this case to choose between the two, I would be just as happy as Rashid for his son and his son's girlfriend if the two of them were to stay together and have children. This is the stupid thing about the concept of identity: that it lays claim to immutability, finality, and exclusivity, whereas love and desire—like life itself—are always in flux, neither coming to rest nor running dry until one's last breath.

RASHID AL-DAIF: In Lebanon Joachim was at ease and I saw he was happy, no doubt about it. Apparently, nothing prevented him from enjoying himself in Beirut and in other Lebanese regions we visited together or that he visited with others. The weather was beautiful. The period between the months of April and May is usually among the best of the year in Lebanon, with daytime temperatures ranging from twenty to twenty-four degrees Celsius and five or six degrees cooler at night. During Joachim's visit, the days were always sunny, the sky blue, and Beirut chock-full of young men. Males in the street were more visible than females and most were brown of skin or verging on it. What could be more attractive for a gay man on the lookout for the boy of his dreams?

As for myself, I frankly enjoy meeting the opposite sex during occasions such as lunches and dinners with friends and acquaintances or at similar functions. I say in all candor that the presence of women delights me, especially if they are free and unattached, and I believe all men, married or bachelor, generally share this feeling. Joachim is blond and he turned girls' heads, which doubtless did something for his pride, but this wasn't what interested him. In considering how to make his stay pleasant and restful, my intuition was to introduce Joachim to some of the rare gay men I knew, but I changed my mind, figuring it wasn't up to me to make things happen, that I couldn't manage something like this and that I didn't like this sort of thing anyway.

Yet many, if not all, of my friends were aware of Joachim's visit to Beirut (newspapers covered our activities), and among these friends were a man and his wife. G. is an engineer and L. a well-known director and university professor whom I had informed about the details of my trip to Berlin. I told them also about Joachim's homosexuality as well as about his friend who lives with him. Their interest and curiosity in this matter whetted my appetite to discuss it, so they ended up being the most well informed about it. I remember talking to L. about Joachim's upcoming visit and the issue of whether it was appropriate to introduce him to gay men in Beirut while we were strolling on the seawall. One of L.'s closest friends is gay, and I remember we were leaning toward introducing them.

The next day, when Joachim arrived, I invited him with L., G., and some friends to dinner at City Café, near the lower gate of Lebanese American University, where we had held a lecture-discussion on our experiences in the West-Eastern Divan program. We sat at a table outside and stayed in the beautiful spring air until late in the evening. When we decided to leave, L. asked me to wait for a minute until Sader, her gay friend, arrived. She'd called him while we were having dinner and asked him to come after work. When he arrived, we had hardly introduced them to each other before they fell into discussion alone together as if they'd known each other for ages. Afterwards, we all got up to say our good-byes to each other before leaving, each to his or her home. I was surprised when I saw Joachim and Sader kiss each other good-bye almost on the lips, their bodies close together. While I was taking him back to his hotel, Joachim confided to me he'd immediately guessed Sader was gay.

Some time later, Joachim related he'd seen Sader on numerous occasions and that Sader had introduced him to gay nightclubs. He filled me in on how much homosexuals suffer in Lebanon and how they encounter insurmountable difficulties in affirming themselves. He told me what I already knew but without having been upset by it before. He was indignant while speaking. He'd already learned Lebanese law permits homosexuals to be imprisoned, that they are whistled at in the streets, and that some fathers who cannot bear their children's homosexuality threaten to kill them if they don't distance themselves from this "habit."

Some rich fathers send their gay children to London to have specialists treat them. He learned that among these are some who despair to the point of suicide. When one gay youth told his family about his sexual orientation, a pall of unbearable sadness fell over the home. The mother isolated herself, the father isolated himself, and they were no longer able to speak to each other or to their son. A deep depression afflicted the youth, forcing him into the hospital where, after several days of treatment and during a guard's moment of inattention, he jumped from the window onto the street below and died. Tragedy!

Without a doubt, my colleague gained a good deal of experience during his Beirut trip and collected much information about this subject, but he is not by nature a Romantic revolutionary in the way many intellectuals are, especially Arabs. They nag and complain about "issues" and proclaim their dissent every chance they get. Joachim, from what I could fathom, rebels only about matters that concern him. This doesn't mean he's selfish; rather that he is a very realistic person who dreams about what he can achieve. No matter how distant his dreams may be from realization, they are of a kind he can achieve. Among these dreams is that of finding a boy. In my thoughts about Joachim, this was a constant and a key among keys to his personality. I noticed how his eyes would follow certain boys. They shine. His vision is ravished.

JOACHIM HELFER: Arabs, as we know, are noble and generous, also with the truth; Germans, in contrast, are realistic and stingy—and so the cliché shall be confirmed: neither was Rashid our host that evening (it was the Lebanese American University), nor was it the first evening after my arrival.

Several days prior to that I had even asked the director, L., a friend of Rashid's whose worldly geniality had done me good, if Rashid's overprotective behavior was typical for Arab hospitality and remarked that I wanted to see more of Lebanon than just what Rashid was willing to show me—for example, I also wanted to look at "old stones," as he called them, and even without him I would view the traces that had been left behind in his country by Phoenicians, Greeks, Romans, and Crusaders.

Admittedly, I added with a grin, my interest was not incessantly and exclusively directed at old stones but possibly once in a while also at more cheerful people than the revered poets of the Café de Paris. I used the French expression *gai*, which, like the English "gay," means both cheerful and homosexual, and I must have made just the right roguish face; in any case, she grinned back at me and promised me relief in the form of a competent guide.

Only after that did the handsome student with the sad eyes, Sader, who was no longer quite sober, enter the scene, with whom I did indeed set out on the following evening. The next morning Rashid became explicit: he had previously attempted to protect our common project and, no less importantly, his own reputation; he had to warn me. He had probably been plagued by nightmares about a mass gay orgy on Martyrs' Square.

In reality I had only had a few drinks with my guide—who, far from being cheerful, was deeply unhappy—in the handful of hidden bars where the not-always-attractive baby fat of Beirut boys celebrates triumphs of pure sensuality. At sunrise we had sat at the sea, somewhat drunk, and told each other about our lives, the suicides of our teenage friends, before we parted with a friendly fraternal hug.

The significance that Rashid—both here and later on—attached to the fact that I kissed a likeable new acquaintance on the cheeks when saying good-bye is amusing: for kissing, not only twice, as I was familiar with from France and Italy, but three times right away is, so to speak, Lebanon's national sport. In Beirut everyone is constantly kissing everyone else, and the only Lebanese person with whom I became better acquainted and still never kissed on the cheek was Rashid, who probably thought the contagiousness was too great.

It was not my business to denounce conditions in my host country, and I did not do this in front of Rashid, who already knew about the distress of same-sex lovers in his world but, significantly, not about their courage: whether he accepted murder and suicide, humiliation, or, in the most favorable case—which one has to be able to afford—emigration to the West with a shrug of the shoulders ("A tragedy!") or as regretfully as one accepts what cannot be changed, I do not know. He had never heard of Helem, the first political-cultural homosexual organization in the Arab world—

founded in Beirut, where else?—although it maintained an office with an informational café, a library, and a website, and had created a sensation with its various campaigns.

RASHID AL-DAIF: I introduced him to a friend of mine, and this friend liked him and wanted to know him better and to introduce him to his wife and children. The friend invited us to dinner at his home the next day. We were six at dinner: the friend, who was about fifty; his wife, who was about forty-two; their son, M., who was seventeen; their daughter, who was about fourteen; and a friend of their son's, who was the same age as him. I don't know if it was an illusion, but I thought Joachim was charmed by M. His eyes never strayed far from the youth.

The mother sat at the table in front of Joachim, and her son, M., sat on her right. The father sat to the right of Joachim, and I was in front of the son. Nobody noticed anything, certainly not M. Only I saw Joachim's eyes move from the wife to her son, with or without a reason for doing so. Nobody present was aware of Joachim's homosexuality. "That's lucky!" I was saying in secret to myself at the time, but not out of prejudice. As a matter of principle, I am completely on the side of those who suffer on earth and of oppressed minorities, including gay men and lesbians, but if anyone present knew about Joachim's sexual orientation the atmosphere would've switched from friendly and welcoming to one of unbearable embarrassment. My friend, the host, once told me, "By God, Rashid, I don't know what I'd do if I found out one day, God forbid, my son was, for example, gay." He didn't say "gay" but rather "buggered" and said "for example" to delay the instant of pronouncing it, as if that would delay a reality behind the words. Then, after a sigh, he added, "I'd kill him!" Naturally, I didn't respond to his statement because I was sure that if his son were gay he'd never kill him. Nevertheless, I was sure it would transform his and his wife's life into a living hell. It would crush both of them.

I remembered the phone call from Thomas Hartmann when he informed me the writer he found for the program was gay. I said to myself that Thomas must have had the right feeling about this and a knowledge about our country from his work in the field of Third World relations. Maybe this knowledge came from his experience in the leftist struggle during his youth, especially in the 1968 period. As I learned later, he was among the student leaders in Frankfurt back then and an activist in Spontis, a group of leftists who believed in spontaneous demonstrations. He worked in the Opel factory organizing workers, and was a founder of the leftist daily *Taz*, published in Berlin. The left at that time was generally supportive of Third World issues.

Nobody at the dinner was at all aware of what was secretly going on, and maybe Joachim himself didn't know his eyes never left the youth. The boy was very brown of skin, a deep and pure brown, and his eyes were penetrating such that you could hardly imagine bearing their gaze. He was riveted by Joachim's conversation, paying attention without being distracted by anything else, not even the ministrations of his mother as she hectored him to finish his plate. It was a habit she'd formed when he was young and would refuse to eat for hours on end, and she'd worry he was dying of malnutrition.

I don't think I'm mistaken about what I saw that evening, and I don't think I saw only what I feared to see. I know when misunderstandings arise with foreigners in Lebanon and Arab countries. I know it from experience since I've lived it for years. My ex-wife, the mother of my son, is French, and she lived with me a number of years in Lebanon and Syria, and we visited other Arab countries together. For example, I believe that building work relations between a foreign woman and a Lebanese or Arab man is much more difficult than between two Westerners. Sex is always an issue between a Lebanese man and a foreign woman and this is soon evident. It is very difficult for the Lebanese Arab man not to misread the free conduct of a foreign woman in dress, speech, going out at night, and interacting publicly. It's difficult for him not to read all this as her sexual availability. Joachim once said to me sex is not the fundamental thing in the lives of German women or men, and from what I have experienced with Europeans and especially with the French, I believe this is to a large extent true.

I always thought we knew more about Westerners than they knew about us, but I have to amend this to say it is not altogether true because our knowledge of them is often superficial and misses the essential. The Western woman is not as cautious in her dealings with men as an Arab woman is, and the Arab man reads this as availability. My wife would go out from time to time to shop, taking our son with her in his stroller. Some workers in the supermarket showed a special interest in our son, and when my wife returned and told me how kind and attentive they were, I listened without offering an opinion or remark of any kind. I knew at the time that two wives of friends lived in the neighborhood and did their shopping at the same supermarket. No workers were "interested" in their children or showed any special kindness toward them. The wives were Lebanese. Then my wife came along one day and said to me the supermarket workers' interest in the boy went a little too far. I narrate this to say there was, without a doubt, a misunderstanding.

That's why I was on the alert during that evening at my friend's house. Many things passed over Joachim's head by virtue of his being German. I saw him notice the woman stretch her arm in front of him to get a bottle of oil on his left. This would never happen in Germany or in France, where polite conduct calls for you to ask your neighbor to pass the salt, the bread, or the oil—if they have oil at the table—not to reach across to serve yourself. As for us, we serve ourselves in order to avoid disturbing our neighbor at the table. It's against etiquette to ask your neighbor to pass you something, especially if that neighbor is a guest. In that case, we are the ones who put ourselves out to get him everything he needs.

I saw Joachim was always confused when he was invited to lunch or dinner. How to begin? With what? We put all courses out on the table at the same time and there is no starter or main course; instead, we put everything out and everybody serves himself. You begin with whatever you wish and reach out to take seconds as much as you want without having to ask permission. A person at the table with us doesn't have to wait for others in order to finish his plate, or to wait for the lady of the house to ask if anyone wants seconds or to pass to the next course. In France, I found it burdensome when I was invited to lunch or dinner to be prevented the pleasure of finishing my meal without waiting for others. It took me some time to get used to this, and I still wait, when I have to, out of politeness.

The issue is not one of intentions but of culture. I remember, as a doctoral student, meeting a French girl at the beginning of my stay in Paris. This girl invited me to spend the weekend at her home in a suburb of the city. Her parents were out of the country on holiday and nobody was home except her older brother. I had not been more than a couple of months in France at the time. In the evening, after the three of us had dinner together and spent some time chatting in the living room, the time came to go to sleep. My friend rose and went to her bedroom; her brother went to work at his desk and I stayed alone sitting, confused, and not knowing what I should do. After about an hour, my friend returned and asked reproachfully what I was doing there. Why hadn't I followed her? I said, "Follow you where?" She responded in amazement, "How's that? 'Where?' To our bedroom!"

"Our bedroom?" I asked, but to myself.

While we were in bed cuddling (on her initiative), I asked, "Won't your brother be upset?" The question surprised her; she didn't understand what I meant, so I continued caressing her just to show her the question was but a passing thought of no importance whatsoever. We did continue making out but I with one eye open.

Joachim cannot imagine what my friend, our host, would have done if he'd known his guest was eyeing his son with such pleasure, such distress, and such insistence. If my friend had known, his mood would have taken a turn for the worse. In the first place, if he'd known Joachim was gay, he would not have invited him to dinner or to lunch.

On one occasion, Thomas Hartmann invited me in the company of my son to dinner at a restaurant in Berlin. The tables were long, relatively narrow, and numerous diners were seated as in a university restaurant. We were speaking French and among us was a certain complicity. The three of us sat at the end of one table and four others sat next to us, two on each side of the table. On one side were a young man in his early twenties and another in his late thirties. From time to time, they would kiss each other as if they couldn't swallow a bite without kissing. Facing them were a man and his wife. Thomas, who heard them easily, mentioned to us that the younger man called them Mom and Dad. I began observing; the scene preoccupied me to such an extent I couldn't tear my eyes away. I can safely say the parents were

124

not delighted, especially when their son kissed his partner. Theirs was not the situation of parents in the presence of their son and his beloved girlfriend. If he were to kiss her, they'd be glad for him and happy for the love that joined them. The three of us agreed on that point but also on the fact that respect for the rights of others means you have to accept what you don't like and don't wish for.

That scene would be impossible in any Arab country.

Then again, everybody at the dinner liked Joachim and found him cultured and amiable, and their daughter found him handsome. As for M., he said nothing, nor did his friend offer an opinion. In the car after dinner, Joachim asked me about M.: his age, his plans for the future, and whether he really wished to travel to Germany to continue his university studies there. M. had asked Joachim during dinner about the conditions of university study for foreigners in Germany, student housing, and what have you. After this flood of questions, I asked Joachim about his friend, the German youth. He responded briefly that the youth was still in a state of self-examination and stopped at that, not wishing to dwell on the subject. I didn't divulge to Joachim what I alone had noticed about him at dinner. I was afraid he'd take it as a reproach and told myself we would doubtless return to the subject in the future.

JOACHIM HELFER: You see what you know, but only if you want to know it: Rashid knew that I could take a liking to such a young man, so he saw that I observed him with favor. He also saw, without wondering what it meant, that this young man seemed to be captivated by my words and focused on me, so noticeably that his mother had to admonish him to finish the food on his plate (which was quite obvious to me even without knowing Arabic!).

What he did not see, because he did not wish to know it, was that this boy quickly noticed and very much enjoyed the fact that he pleased me and also made great efforts to please me. What neither Rashid nor the boy's father wanted to know was the most obvious thing: if there had not been a certain fineness and sensitivity noticeable in his manner—in Rashid's alphabet it might be called "femininity"—then why would his father have expressed concern about his son's sexual development?

I am almost certain that Rashid was the only one at the table who
believed that he alone saw the obvious—but what was obvious? That I
was about to forget all my table manners—oil jug or no oil jug!—and
throw myself on the boy right then and there? Did anyone besides
Rashid harbor the suspicion of secret trysts? Is it conceivable that
I believed this boy wanted to signal his homosexual orientation to
me, even his sexual availability, in front of his entire family?

He never would have acted as he did in front of this father with
his dark views if he had been aware of this. If his easygoing behavior
suggested anything it was that his father's fears were, at that time in
any case, unnecessary; the spawn of the usual automatic equation of
effeminacy and homosexuality.

The only obvious thing was the natural tension between an
adolescent looking for role models and an adult, each of whom,
through the glass walls of the years, recognizes something of himself
in the other, of his own desires and inclinations: the man recognizes
their beautiful latency in the boy, the boy their tangible realization
in the man. Only in this case not a soccer player or rock musician
but an author, on top of everything an incarnate author who likes to
provide information, who takes him seriously and notices him, and
who comes from the country in which he himself wants to study. This
tension, which is a part of every good teacher/student relationship,
is undoubtedly erotic in the broadest sense of the word, but only
becomes sexual in exceptional cases. Its compulsive sexualization
arises from Rashid's image of the rampant homosexual, for after
all, he would probably not interpret every kind of sympathy between
himself and his female students sexually—or would he?

His first novel depicts how a professor of literature, during a bomb
attack on the university in the civil war, had sex with a female student
who remained faceless for him during the act after the lights had gone
out in the shelter and all the occupants had huddled together in mortal
fear; afterwards he almost goes crazy having to wonder whether every
female student in every lecture and seminar might be the one whom
he embraced so passionately in those exceptional circumstances.

Especially for a university instructor, which Rashid remains
to this day, writing this book was undoubtedly very courageous—
incidentally not only by Lebanese but also by German standards,

126 to say nothing at all of the U.S., where erotic contacts between teachers and learners are strictly forbidden at many universities and lead to immediate dismissal or expulsion. I do not know whether he ever suffered the hostility of female students or their fathers for this literary provocation. If he did, he would certainly not consider this reaction of the people's sensitivities to be acceptable, let alone correct; on the contrary, he would consider it to be stupid.

Poets and thinkers must violate convention where it is the custom to make sweeping judgments about human beings and their actions on the basis of identity, founded in whatever attribute, instead of based on situation and cause (i.e., morally in the truest sense of the word); they must, whether in word or deed, offer society the opportunity to recognize this convention as evil rather than good and to discard it. This is what Rashid does and this is what I do.

RASHID AL-DAIF: The next day, I showed him the cedars, the famous cedars of Lebanon in the north of the country, above Bsharri, the town of Gibran Khalil Gibran. We talked about diverse things while roaming around this forest, pausing for a long while on Joachim's attachment to his favorite poet, Rainer Maria Rilke. He recited for me some passages of his poems and commented on them. Then he moved on in a rather surprising way to the subject of his German friend with whom he read Rilke and whose answer he was awaiting. He informed me the young man had decided to stay with his girlfriend because he could at last have sex with her, and he was very happy in this relationship, which had deepened and had convinced him beyond doubt that he was not gay. He told me all this with pain and mentioned they had agreed to meet on Joachim's return to Berlin in order to discuss the matter face-to-face. When I asked him if there remained any hope, he raised his hand to the sky!

Here I remembered the day he'd invited me to visit "The Lady of Berlin." He told me, "Today I'm going to show you the Lady of Berlin." I asked him who she was and he said, "I'll show you!" so I submitted without too many questions and let him lead me wherever he willed. I eventually found myself in a museum of ancient Egyptian art in Charlottenburg, Berlin, face-to-face with Nefertiti. He announced that this was "The Lady of Berlin" as if to say, "You always go on about your desire for women, so take this one! Look at her. Doesn't she make you feel you don't need any of the others?"

I was indeed taken aback. This was a beautiful woman for all time. It was as if her lips, her eyes, her eyelashes and eyebrows were the work of the greatest makeup artists of today and her clothing revealed her entire perfect neck. Everything about her was magnificent today, just as it was certainly magnificent in the past, maybe more so. She really is a lady, not only a work of art. She is a woman who shows you her face and knows of your existence in front of her or next to her as you contemplate her with pleasure. She is truly a woman, the quintessential woman. What is the secret of her beauty that makes it persist throughout time? Intelligence radiates from her; her arresting presence imposes itself. Blessed is he for whom she cares.

After the shock, I said to Joachim, "This is a woman," and he responded, as I expected him to, that this was woman in art. It seemed to me in the context of the discussion that if Nefertiti in the flesh had offered herself to him, she could not have displaced a young man in his feelings and interests. "This is a work of nature," I said to myself, "and you can't do anything about a work of nature."

He told me about the young man's decision in the cedar forest at an elevation of two thousand meters above sea level. It was springtime and the weather was misty, which made the already majestic place even more so. The mountain cedars have been a part of our education through many sources, among them the literature of Gibran Khalil Gibran, author of *The Prophet* and son of these valleys and hills that have sheltered monks devoted to God and are free of all filth and unseemliness. The cedars are a small forest consisting of a few hundred trees, among them some great, astonishing ones they say are thousands of years old. They have a history and many Lebanese think of them as mediators with God. The image of the cedar at the center of the Lebanese flag was taken from one of these cedars we were wandering under.

It was in this holy place he told me the bad news. I asked myself if I felt a sort of contradiction between the sacredness of the place and the worldliness of the subject. In the holy atmosphere replete with

"Gibranic" charm, romanticism, and mysticism, I felt sympathy with Joachim. I was sad for his failure to build the relationship he'd hoped for from the depths of his heart and of which he dreamed perhaps every day. This was in spite of the strangeness of thinking about such a relationship in that place. We had gotten used to hearing about such things in cities and especially in "grindstone" cities that sharpen their inhabitants' desires to such a point that no barrier can block their realization. The sincerity that emerged from Joachim's conversation put him in harmony with this place in spite of the peculiarity I mentioned or maybe (why not?) because of it. Joachim displayed his desire for a man twenty years his junior as if it were of a mystical nature because he deeply and fervently believed in a kind of providence, which believers would call God, that shepherds this world and would not forsake one who dreams of giving all. It had not forsaken his roommate, N., who also had a great desire to give. He gave and was given.

JOACHIM HELFER: Whoever sees what five thousand years of civilization have left of the erstwhile primeval forests of the cedars of Lebanon, which have been crafted by carpenters into everything from the ships of Pharaohs and the Ark of the Covenant to the chess sets of the Ottomans and the French, can hardly believe that human beings are no match for nature. The reason I began quoting Rilke up there, under those almost unbelievably majestic giant trees that stand directly on the tree line in nearly eternal snow, was that I was able to do so in French, whereas I would have had to improvise a translation of Goethe's "Über allen Gipfeln ist Ruh" (Over all the treetops is peace) or Hermann Hesse's "Seltsam, im Nebel zu wandern" (Strange to wander in the fog).

Susceptible to the magic of the place, which had given me a need for harmony and communication, I wanted to try again to approximate for Rashid what I had not been able to do in Germany in spite of several attempts. After all, he was explaining to his German guest the magical-mythical relationship of the Lebanese, especially of the Maronites, to their sacred cedars in a way that gave the impression that this notion must be completely foreign or even appear bizarre to him; as if the relationships to linden trees and oaks in the land of St. Boniface, the lumberjack missionary, up to the present political explosiveness of reports on the dying forests, were purely a matter of forestry and not also mystical in nature.

Rashid is correct to warn himself and others of the fallacy that just because one speaks a Western language one knows much more about the West than Europeans like me who speak no Arabic know about the Middle East. While he himself is familiar with the technical exterior of Western Civilization, he is hardly familiar with the cultural history from which it has arisen and that propels it to this day.

On the icy, wind-swept, broad, and straight streets of Berlin, metropolis of a modernity that is as powerful as it is violent, it was difficult to demonstrate why Berlin is Germany to an even lesser degree than New York is America. So I took advantage of our excursion to Munich, interrupting the trip in Bamberg to show him the Romanesque cathedral that Saladin's ambassadors to Barbarossa had already seen, as well as the row of houses on the bank of the Regnitz River that still look just as they do in one of Dürer's watercolors, which introduced sensitivity to landscape into European painting.

"*Ça, c'est l'Allemagne!*" I remarked upon viewing the rooftops with their nooks and crannies and the alleyways at the foot of the cathedral hill. Whoever wishes to understand German society, with its guilds and niches, the cleanly paved labyrinthine paths of German politics and administration, and the German temperament, with its penchant for pretty trifles and a warm hearth, must keep in mind that the streets of Berlin—like those of Paris and London— were copied from the Romans and are therefore an exception, whereas the alleyways of Bamberg are the rule. Rashid smiled at my enthusiasm, returning it only when we continued our journey on the ICE, the high-speed train that could also solve Lebanon's traffic problems: "*Ça, c'est l'Allemagne!*"

Yet, finally the cedars were silent in a language that we both could understand. What could have been more fitting up there than to speak of the highest act that human beings are capable of: love? So I murmured, "Daniel is happy with his girlfriend . . . ," with a generosity of spirit similar to that with which I brought Rashid to see Nefertiti, the "most beautiful woman of Berlin," as I put it, which, interestingly, he turned immediately into its "mistress" (*Herrin*).[4] You are always telling me how much you love women, so look at her: just a head, no body at all, and yet more woman and a better woman than everything that you are able to see in women in the flesh, the way that you look at them!

I had fallen hopelessly in love with a boy, and was happy again with my life since the desire had been transformed into tender concern: the only hope that I left behind in Berlin with Daniel was that he would be happy. When he mailed me Botticelli's *Birth of Venus* in Beirut, too sensitive for indiscretion and too intelligent for ideologizing, I was happy for him! What I felt was the harmony with life, the profound trust in its hidden meaning that Rashid refers to as my belief in Providence. Daniel's declaration of principle, my concern, my alleged wish to discuss something after my return, and my disappointment—all that was added by Rashid from his own alphabet.

If Rashid were French I would attribute this misunderstanding to my German peculiarity of becoming silent not from sadness and not finding silence to be sad, of not hearing in it the nearness of death but the nearness of God: my friends in the South of France always thought that they needed to be concerned about me when, after a day filled with conversation and social obligations, I was finally allowed to sit silently aloof and gaze into the unspoiled countryside, immersed in both myself and in the contemplation of creation, hence completely happy—"*Mais vous êtes si triste ici!*"

I was never closer to Rashid, however, than when we fell silent next to one another before the breathtaking view of the sea offered by his country house from an elevation of fifteen hundred meters. After, at most, half an eternity, I found the panorama to be "Like a bird!" simply to allow him the enjoyment of adding "Like from an airplane!" Rashid is held prisoner perhaps less by the country in which he lives than the time, the old but certainly not eternal presence of the either/or logic, the structure of power, ambition, and such missionaries who can only erect their church from the

4. Helfer cites the German translation of Rashid's original Arabic text here, in which the word *Herrin* is used.

wood of sacred trees; in contrast, love, to which the future belongs, like freedom and tolerance, always inhabits the logic of "this but also that."

RASHID AL-DAIF: It's strange on my part, this feeling of sympathy I have for Joachim. It even occurred to me, for instance, to ask him about his friend N., whether he knew about Joachim's desire, his attempts to fulfill it, and whether this would hurt N. in any way. It would've put me at ease, but I decided against it. It crossed my mind to help him, but then I asked myself, "How? How can you help anyone in a personal, intimate matter like this?" If it was a question of a relationship with a woman, it would've been easier, but it was a question of a man—a male. How can I ignore this when in our culture, if we want to describe a liar with no conscience who is capable of weaving conspiracies and planting chaos, we would say he's "sticking male plugs together"? Nevertheless, I tried. I tried without saying anything about it and without alluding to anything.

I tried following the example of Zubayda, the wife of the great Arab Caliph Harun al-Rashid and mother of his son, the Caliph al-Amin, who was replaced in the caliphate by his half-brother al-Ma'mun after a war between them destroyed Baghdad, the capital of the empire, and left some tens of thousands dead. When Zubayda saw her son, the Caliph al-Amin, preferring young boys, she wanted to steer him in another direction, so she bought for him some early-adolescent slave girls and dressed them as boys, cutting their hair like that of boys. She offered them to him as a gift for his sexual needs, so he'd take his pleasure in them and give up young boys.

I invited Joachim to dinner at my house with a number of friends and acquaintances who I thought would be good for him to know. I invited, at the same time, a girl of twenty-six who was beautiful despite a clearly masculine aspect no one could miss. She was short of stature and anybody would say she resembled a young boy. She arrived before Joachim and sat on a love seat. When he arrived, Joachim spontaneously sat down next to her and stayed there next to her the entire evening, talking with her and she with him. I noticed her once rise to go to the kitchen and bring him back a glass of water, which he accepted while looking into her eyes, surprised. He mentioned later she'd sensed he was thirsty without letting on, so she rose spontaneously and brought him a glass of water without him having asked her anything and without her asking him if he wanted anything. Then she sat down and continued the conversation with him as naturally as could be, as if she hadn't paid attention to what she'd done. At the end of the evening, when everybody was saying their good-byes, he kissed her near the lips, and she blushed from shyness or from nervousness or from both at once.

I wanted to know if he'd set a date to see her again or if she'd left an impression on him or moved him in any way. I asked him at the end of the evening when only he and I were left in the house. I asked him clearly and precisely, mentioning I had noticed this girl's interest in him. He responded immediately with the honesty I had come to expect from him and that I quickly discovered was one of his distinguishing features, "You're right! I noticed, too. I found myself taken by conversation with her. The truth is she caught my attention. It's impossible to find a woman in Germany who'd bring you a glass of water! We all (he meant Germans, of course), men and women, learn to serve ourselves. She surprised me, this girl, by her initiative. She was very nice. It was a good thing you invited her. A beautiful surprise." I hesitated but had to ask him whether he'd made a date to meet again. He said, "No," but it seemed to me he said this with some pain and regret.

He mentioned he'd become used to girls finding him handsome. He always heard this from them—he is confident of his beauty—but there was something different about this girl who found him handsome that evening and doubtless loved his beauty.

JOACHIM HELFER: It is not astonishing that different societies have different ideas about gender roles. It is hard to comprehend, however, that the expectations and ideas that Rashid takes for granted, presumably representative of his society to some degree, are themselves so contradictory: if he considers me, as a homosexual, to be a woman rather than a man, why does he interpret it as an erotic sign and not as an attempt to avoid such a thing when I behave as a woman would in his society and sit next to a strange woman rather than a strange man?

I followed my instinct and simply sat down next to the person who seemed the most congenial to me of all those present: a young woman whose behavior had caught my attention, not because it would have been unusual in Berlin but because it differed from the behavior of most women in Lebanon. Just like me, she seemed to attach no importance to emphasizing her sex—i.e., to alluding in her hairstyle, clothing, makeup (or rather lack of makeup), in the way she sat, stood up, and walked that she was by no means simply a human being but first and foremost a woman.

It was the absence of all connotations of sex and power—and these are inseparable in Rashid's world!—that impressed me about the manner in which she handed me a glass of water, just because she had noticed that I was thirsty and it was less convenient for me to reach the kitchen from where I sat than for her. Precisely because she had grown up in a society in which women serve men, it was a utopian moment when she could hand me water *without* making the impression of recognizing this hierarchy.

Rashid interpreted my observation to mean precisely the opposite: When I deplored the fact that it had become rare in Germany for anyone to bring anyone else a glass of water because, in a society that does not distribute power simply according to sex and age, every human gesture is interpreted as a symbol of subservience, I did not mean to say that I longed for a return to the subordination of women to men that is natural for Rashid. On the contrary, I longed for a world beyond it in which the thirsty are sated by those who sit at the source. But returning to that evening: as a narcissistic teenager I had sat at the source long enough not only to sense but also to enjoy the fact that this young woman to whom I had taken a liking also took a complete and total fancy to me. At the age of sixteen or eighteen I would not have hesitated for my part to slake this thirst, for at that time I did not care whom I embraced as long as I saw my reflection in his or her eyes (and who can discern one's sex from the eyes!) and recognized myself in the pleasure that I was able to give.

In choosing my partner, however, I had, after a perhaps excessively eventful youth, consciously decided on firm hands and a life dedicated to the mind rather than the body. Identified through this relationship as gay, women left me in peace, even when, after more than a decade of sexual fidelity but before the encounter with Daniel, I began occasionally to have the kind of nonbinding affairs that, differently from the ones between men and women (or women and women!), according to my experience not only do not shatter a relationship but, on the contrary, give it the first real stability.

Even in Germany the equalization of gender roles has not led to a complete lack of distinction between the behavior of women and men. Flirting with a woman like that friend of Rashid's, who did not realize that I was gay, perhaps because she had never consciously had anything to do with gay men before, and who was single and at the age in which, if she wanted to have children, she would have to look for their potential father, would even in Germany have been more dangerous than the sexual act with a man—and this was Lebanon!

The risk lay in giving her the false hope of having found the man she perhaps had been looking for for a long time and would not find so quickly in Lebanon: not because he was blond but because he did not perceive her as a "defective" woman precisely because of her "masculine" manner—but as a human being. So I kissed her good-bye, like you kiss a sister whom you are wishing luck. If I had already known at that time that Rashid was playing a game that perhaps was no game at all for this boyish woman, I would not have been angry for myself but for her: Rashid's role model Zubayda, mind you, had used *female slaves* for her purposes!

RASHID AL-DAIF: Before asking him, "Why didn't you ask her for a date?" the thought of his friend, N., occurred to me, and I said to myself I was stabbing him in the back without there being any enmity between us. I remembered something I'd never really forgotten when I was in Berlin: I sometimes felt I was preventing N. from spending as much time with Joachim as he'd have liked.

I remember in particular an afternoon when we visited the Jewish Museum in Berlin and planned to go to the Literaturhaus to have dinner. Joachim hesitated before agreeing to my suggestion to have dinner there. He said to me first that he couldn't because he had to return, then fell silent. I considered the matter closed and was planning to have dinner alone and wait for a reading from a recently published novel in German, translated from French. Joachim returned and when we reached the Literaturhaus, he said, "Let's have dinner here." I noticed at that moment he'd been on the phone longer than usual, but I didn't take the thought any further or try to explain it. Right after dinner, we had to go up to the room where the reading would be held. Suddenly, he said, "I have to return home. N. likes me to be with him in the evening." I realized then the meaning of the unusual telephone conversation. It also dawned on me that I was dealing with a person in a relationship and that this was something I hadn't before fathomed. I noticed the relationship between two men had its obligations. The man had to return in the evening to the other man in this relationship just as a man in a marriage has to return to his wife. I noticed I didn't ask him about his partner as I would ask any other married man about his wife. I noticed I behaved with him as if his conjugal commitment had no existence, as if he were a bachelor and not attached. Such concerns didn't exist in my culture. The intimate relationship between two men in my "spontaneous" culture was secret, not public. I realized I now had to take into consideration this relationship, not to forget to ask about N. from time to time and to suggest he accompany us when I invited Joachim someplace, or when we decided to do an activity, just as I would with a married man. I'm not used to such behavior. I say in all frankness, in our countries this behavior would immediately cause laughter and make one feel embarrassed. It's something almost impossible, except perhaps in extremely limited and isolated circles that resemble an underground.

Joachim seemed somewhat sad and embarrassed when he withdrew from the reading to return home or, as we would say when talking about a man and wife, "to return to the arms" of his partner. I asked myself at the same time whether I projected this into his behavior and his face or if he really was like this. In other words, was I reading according to the alphabet I knew how to read—or was I reading according to the right alphabet?

When Joachim left the room a few minutes before the reading began, I wanted to ask him to send my apologies to N. for delaying him that evening from his appointed return, but I didn't because this had simply not yet become a part of me. In addition to other questions, I asked myself after Joachim's departure whether N. felt jealous about Joachim spending all that time with me, working for the most part. I imagined what might happen between them by way of reproaches, give-and-take, and accounts to make—all because of me. I was embarrassed. Yes, in a way, I was embarrassed such a thing could happen. Then I blamed myself for being inattentive to the matter of their being a "married" couple and completely like man and wife or maybe even much more so. The link that bound them was more profound than the link between a man and a woman because society had made them suffer for it until it finally accepted them for who they are. Maybe they paid a very high price for their established situation, so what they had between them was no joke but rather serious—to the point of tragedy, perhaps. Maybe to this day they continue to suffer from numerous obvious and subtle discriminations and exclusions.

I remembered here that we would read anecdotes about homosexuals as curiosities in books of Arab literary history. It's not at all a curiosity, as anyone who consults the account of Ibn Munadhir in *al-Aghani* (*The Songs*) by Isfahani can see. The matter is certainly deeper than that. Ibn Munadhir was one of the most eloquent poets, knowledgeable and well versed in the Arabic language and an inspiration for its finest practitioners. He was enamored of Abd al-Majid Ibn Abd al-Wahhab al-Thaqafi, a brilliant expert in the Hadith, who was cited by the greatest Hadith scholars. It is said of them that one evening after prayer Ibn Munadhir left the mosque in Basra and Abd al-Majid followed him, and they conversed all night until dawn. If Abd al-Majid left to go home, Ibn Munadhir accompanied him until they reached Abd al-Majid's home, then Abd al-Majid would accompany Ibn Munadhir back to his home. Neither could bear to leave the other until morning!

It was also told about them that Abd al-Majid "was very gravely ill in Basra and Ibn Munadhir took care of him, nursing him and serving him himself, scorning to delegate tasks to anyone. A visitor who saw him with his own eyes reported: 'I went one day to visit Abd al-Majid. Ibn Munadhir was there and had heated water for his friend to drink, but his condition only worsened and he moaned, "Ah!" in a weak voice. At that, Ibn Munadhir plunged his own hand in the hot water to share Abd al-Majid's pain, scalding his hand almost to the point of it falling off before we managed to pull it out and cry, "Are you crazy? What are you doing? Does this do any good?" Ibn Munadhir only replied, "I'm helping him! This is the least I can do!"'"

It worried me to think I might come between a married couple, untying a strong and precious knot between them, but I said to myself that I shouldn't get mixed up in these concerns. I came to do a job that must be accomplished to the best of my abilities and that's it. I didn't have time or energy to manage sentimental issues and especially an issue of this nature, about which I am totally ignorant. Therefore, I felt something akin to guilt after the dinner during which Joachim harmonized so well with this girl. I vowed to stop my interest in this business and leave him alone. It was up to me to stop feeling the responsibility (I almost say paternity) I acquired as a result of the confidence and friendship that was quickly established between us as a result of his openness and natural goodness. Moreover, I was certain he would refuse the expression of such feelings.

I couldn't keep myself from asking, "Does N. know about everything you're doing?" He said, "No," which surprised me and I didn't attempt to hide it. Joachim doesn't tell N. everything, but one way or another N. knows everything. He knows the broad brushstrokes if not the fine lines. The relationship between them, as it appeared to me and according to what I understood from Joachim, was more complicated than it seemed at first blush. The appearance gave the impression of considerable simplicity; the truth is—and this was a surprise for me—that they have been sleeping together in the same bed for twenty years but as far as I could tell, and I don't think I misunderstood, they have not had sexual relations for ten. It seems that the elder partner is no longer aroused except by youths and that outside this sphere he remains neutral. It also seems that the pleasure of the younger partner has changed, as pleasures of all sexes and persuasions will change. Pleasure decays with time.

JOACHIM HELFER: The fact that Rashid systematically cites ideas and observations that are mutually exclusive must mean that they are a stylistic device to portray the inner conflict he feels between observation and tradition. While, on the one hand, the Arab legacy provides a tale of how love between men can not only transcend physicality but can also lead to downright contempt for and mortification of the body, on the other hand Arab prejudice claims that gays only think about sex: an understandable misreading of the Western gay subculture, which is striking first and foremost for its flagrant exaggeration of sexuality and its significance. Rashid would have to know more about its history and take a look behind the lurid scenes in order to recognize this brazenness on display as a strategy of emancipation from shaming as the primary means of oppression.

Yet, the contradiction between beautiful literary models of soulful love and the reduction of partnership to sexuality in everyday life seems to me to be characteristic of Rashid's view of heterosexuality, which is at the very least not atypical for his society. In any case, with the single, welcome exception of the film director and her no less congenial husband, the engineer who visibly adored her, I never experienced Rashid's friends and acquaintances in Lebanon as couples or parts of a couple, but always as apparently unattached men who never gave the impression that someone was waiting for them at home.

This impression, emphasized by the demonstratively spontaneous and extravagant way they deal with time, was no doubt false in most cases; as is so often true, we differ less in practice than in the image we present of ourselves, wish to present, or believe that we must present. My suspicion is that Rashid would have found it no less strange if on that evening my *wife*, who was feeling neglected, had asked me to come home—or rather, if I had not attempted to conceal from him the fact that I had complied with this request and thus admitted having shown consideration for a *woman*. After all, one can still "return to her bosom" after an evening spent chatting with friends in the café.

In reality, on that evening I was torn between my need to discuss my day with my partner and my concern that I would do injustice to Rashid if I told everything at home in the way it had happened and had bothered me. For it was the evening after our visit to the Jewish Museum, and I freely admit that there I perceived Rashid's alphabet—different from my own in many ways—for the first and actually only time as an illiteracy that was almost unbearable.

"*Six Millions—c'est vrai*?!" he asked with an impressed look on his face, his ear pressed to one of the multilingual information terminals for basic facts. After walking through the exhibit of the not exactly copious material remains of Jewish life in Germany, he asked me how many Jews had lived there at that time. When counting Germany and Austria together I indicated six hundred thousand, a flash of recognition went through his face: "And why then does one speak of six million?" Especially since most of them came to Israel!

Although I spoiled his satisfaction in having uncovered yet another of Zionist propaganda's lies, I no longer wished to explain why I had tears in my eyes in front of an exhibit that could have come from the biography of my partner: a map of the world drawn in crayon by a boy born the same year he was, on the eve of the tide that would sweep him too to South Africa. If *that* was his political-historical consciousness, then I preferred to talk with him for the remainder of our exchange about something as harmless as sex!

For that reason I also did not ask him in Lebanon when he brought me to see the former Israeli military prison al-Khiyam in the southern part of the country temporarily occupied by the Israelis, which Hezbollah had turned into a memorial site, why he had not wished to see a concentration camp memorial site in Germany. In consideration of his feelings I also refrained from commenting that the two deceased among more than ten thousand prisoners in several years of war, who were honored there as so-called martyrs, did not exactly attest to their Israeli adversaries' will to annihilate them. Sometimes you just have to hold your tongue in order to continue a dialogue.

And so I returned that evening to the arms of my partner, who always sees and knows everything that goes on in my soul without wanting to know precisely or monitor every little detail of my everyday life.

RASHID AL-DAIF: The truth is that every time I decided to get out of this sphere of interests and to limit my attention and conversations to politics, society, culture, literature, and the novel, I saw myself drawn more and more deeply into it. You can't forget your colleague is gay. This is a matter that keeps cropping up in your mind in a most vivid way, refusing to sink below the surface of consciousness quickly or easily. That's what I discovered about myself, and I don't think it's a personal quirk peculiar to me alone. Indeed, I'm almost sure it's a cultural matter characterizing people generally in our countries. If I can't be sure about the situation in Germany, I am sure I never spoke with anyone who knew Joachim without his homosexuality featuring prominently in the discussion in one way or another.

In addition to that, Joachim, by nature, will help you to stay within this train of thought and not to forget it. I'm little acquainted with persons like him who have no secrets of any kind and who take the position (with me?) that personal and intimate relations are not secret; rather, they can be discussed as if they were a public matter. Joachim is a person who has conquered his shyness, and this is why, in this situation, he conceals nothing and talks about himself as if he were talking about a character in one of his novels. To a large extent, he's capable of speaking about himself from a distance as if he "himself" were independent from the speaking "I."

I, too, am the kind of person who enjoys distancing himself from what is close to him in order to discuss it as neutrally as possible and who enjoys also even distancing the "self" in order to narrate it. That's my nature. This of course doesn't mean I don't like anything close or that I don't like myself. On the contrary, I'm one of those who always say human beings can love someone, a group, or a religion to the point of martyrdom while remaining at the same time critical and neutral toward it. To keep from going blind.

In any case, I return to Joachim's relationship with the girl I invited to dinner for him. He didn't ask her for a date, but I understood from him that it was possible to ask her out and that it was maybe even incumbent upon him to get to know her, be it out of mere curiosity.

Joachim's sentimental "preoccupations" were certainly not the only subject of our conversations. We discussed various topics, and the program's list of prescheduled activities was full. In addition, outside the parameters of the program we decided on the spur of the moment to undertake various cultural, social, sightseeing and entertainment activities. Everything whetted our appetite for conversation. We talked about driving in the streets of Beirut, the weather, the mountains, the coast, and countless other things. We gave talks at Lebanese American University, the American University of Beirut, and St. Joseph University, as well as at the Antelias Cultural Union and the University Students' Club in Tripoli. We had meetings with writers, poets, and journalists. We visited places I assumed would help Joachim to form as complete an idea as possible of the situation in Lebanon and in the region, from Khiyam Prison in the south where resistance fighters were tortured to the cedars in the north by way of the Sabra and Shatila refugee camps—famous, unfortunately, for the slaughter that took place there. Among other activities, we ate home cooking and in restaurants throughout the country and sat in the famous cafés of Beirut.

JOACHIM HELFER: What we did *not* do is more enlightening: make an appearance at the country's largest university, the Arab one, as we did at the three smaller, finer, English- or French-language universities (the professor most likely did not wish to be seen with a homosexual in his own domain), although, in contrast to the other three, it even had a German department. Conversely, it was characteristic of my naïveté that I interpreted Rashid's failure to pass on my offer to make myself available to the students of German there for a reading and discussion, without honorarium of course, as Middle Eastern sloppiness.

Nevertheless Rashid observed correctly that the greater tolerance in the West in no way means that there are no longer any reservations there. What distinguishes us, whether truly as a result of the Enlightenment, as one likes to believe in the West, or rather in reaction to a history that is unimaginably painful by Arab standards, is far less tradition than a small head start in development.

Thus, Paragraph 175, in the stricter version of the Nazis, was not liberalized until the twentieth year of the Federal Republic, the fifth year of my life, and not completely abolished until I was an adult. Courts of my country refused compensation to the few thousand survivors who, on the basis of this paragraph, were tortured and castrated in concentration camps but not killed like ten thousand more, with the argument that justice had been done to them.

My generation, different from Daniel's, is still conditioned by the fear we felt, at least in our youth, of being identifiable as homosexuals—not to mention my partner's generation, which still suffered genuine persecution. In contrast, in the West there is, specifically in regard to our relationship, which is more Greek in the classical sense than modern precisely because it transgresses generational boundaries, an almost universal societal reservation that is getting even worse and is also shared by the gay subculture. And in Germany whoever writes about all this quickly lands in the ghetto of gay books. No, we are still far from having an emancipated and enlightened relationship to sex and sexuality.

The more interesting question is why indeed did Rashid wish to forget my sexual proclivities? Does tolerance, for example, consist perhaps in forgetting the difference of those who are different—rather than, in fact, consciously putting up with it? Apparently my sexual orientation played no role during our visit to a Palestinian camp—or perhaps it did? For I had traveled, after all, as an indivisible human being, had taken my charisma and receptivity, including the erotic kind, along with me to the Middle East and had noticed the glances that I attracted as much as the ones that I cast.

Rashid's wish to banish the fact of my being like that from his consciousness by way of political discussions arose by no means from the intolerance that he grew up with and from which he had already emancipated himself as a high school student, but from the concept of tolerance of the post-totalitarian West: as false as it is comfortable, it simply denies all differences.

To relinquish the basis for moral judgment by foregoing all distinctions may be understandable in light of the many human beings who are tormented in the name of a false morality; the old false moral judgment is not revised in this fashion but instead, so to speak, only suspended. I, however, have never harmed anyone in any way with my sexuality, having at all times moved within the boundaries that have been drawn rationally by morality—and have no need for anyone to look away mercifully.

The question is how many people must be murdered on the streets of Europe before the West, and with it also its admirer Rashid, comprehends how life-threatening it is when one looks away in pseudotolerance and that no society can endure without binding concepts of right and wrong. Homosexual and heterosexual love can flourish alongside one another in mutual acknowledgement and respect, no different than Jewish, Muslim, and Christian communities; rule of law and vendetta, equality and patriarchy, tolerance and intolerance are mutually exclusive.

RASHID AL-DAIF: Amidst all these activities came a phone call from a woman who worked in the Beirut Goethe Institute. She said a journalist from an English-language Beirut daily wanted to interview us. I told her that I couldn't hold a conversation in English, but she said the journalist spoke French and had a bit of colloquial Arabic and that she had German origins and German was virtually her maternal tongue. With Joachim next to me as I spoke with the woman, we settled on four o'clock in the afternoon of that same day to meet at the Goethe Institute.

At the main entrance to the Institute we met a woman whom Joachim approached, thinking she was the journalist who was waiting for us. She soon made it clear that she was a German journalist living for some time in Beirut as a correspondent for a Berlin daily, but she wasn't waiting for us. This journalist was shorter than Joachim, which was obvious to me when I saw them shake hands. She smoked. She wore a long dress that reached down to the middle of her shins and athletic sneakers that didn't go all that well with her dress. The strange thing about this is I found myself trying to see this woman through Joachim's eyes. This was impossible. How could I do that? What attracted my attention to her was her backside; it continued straight down from her back and the cheeks were not round or protuberant. Her hair was also cut *à la garçonne*. It was very short.

Her body was straight, like that of a conquering general who had won historically decisive battles. She stood proudly—why? I couldn't understand what motivated her pride—and with something haughty and maybe challenging about her also. Her head was lifted slightly back, as one who is trying to see the tip of her nose. Maybe

144   because of this, she had an influential presence. It was a strong presence. After a short time, an employee of the Institute arrived and informed us that the journalist who wanted to meet us was waiting on the second floor, so we went directly up, but I noticed that Joachim lagged behind me a little, talking with the woman who was with us.

The journalist who worked at the English-language Beirut daily asked us many questions and we responded, Joachim in German and I in French, with Joachim or her translating for me what the other was saying in German. She asked us about our writing styles and subject matter and our points of view on the things we saw together. After she asked all her questions and it seemed to me the interview had ended and our conversation had morphed into a trading of comments on various topics, I indicated my desire to leave. Joachim did likewise, but (Coincidence! Coincidence!) at that very moment the director of the Goethe Institute entered and suggested to all three of us that we attend the vernissage of a Lebanese artist's work. I declined because I was really feeling tired and needed to get home to rest, but Joachim accepted the director's invitation and so did the journalist. I excused myself, said good-bye to everyone, and asked Joachim to call me after the vernissage, mentioning I was prepared to accompany him that evening if he wished.

Joachim didn't call that night. I wondered to myself whether he hadn't seen Sader, the gay Lebanese whom he'd met the day after his arrival in Lebanon. I always thought he was with Sader or on that track when he didn't show up without giving any sign.

JOACHIM HELFER: Hm, if I don't hear jealousy in those words . . . In any case, Rashid always wanted to know exactly where I was at all times, what I was doing, whom I was meeting, preferably via hour-long telephone conversations, whereas in Berlin I seldom arranged to meet him more than three times a week; after all, we were not a married couple. I attributed it to a different understanding of hospitability, reinforced by the difference in our ages, which might in fact have caused him to feel an almost paternal responsibility for me. It never occurred to me that he might be less concerned about my security than my chastity.

Thus, I engaged in such lecherous adventures behind his back as a trip to the old stones of Baalbek by taxi over High Lebanon and across the Bekaa Plain. When the lights went out in the exhibit hall furnished by a German archaeologist beneath the two temples of Hellenistic Heliopolis (because the electricity supply had broken down, as is often the case in Lebanon), I finally allowed myself to do what I had always wanted to do but never could have done unseen in the ancient collections in Europe: I placed an admiring hand on the marble behind of the Torso of Apollo.

One sees not only with the eyes—but also just as much, at least, with the mind: when in Berlin's Altes Museum I led Rashid to the Greek bronze of the boy raising his hands in adoration of the sun, which had already enchanted old Fritz (Frederick the Great) and radiates a sensual aura that eluded not even Rashid, he asked me, "*C'est un garçon?*" (Is that a boy?). The genitals, albeit still those of a child and slightly under standard for the classical ideal of beauty, are nevertheless clearly male and were close enough to touch!

This time, instead of turning away in disgust he walked as if he were being pulled against his will around the sculpture, which more than satisfies Hellenism's aesthetic requirement that the object be beautiful from every angle—which it is from behind in more of a female than a male way. Relieved, after all, not to have found a boy to be erotic but, seen in this way, a girl, he drew the conclusion when leaving—as generous as it was conciliatory—that upon seeing *that* even he *himself* could almost understand what Plato was writing about in the *Symposium*!

Using the same procedure, only in reverse, he also saw the journalist through my eyes—which could only mean, through what he considers to be my eyes. Just as he castrated the Berlin boy using the scissors in his head in order to delight unhindered in the girlish figure, he also excised all curves from her athletic but by no means unfeminine figure, assuming that they would bother me.

What he himself must have found unsettling was precisely her imposingness; hence the strange assertion that she was smaller than I was, which in relationships between men and women, especially of the same ethnic background, is statistically the norm and hardly worth mentioning. Only, she was not smaller than Rashid, even in flats (they were sandals)! The fact that she, as a German, was able to conduct an interview for an English-language newspaper in French, and in addition spoke literary Arabic and understood the Lebanese dialect, must have aggravated his anxiety.[5]

But above all, her body language must have intimidated him: this was indeed not a girl or a little woman, this was a young woman of the tribe that had already given the Romans the culture shock that women can also take up the sword when freedom must be defended; Rashid took flight . . .

RASHID AL-DAIF: On the morning of the following day, we had a date to go to my house in the mountains in Ehden, at fourteen hundred fifty meters above sea level and a hundred kilometers from Beirut. He arrived at the appointed time and everything seemed normal, but this normality was mixed with something else. He tended toward silence in the car, my car that I drove myself. When we arrived in Junieh, some thirty kilometers from Beirut, I asked him, "What's bothering you? Tell me."

So he told me.

I could never have guessed what he was about to tell me. He said: "As of last night, I'm a father!" and went on, "During the vernissage yesterday evening, I saw the German journalist we'd met at the entrance of the building and who I thought had been waiting for us. Afterwards, I remained at the Institute talking with her, and then she suggested we go somewhere to have a beer. I accepted. She took me to a nice place in Monot Street well known for its nightlife. She knows Beirut and its nightspots well. We drank beer like two Germans and at the end of the evening continued on to her place nearby, and we ended up in bed together."

"Naked?" I asked in naïve surprise.

"Naked."

He said, "When we reached the critical moment, she got up and left the room, to come back shortly afterwards and state: 'I don't have a condom.' I replied without thinking for an instant

---

5. Rashid al-Daif's text indicates a female journalist other than the woman we will come to know as Ingrid conducted the joint interview. Joachim Helfer's text explains that Ingrid conducted the interview.

about what I would say, 'I'll be a father,' and that's how I became a father."

I said, "Wait a bit to see if it's so," but he replied, "Waiting won't change a thing."

"Oh my God," I said to myself. "What's happening? Has Germany been restored overnight? So has the German come back to his senses?"

He said, "This was the first time in twenty years or maybe more. This was the first time I slept with a woman!"

A wave of questions swept over me, and I couldn't decide which one to ask first. The event stirred an irrepressible curiosity in me. I was before a "literary" truth, as it were, one of those truths that seem tailor-made for writing. I asked him first if he'd enjoyed being with her as he enjoyed being with a man, and he responded in the affirmative. The point of my question was clear to him; I wanted to know whether the pleasure with her was superficial and ephemeral or authentic, genuine, and capable of lasting, so he added, "I had much and deep pleasure with her." I said to him, joking, "Germany has returned to its senses, then?" He smiled and said nothing.

"What attracted you to her and changed the course of your life?" I asked. He replied, "I don't know."

They talked a lot together, and she was attracted to him in particular after a few experiences with Lebanese men who didn't treat her as she liked to be treated or according to required conduct. There was, according to her as a German, something boorish in their behavior. It was as if they were simply emptying the contents of their scrotums and then leaving. Joachim remarked, "She saw something different in the way I treated her, an interest, a tenderness, and the like." Did he say "tenderness"? I didn't comment on what he'd said, but his remarks reminded me of a comment a Lebanese friend always made when he talked about relations he'd had with married women, "Her husband is inadequate," although he'd say it in the colloquial, "Hubby's not up to scratch!"

He said the probability of pregnancy was very high because she was in her fertile period, and she was in agreement with him that they would continue their encounter without a condom. She smiled when he told her, "I'm a father," and stretched out next to him on the bed, clinging to him, free of all constraints, free of all embarrassment, free of all calculation. A transformation had occurred over the course of a few moments. What had happened between them became more serious and acquired continuity. Together they initiated a continuity. The moment embraced the present and the future together.

Joachim was agitated as he related all this, and the thought crossed my mind that he was on the verge of tears as he asked with a wistfulness he could not conceal what his mother's feelings about this would've been if she were alive and he could tell her. He wished she were still alive; she'd have been delighted. It surprised me he remembered his mother. I'd have expected anything but for him to remember his mother at that particular time. "How ugly clichés are!" I thought. How is it Germans are said to be cold? I remembered when my wife was pregnant, I didn't think about my mother at all— or my father, who had died more than twenty years before.

Joachim spoke as if the pregnancy had occurred and giving birth was a sure thing after the required interval. On the road to Ehden, he chose a name for his son: Sebastian. I told him in jest, "Call him by my name, Rashid, then you'll become Abu Rashid. That will be your nickname in our countries." He wasn't convinced, so I said, "Then call him Lebanon, the name of the place that changed your life," but this suggestion didn't meet with favor either. I corrected myself, "Unless maybe this event didn't change the course of your life." He didn't respond. He liked the name Sebastian, so I started to call him from that time on "Abu Sebastian," according to the Arab custom I explained to him of calling the parents by the name of their eldest male child.

He said he'd tell his son early on of his father's homosexuality. He said he was confident that human beings could accept anything when they're young. "And what if your son grows up to be like you, gay?" I asked. "I can't do anything about that," he said. "That will be his lot and destiny, and it's not up to us to try to oppose it."

Joachim was agitated but there was no crisis. No psychological crisis. No financial crisis. No procedural crisis even. The matter seemed simple to him and this surprised me. Once again, I asked myself, "Am I reading this according to the right alphabet or according to the alphabet I know?"

JOACHIM HELFER: Rashid is by all means a master of the novelist's craft: the tweaking and deleting that first make one of life's contingencies into an event worthy of literature. Part of this consists in making real people into characters by embellishing or inventing things that they never really said in so many words, although they could have—even should have—said them in an interpretation of their own stories. This is acceptable. The meaning of this dialogic experiment can lie neither in unveiling the truth of my private life to a marveling audience nor in my literary treatment of it, but solely in unearthing culturally conditioned differences in our two views of it.

I wish only to point out those distinctions between life and literature that indicate how different our ideas of sexuality and gender roles are. This begins already with the point in time: with the exception of a few passages, the drive to his country house happened approximately the way he described it—only not on the day after our meeting with the journalist, but rather several days later.

This is important because the image of the Western woman with whom you somehow inevitably end up in bed—as a nightcap, so to speak—is an Arab cliché comparable to that of the beer-drinking German; I did not, after all, revert immediately to *all* of my discarded school habits in Lebanon to the extent that I would have drunk beer for one evening instead of wine. She had asked me what Rashid and I actually discussed with one another the whole time, and in her apartment I discovered the bookcase of a sociologist and Arabist who was interested in gender studies.

Thus, we talked until the break of dawn about men and women, love and sex, hetero- and homosexuality, about my happy gay life with a longtime companion, as well as about her relationships, which never succeeded in the long run, the fear of commitment of her Prince Charmings who were not turned into frogs by kisses but indeed by the mere mention of the word "child," about the loyalty of her gay friends, and about her lovers, who, since they were men (especially Arab men!), Rashid, himself a man, most likely believes always promptly abandoned her—the woman from abroad—whereas I told him exactly the opposite: that it was Ingrid who threw out her lovers, whether Arab or German, as soon as they began to play the tough guy.

If there was anything in particular about Lebanese men that got on her nerves, it was not a lack of consideration, as is reported by Rashid's character "Joachim," but rather precisely the controlling and dominating behavior that masks itself as concern—I was familiar with it from Rashid. In contrast to him, she had noticed how shaken up I was at that time: my partner had received a disconcerting medical diagnosis. It was not yet confirmed and, in any case, without immediate consequences, which is why he was able to persuade me to fulfill my obligations in Lebanon instead of following my impulse to return home at once.

But also, because of the unusually long separation, I was overcome for the first time by a foretaste of the solitude that at some point awaited me. This was our mood, the sudden horror of children in the face of time, a horror of the fact that they have long since ceased to be children; in this mood we talked about our childhoods, about the families in which we grew up, her relationship with her parents, the fact that I had still not come to terms with the death of my mother a few years previously, about my father, who had long since passed away and had been my father almost exclusively in the biological sense.

Apparently, we were very compatible in terms of our backgrounds and many basic characteristics and values; we could quarrel with each other like siblings; there was a certain kinship, in the nonbiological sense, even if at that time we did not yet know that our parents had actually known each other since college and certainly not that my father had once proposed to her mother before he married my own mother—if I really believed in something like Providence I would have a reason to do so . . . In brief: we liked each other, and the silence we maintained about what we were missing in our lives became clearer and clearer; or rather, the silence about what we wanted to give back to life.

When, after kissing each other good-bye, we soon made another date and she finally came along to my hotel room, we were both conscious of the reason. For that reason we did not use a condom and not because neither one of us had one in our possession—and indeed, we never mentioned it once. In the nature of things, my certainty of having become a father could only mean the conception

first carried out in my mind (i.e., the irrevocable "Yes!" to the idea
of creating life, or rather passing it on, that I heard in myself when
I noticed that we had omitted what we—two enlightened children of
the AIDS generation—never would have omitted otherwise or would
ever consider omitting).

Yet there was a profound pleasure in this "Yes!"—although the
claim that it had been "the same pleasure as with a man" would hardly
be compatible with Rashid's view of how I had come to my senses!
For the order that he was talking about appeared not to consist
in passing along life: Why else would he ask me if my fatherhood
might possibly have changed my life? He cannot have meant: Will
you not be a father when you are a father? Even the worst father is
and remains irreversibly a father—precisely this existential truth is
poeticized by the paternal Arab names that he cited.

He can only have meant: Will you be a man from now on? What
appears to be important for Rashid is the act itself, which needs to
be neither an act of love nor procreation in order to restore order
(i.e., the subordination of woman under man). "I have become
a father!" would therefore merely be a by-product of what really
counts: "I have become heterosexual!"—which was not a question
because there can be no question of that.

RASHID AL-DAIF: What made matters easier for him was that
his partner accepted the idea even though she hadn't expected it.
Doubtless, she felt a need for a child but not a pressing need, and the
notion hadn't crossed her mind that this would happen to her now
at this particular instant. I translated for Joachim on that occasion
the Arabic saying that coincidence is better than an appointment.
What also made this risky matter easy for Joachim was his partner's
apartment in Berlin and that she could count on her parents' support
since she was an only child and they were well off. They could support
their daughter and her child even if their daughter was forced to
remain out of work for a long time. This put Joachim considerably
at ease—the apartment and the support (or at least partial support).

The concern for the apartment was very understandable
because he'd lived with his partner for a long time and didn't
imagine himself one day outside this partnership, this home, or

152 this couple. The apartment permitted him to have perhaps two houses. More precisely, the woman's apartment represented for him something of a temporary escape in order to catch his breath and make decisions without hurrying and without the pressure of having to find a quick solution. Joachim didn't yet have time to think about these things and wasn't yet used to looking at them from all angles. He was still under the influence of the initial shock and had spent only a few hours in this stage of the metamorphosis. Pregnancy, parenthood, the child's home, responsibility for its existence, and everything resulting from a person's saying yes to having a child, he consciously accepted—even if he was quick and impetuous about it. He'd have to face all these issues in the near future. That's what I said to myself and what I tried to get across to him as much as our conversation permitted. He didn't yet know what he was going to do about all of this.

I remembered on that occasion an autobiography, *The Secret Life of Salvador Dalí*. I was astonished when I read things in it that applied to me directly. Dalí writes that a person cannot know in advance where his feelings will lead, as if he were riding them and they were leading him wherever they pleased, sometimes independently of his will. He relates events that happened to him as illustrations, such as how, when he was a boy, he once pushed a visiting friend his own age from a bridge a couple of meters high and without railings. The boy, whom Dalí loved, fell, broke bones, and almost died. This is something I have a personal knowledge about. I mean I've lived it, I live it now, and I know that I'll live it in the future—according to my nature, not according to Salvador Dalí's, of course. I think this is what was happening to Joachim.

He mentioned many things and revealed many feelings to me on the way to Ehden that day. We talked about everything the event evoked in us without limits and however the thoughts came to us. We had plenty of time because of a traffic jam choking the northern exit from Beirut and because the automobile is an intimate place conducive to conversation. We didn't talk about whether Joachim would tell his friend, N., which surprised me a great deal because I had expected that to be the first point we'd discuss. I waited in vain for the appropriate moment until I finally asked him, "What about N.? When are you going to tell him?" He didn't say, but he did say, "I'm trying to imagine what his reaction will be." He was wondering whether he should tell him by phone from Beirut or wait until he returned to tell him face-to-face. He was leaning toward telling him in person.

Events were rushing ahead and he'd not yet had time to catch his breath. He couldn't escape, and in any case he didn't want to. He feared leaving N., who had become elderly, to old age and loneliness. Or maybe he didn't fear so much as reject it. I don't know. When I see something, I always ask myself which alphabet I'm reading it by.

I recall a French friend married to a man twenty-five years older than she. She was around fifty when he reached seventy-five. As he grew old, she became free to have sexual relations with others. She didn't tell him about these relations, but she insisted on being with him to give him his medicine and on being in the house at his bedtime, around ten o'clock. She told me he'd been her professor and had taught her a lot. She fell in love with him, married him, and gave him two children, but he'd become another person "to a certain extent," she added, and said she was committed to him and could not stray from her commitment.

It seemed to me that Joachim's imagination couldn't admit the possibility of living outside the home of his partner N. Would N. accept Joachim's friend and a newborn to live with them? I don't think Joachim knew in advance whether N. would accept this. He might not even have asked himself the question yet.

JOACHIM HELFER: Well, I think it makes a difference whether you jump into the cold water yourself or push someone else from the bridge: for the unforeseen opportunity of still becoming a father I would have taken the risk of a hard, gravel-bed landing because the stream of love had unexpectedly run dry, but I would certainly not have risked breaking my partner's heart. Is it a legacy of the Greeks to intensify all conflict to the point of tragedy when real life is much better suited for drama and comedy?

Yet, it is by no means a Middle Eastern tendency but a Western one to make the most natural thing in the world artificially more complicated, to understand children not as part of real life (which, after all, is never perfect but always temporary, cobbled together from all sorts of considerations and compromises) but to imagine them instead only in the ideal sphere of the nuclear family from the margarine commercial: perfect, uncompromising, happy, and absolutely deterring. Or rather, this split in consciousness is typical of the West, especially of Germany; it gives rise to family policies that are still today oriented toward an ideal image that everyone knows is increasingly rare in reality, while more and more real households of children and adults are disadvantaged in comparison to childless married couples, for example in tax law.

Rashid, the Western-oriented Arab, reproduces this schizophrenia in his concerns for me: for it is known that his own child grew up with his mother in Lyon, completely without his father, and not because Rashid would not have been allowed to move to France but because the mother wanted it that way. Perhaps, in the long run, Rashid's proximity and constant physical presence would have annoyed her just as mine would have annoyed Ingrid—in any case, it is significant that Rashid does not compare the two cases, which in terms of their outcomes are not dissimilar. The only noticeable difference for the child consists in the distance between the parents, both emotional and spatial: in his case, the bitterness of divorce and a five-hour flight; in my case, heartfelt understanding and five stops on the subway.

Rashid does not, however, seem to be concerned about the child and its practical living conditions, or indeed about practical matters at all, but rather about the theory and symbolism of a relationship structure that is foreign to him: the fact that it goes without saying that I will continue to live with the man of my choice, but without wife and child, because I need the male spirit of our partnership to live like I need air to breathe, whereas in the long run I would suffocate in what Thomas Mann called *Weiberluft* (women's air); the fact that Ingrid would live in her own apartment with our child but without its father, not as a sacrifice but because she did not wish to burden her parenting with the risks of a relationship in which, as she knows from life experience, she would sooner or later feel restricted—this appears for Rashid to be the cultural fault line.

Yet Rashid's apartment, mind you, is also not kept up to snuff by a girlfriend but by a housekeeper, and whoever imagines the life of an extremely productive novelist who earns his living as a university professor can hardly believe that much time and space remain for wife and family. The fact that she, especially as a woman, acts according to a logic consistent with the incompatibility of men and women provokes the Arab male, even making Rashid spiteful toward the character Ingrid, whom he ought to elevate to the status of goddess as the savior of my soul for heterosexual heaven.

What he appears to resent is that she is neither simpleminded nor naïve. Above all he resents that, rather than passively tolerating events, she actively takes initiative, that Ingrid finds Joachim to be the most suitable father not out of ignorance and not in spite of, but precisely because of the irreducible fact of his being like that and not otherwise, and precisely because he lives in a relationship that also allows her freedom (while she does not have to share him with other women).

Horrified by how independent a woman ultimately can be, he also prefers in matters of support to think back to the ideal material dependency of the family than to recognize that a college-educated and employed woman may need the assistance of the father for raising and supporting the child but not for her own livelihood, in spite of the fact that there are self-supporting women in Beirut, particularly in Rashid's progressive circle; here, too, Rashid's imagined roles correspond less to the society in which he lives than to the one in which he wishes, or rather does not wish, to live. In it, Joachim, his partner, and Sader are only embarrassing; Ingrid, however, is a genuine annoyance.

RASHID AL-DAIF: When we were on the road to Ehden, Joachim mentioned several times a desire to contact his female friend when we arrived. As soon as we entered the house, he asked permission to use the mobile phone and went out on the balcony for privacy while he spoke with her, even though they spoke in German and I wouldn't have understood a thing if he'd stayed with me. Actually, I would have. I'd have understood a lot—in fact, everything. Even if he was speaking with her in German, his proximity to me would've meant that he wasn't alone with her. "That's love," I said to myself.

Is it possible? Did Joachim fall in love with this journalist whom he'd met only yesterday? Was it love at first sight, *un coup de foudre,* as the French would say? After the first call, it wasn't more than two hours before he called her again. Each time he had to ask my permission because he'd left his own mobile in Germany. I grew annoyed with myself because I'd become like a warden to him, so I placed the phone on the table we were sitting at and told him to make himself at home and use the phone without asking permission whenever he wanted.

We'd agreed to stay in Ehden as long as we felt like it, but he indicated a desire to return to Beirut the following day, so we returned the next day in the afternoon. I dropped him off at the hotel, leaving him free to contact me for dinner and an evening out if he wished—or not if that were his pleasure. He didn't call until the following morning, when he informed me of some bad news, the gist of which was that N. had skin cancer, was very anxious, and wished that Joachim were by his side because he'd had medical tests and was awaiting the results that would show if it was malignant.

This bad news pained Joachim greatly and he felt somewhat guilty for being far from N., but he did not decide to cut short his trip and return immediately to Berlin in order to be at his friend's side, as N. had wished and as Joachim would've wished if he'd not been committed for two more weeks. Since his arrival in Beirut, Joachim wouldn't leave his hotel room without first speaking with N. It was N. who called every morning, but Joachim began to call him sometimes during the day to check on him. He spent the next few days worrying until the test results came back. Finally, the tests showed no call for alarm. The matter was serious, requiring treatment and follow-up, but it wasn't the dire fate it had seemed at the beginning.

Once Joachim was reassured about N., I proposed that we spend the following weekend in Ehden and that he invite his journalist friend. He welcomed the invitation but said he'd have to consult with her before he could say yes or no. I told him it was natural for a man and woman to consult with each other, especially at the beginning of their relationship. His friend declined the invitation because her work required her to stay in Beirut for the municipal elections that were taking place at that time. "And you?" I asked. "Would you like to go without her?" He said, "No, I'd prefer to stay."

I don't remember a day that passed since his friend's pregnancy without our talking about it or something related to it, if only in passing. He anticipated the time of her period with worry and impatience. He didn't want to announce the news before being completely sure she was pregnant, so he asked me several times to keep the news of their liaison secret. He said this was her will; he didn't tell her I knew about the relationship and its details. Even so, she wasn't so simple as to not suspect I knew.

Matters stayed so during the time remaining in Joachim's trip, and we continued our activities and performing our duties for the program that united us. We also discussed this unusual event as the time approached for his return to Berlin. With some Lebanese and German friends, I decided to give him a farewell dinner on the evening of his departure. We invited him and his friend. Before the appointed time, I passed by the hotel where he was staying to pick him up and take him to the restaurant. She was with him and came down from his room with him. Naturally, I wasn't surprised by this; on the contrary, it was to be expected (by me anyway). What surprised me was something else—the presence of Sader at the dinner.

I didn't expect Sader to be among those attending the dinner. In fact, I surprised myself by feeling as if I were disturbed by this presence. I didn't ask Joachim who had invited him. That question, as I said to myself, would seem as though I were sticking my nose into his business, and maybe he'd take it as an implicit reproach and be embarrassed by it. It would look as though I were saying to him that since he was now awaiting a baby, he should adopt a more critical posture and not permit himself such transgressions. That's not what I wanted to do at all. It was not my intention. Of course, I wasn't naïve to the point of claiming I expected him to change his behavior after his friend's pregnancy. But I surprised myself that I behaved as if I aimed for this, or as if I were driven by this desire without being conscious of it.

I didn't ask him then who invited Sader to the evening's dinner, but I guessed that it must have been him since who else could it have been? I observed his friend, who seemed as if she was alone most of the time even though she was among us and with us. She carried a glass in her hand as a princess would, observing, not waiting for anybody and not expecting anything from anybody. She observed as if she were in the party and above it because she was several days pregnant and self-contained. As for Joachim, it was clear that he wanted to be with her but Sader occupied him much. Finally, he returned to her and remained by her side, and they began talking between themselves or with others, and to Sader, of course. I asked myself whether he'd told her anything about Sader, and in truth I know nothing about his relationship with Sader—I don't even know if there ever was a "relationship" in the first place. Joachim didn't tell me anything about it, and I didn't want to ask.

Of course, Joachim told his friend about his relationship with N. It was inescapable and impossible to hide even if he'd wanted to. Yet he could have hidden his new "relationship" with Sader. It was clear to me that Joachim sought to consolidate his relationship with Sader, and it was clear that he wanted this relationship to continue. At the same time, next to him was a woman, pregnant by him, who no doubt knew about the relationship. He told me himself that he'd told her just about everything, so she was doubtless in agreement with all these relationships and had no problem with him seeking out men while she was pregnant by him. She wanted from him only that drop of semen and nothing else. This phenomenon is becoming well known in Europe and the West, generally, where women have relations with men in order to become pregnant on purpose, telling the men only after becoming pregnant, or telling them after the baby is born, or not telling them at all. They want the men to stay out of their lives, informing them only because they should know. A French woman and friend who works as a psychoanalyst in Paris told me that she knows of many such cases.

Between two environments, the German and the Arab, much discussion must take place in order to clarify things. That's what I kept repeating to myself. At the end of the evening, Joachim remained with his friend and Sader and told me not to worry about taking him back to the hotel, that he'd manage a ride back. I said good-bye and left.

JOACHIM HELFER: The uncertainties—not to mention the chasms that open up here—do not separate life worlds as much as emotional worlds, worlds that I do not like to consider typically German or Arab: if my partner had wished, as Rashid portrays it, for me to return ahead of time because of his health concerns, I would have flown immediately; if I had had my way I would have given in to this impulse; I had already prepared the director of the local Goethe Institute for this contingency.

Ultimately, my reason for remaining was not the program and not even Ingrid, but solely the fact that the man I loved explicitly requested me to do so: what he wished was as much normality and as little panic as possible. In his portrayal, which mixes up the sequence of events, Rashid represses the fact that I was in a state of panic, that it was only the shock caused by the knowledge I had repressed more or less for twenty years that I could not remain for my whole life a young lover, a "son" in a certain sense, that allowed me to recognize and seize the opportunity to become a father (i.e., Rashid represses the vital relationship in which I found myself, and thank God, still find myself).

Rashid too wishes above all for normality, be it at the price of veracity and humanity. Hence his coolness toward "N.," which was already noticeable in Berlin and remains even in his report (all other main characters of his narrative are given names), which is not personally directed at N.'s real life model but indeed at his life by my side. Hence the gushing misinterpretation of what happened between Ingrid and me as a renunciation of my previous life and a return to normality, or rather *his* normality—which at the same time diminishes it from something marvelous to something conventional.

And hence his resentment of poor Sader; of course I invited him to my farewell dinner (of which, by the way, I was the host): on my last evening I wished to bring together at the table those of the many acquaintances I had made in Beirut to whom I had grown close, those people with whom it was a joy to dine and not a labor. To this group belonged also the student with the sad eyes who had shown me his city, told me his story, and in the process had also—of course—shared a moment of tenderness with me; the fact that this encounter, which Rashid even claims to have helped initiate, would remain fleeting for lack of greater common ground does not mean, however, that it was dishonorable.

One might ask how Rashid handles his own affairs when he, on the one hand, assumes that Sader and I had sex at every moment in which we were unobserved by him, but on the other hand is annoyed that I invited him to my going away party; but that is his problem. Getting along without a double standard is part of the freedom of *my* moral conduct: whoever is good enough for my bed is also good enough for my table.

RASHID AL-DAIF: Joachim doesn't like calling on the phone, and I don't like writing letters, so after his return to Berlin we exchanged only a few emails—not more than eight—and fewer phone calls. The first email I received from him was on the day of his return. He informed me of his safe return, thanked me for the hospitality, and said that he was reassured regarding the state of N.'s illness, which in spite of its seriousness was not as dramatic as it had first seemed, and this put him considerably at ease.

Joachim left in the middle of May. In mid-June, he wrote informing me that he'd visit Beirut in the second week of July and that he'd stay with his friend. In the same email, he wrote in parentheses that his friend "was not pregnant . . . not yet!" It wasn't difficult for me to grasp that the first attempt had failed, that he was coming back for a second try, and that he insisted on having a child.

Did he come upon just the right woman to achieve his desire for a child under the conditions that he wished? I don't know for sure what these conditions are, and I don't know, for that matter, whether he has a clear notion of them himself; but from our conversations, I was able to glean the essentials: a woman of independent means and housing who is content with the child and demands of him nothing else, materially or emotionally. Did Joachim insist on this return to Lebanon simply to impregnate his friend or to be a parent or both together? Did this woman touch a hidden nerve in him and is this what made him return?

Joachim decided then to return to Lebanon and to stay a week in order to give it another try with her. I reveal in all frankness this surprising news made me very happy—it "stirred" me. As they say on such occasions in the English language, *It was exciting!* I think this is a suitable expression. The news stirred me for several reasons, no doubt. I tried to resolve the matter within myself: did I want his visit to Lebanon to form a turning point in his personal history?—"in the history of a German writer!" Look closely at this expression, as if it were taken from a book. Did I want the discussions we had between us to leave a trace in him and to help push him to choose a "normal" life that I can understand? Am I traditional to such a degree? This was a way of life very far from us and not only outside all the usual but outside all acceptable possibilities in our environment. It wasn't in reality a matter entirely foreign to me personally.

I don't know for sure what pleased me or stirred my interest to this extent. It could be simply that I was before a narratable event and a truth that interested me in a literary way. This was largely because it was an unusual truth that broadened horizons and pushed back borders, and this is in the nature of literature as I see it.

Joachim decided then to return to Lebanon within two months of his departure, and I decided to welcome him as I would a close friend. A few days before his arrival, I visited a dear friend of mine who was recovering from lung cancer. We talked about everything, and I told him about the visit of a German friend the following month. He wasn't aware of the program that had brought us together or of the activities we had undertaken in Berlin and Beirut, because he'd been undergoing difficult treatment. I told him my colleague was gay and that he had met a woman here in Beirut, and began a relationship with her that was the first he'd had with a woman in twenty years. He said in the tone of a princely commander: "Then throw him a party! Give him a wedding! Make a feast!"

This friend is a theater director who studied direction in Moscow during the time of the Soviet Union and whose works were marked with distinction in the Lebanese and Arab theaters from the late 1960s through the late 1990s. He was married to a woman of a different religious community and permitted his children to adopt whatever creed or religion they desired—or not to adopt a creed or religion. He was open to the furthest limits in all political, social, and moral matters. In addition to being an avant-garde director, he was also an avant-garde human being. So he told me: "Throw him a party! Give him a wedding! Make a feast!"

I thought a lot about what he said, turning it over and looking at it from all the angles, and I thought about his motives for saying it. Many scenes in my friend's plays feature epic moments: diverse celebrations and, in particular, weddings, funerals, and fateful moments. I thought about what he'd said and asked myself whether it was a result of an overwhelming desire for joy and for life because this rude illness had depleted his energy and he was now at the stage of recovery.

So I threw him a wedding party. I invited Joachim and his friend to Ehden in July—a beautiful period of mild temperatures and deep, close skies that yield the best fruits of the summer. Ehden increases in beauty and brilliance at this time of year, especially if you compare it to Beirut in the summer months where the heat and the humidity are lethal. I invited him then to Ehden but didn't tell him what I had planned for him.

In the evening, we headed for a small outdoor restaurant near the source of a spring. I had previously agreed with the owner that he would prepare for us a wedding table and had requested that he find us a singer adept at playing the oud and singing classical Arabic and regional songs—anything that delights the heart and makes the earth shake under listeners' feet. I invited a number of friends among those who like this kind of evening entertainment, including one friend who lives to dance and to lose herself in dance. I began to organize this whole evening from the time my friend, the director, advised me to throw him a wedding party. I say throw "him" and not "them" because in truth, I didn't know her or her likes and dislikes. This is why the initiative was intended for him, not her.

Our dinner began around nine in the evening. It was a beautiful evening—a person could not hope for one more beautiful. The sky was so pure you could pluck the stars from it, and the wind was but a mild springlike breeze. Flowing water from the spring nearby was audible, and from within this wild calm, humans and jinn are altogether awestruck. The restaurant was deep in a forest classified by UNESCO as a protected natural area for its rare plants and trees. In addition to all this, the security situation in Lebanon was calm and would not worsen for a few months yet.

We drank, sang, and danced. The singer the restaurant owner had hired sang with all his heart as if he wanted to convince the "foreigners" among us of the genius of Arabic song and of his ability to entrance the mind. In this task, he succeeded brilliantly. The "bride" danced in rhythm to his songs, imitating the friend who really did lose herself in raptures of dancing, cutting loose as never before. The "bride" began shaking her belly, hips, and chest—she didn't really have a chest for the occasion, it being almost flat—and the shy and cautious "groom" also danced. I, too, danced and that is a rare event. My God, how the success of that evening made me happy! The party lasted to the wee hours, until the couple tired of dancing and had quenched their thirst for drink.

In the house everything was ready for them: the bed and the snow-white sheets just as in bygone days. At fourteen hundred fifty meters above sea level, near a window giving onto the holy Qadisha Valley and from there to the Mediterranean Sea and the world, I lit for them incense from the holy trees of Lebanon: cedar, pine, and larch. Before they entered the bedchamber, I prepared for each a cup of herbal tea made from July wildflowers, herbs, wild thyme, mint, and a drop of orange petal essence in each cup. They savored the delicious infusion.

I feared at first that Joachim might be one of those boisterous city dwellers who soon feel bored and cramped in these natural settings, but he was quite the opposite. He resembled me and yearned for a home in the mountains or in the countryside, far from the city, where he could work or take refuge when he needed solitude.

The next day, I rose before they did and prepared a special breakfast for them. I knew that Joachim didn't eat in the morning, but I was sure that this time breakfast would please him. I prepared them a breakfast, not for two but for many more: yogurt, local cheese, green olives, black olives, eggs fried in local olive oil, fresh breads topped with meat or dried thyme in olive oil, a pot of tea, and wild honey. I placed all this on the balcony table that opens to the whole world, and took leave of them, so they could have the house to themselves. I knew that Joachim always desired conversation with his friend. He made an effort to speak in French with her in my presence, which was very polite but I wanted to free them of my presence.

After a few days, Joachim returned to Berlin, leaving his seed to grow within his friend in the beautiful land of Lebanon. The probability of his friend's getting pregnant this time was very high since they'd no doubt chosen the right time.

JOACHIM HELFER: When an Arab writer begins to spin a yarn, no one should contradict him—who wants reality (hummus, curd cheese, and kebabs with pita bread for the three of us) when you can have such a poem about a wedding banquet! The Western reader who has made it this far in the text will, in any case, already have noticed that Rashid's truth is not always mine. Friendship and hospitality compel us to take a seat at the richly set table of the storyteller without protest, especially since Rashid is a generous host not only in literature but also in life: on several occasions I was allowed to pay him the honor of eating what he put in front of me . . .

Thus, Joachim tastes all of the sweets from the kitchen of the Arab poet, although he knows that they cannot possibly be good for his figure—happy, as long as he is eating, not to have to dance any absurd fertility dances with a breast-amputated Ingrid. At some point, however, he is full, clears his throat, and drinks a sip of courage from the arak:

> I do not wish to spoil this beautiful celebration; I too love
> *The Thousand and One Nights* and have nothing against bringing
> poetry into life—on the contrary, I am all for it: allowing
> ourselves to be encouraged by poets to approximate as closely
> as possible the courage and grace of the ideal characters of
> poetry in what we ourselves do in everyday life.
>
> But no one should be unwelcome at this celebration
> of life. This is the eternal beauty and truth of what
> Scheherazade narrates: that there is room for everyone—
> man and woman, rich and poor, young and old—and it goes
> without saying also for the men who, as she paraphrases
> with Middle Eastern delicacy, prefer bananas to figs; and

for a woman like Scheherazade herself, who is immortal
not because of her breasts and thighs . . . of course, there
must be room in life for children! Where there is no room
for children there would be nothing to celebrate; life would
have no meaning and humanity would have lost its dignity.

As long as Sader, your friend, neighbor, and son, is not
allowed to take a seat at this table—or is at most tolerated
at the children's table, but is not allowed to eat and drink
among you accompanied by a male lover, to laugh and to
dance when you are in good cheer while he perhaps almost
kills himself from worry—then you are not celebrating life
but jeering at it; you are not bringing poetry into everyday
life but are driving humanity out of it.

Rashid, esteemed colleague, you are right: it is a question
of deciphering life correctly. We find the alphabet to do
this in the texts handed down to us, whether those of
religions, poetry, or the unwritten book of tradition. The
meaning and dignity of life are not, however, in the letters
but in life itself, which is always right because it is the text:
sacred precisely because it is not chiseled in stone or cast in
lead but is alive. When we can no longer decipher life with
the usual letters we must not censor its text but must learn
to read anew. Life means learning to read.

Take the man whom you call "N." and I call my life
companion, which is also an abbreviation for the many
things that he was and is to me: lover, partner, friend,
teacher, father. You did not reserve a place for him at
the table of your Arab showcase wedding—or do you really
believe I would have returned to Lebanon without his
blessing? Can you imagine how difficult it was for him to
begin this new chapter? To read it with his old eyes, as life
intends it: not as loss or betrayal but as joy and gain?

He, who, with all respect, exceeds you not by a little in the
dignity that only lived life heaps on us, is young enough to
learn to read anew; why don't you grant him the place of
honor at your celebration of life that he deserves? You can
read well enough and are Rashid enough (for Rashid means

"the wise man") in order to recognize that there is a gaping abyss between what you read in my life and what is written in tradition; then, my friend, be no less courageous than (just to name her by name . . .) Ingrid: jump across your shadow!"

This, with a mouth full of Arab sweets and anise liqueur, from Joachim.

RASHID AL-DAIF: On the eighth of August, less than a month after the "wedding" party, I received one of Joachim's rare emails. It was signed "Abu Sebastian," from the name he'd chosen for the child if it were a boy. So Joachim was now sure that his friend was pregnant.

In the same letter, he apologized to me for something that stirred many questions within me. He apologized because he'd delayed in writing owing to tension in the relationship with his friend and therefore with "all of Lebanon," as he put it. He added that the matter had been resolved and signed "Abu Sebastian." At the end, he asked me to keep the matter between us and let it go no further. I wasn't fully aware of the reason for this tension between them that necessitated he refrain from writing me, but I was confident we would discuss the issue at length when we met in Frankfurt the following October. I was invited there with a number of other Arab writers on the occasion of the "Arab World" being chosen as the principal theme of that year's annual Frankfurt Book Fair.

On the thirty-first of August, Joachim wrote me a letter devoted to a subject I'd asked him about in a previous letter, and he ended it with four words he put in parentheses—"(Ingrid lost the baby)"—and signed the letter, "Joachim Aggrieved." The news shocked and saddened me. This was the last letter Joachim wrote me before our meeting in Frankfurt some two months later in October at the Book Fair.

When I met Joachim in Frankfurt, his friend Ingrid was with him. I asked him about N., who had stayed in Berlin. He said his health was fine and that he sent me his greetings. I asked him about his friend, the young man, and whether he saw him. He replied there had been some new, unimportant developments, but there was no time to talk about them just then.

Time was short in Frankfurt. We were not able to talk together as we'd have liked, and his friend Ingrid accompanied him most

of the time, which of course kept us from speaking freely in man-
to-man "collusion." We did meet alone one time for lunch in one
of the restaurants at the Fair, where we talked at length about our
experiences in the West-Eastern Divan program that had brought
us together. The main idea that emerged during the discussion
was that I would write about his experiences in Lebanon as I saw
them from my point of view. In particular, I would write about
his experience of meeting a woman (Ingrid) and of his desire to
impregnate her or to see her through the birth of a child, or both,
after life as a homosexual for twenty years. We also agreed he would
write about this same experience but from his own point of view.

It wasn't strange to his nature or habits—or to mine for
that matter—to agree to this plan; nevertheless, our agreement
was a surprise to me. I felt somewhat embarrassed because what
had happened with him was a very personal and intimate affair.
It embarrassed and annoyed me a bit to write and publish what
I saw, and what I saw might have been different from what had
really happened because I had to read it through the alphabet I
knew, and see it through my eyes, and hear it through my ears.
However, I conquered these feelings and decided to implement
our agreement regardless of any potential problems. Joachim's
only admonition was not to hurt his friend Ingrid's feelings, not
to touch her personal dignity, and to refrain as much as possible
from publishing things about her with a frankness and clarity that
might be damaging.

The last time I saw him before my return to Beirut, Ingrid was
present. I wished to speak with her about just that subject. I wanted
to ask her about her view of this relationship and whether she was
in agreement. Many other questions crowded my mind as well, but
it was almost impossible for me. How to begin, and from where?
Would she accept such a discussion? Did she have a specific desire,
like mine, to talk and respond to my questions and preoccupations?
I wanted to talk to her and to listen to her in order to know what she
was thinking about, what she felt, and how she saw the present and
the future. I wanted to hear how she decided to become pregnant
by a gay man in a long-term relationship, a man who was trying to
establish a lasting and fated relationship with a young man, a man

who at the same time pursued men like Sader—or let himself be pursued by men like Sader? Was she really in agreement with all of this? Or did she want from him only that drop of semen?

While bidding them farewell, I said to myself that much discussion must take place in order to achieve a clear understanding between Arabs and Germans. Much discussion—and a fervent desire for discussion.

JOACHIM HELFER: Rashid was noticeably much too fascinated by what he witnessed not to write about it; and why not? We are writers, obligated to bear witness. My request for consideration for third parties referred, of course, to *all* participants; he fulfilled it as well as he could. I only removed, with his consent, a few clauses from his text that seemed to me to be unnecessarily hurtful. We are both aware of the fact that this dialogue nevertheless violates the boundaries of good taste; it can be felt to be obscene, monstrous, because it lifts the curtain on living human beings rather than characters. Third parties who are recognizable or identifiable through their association with me would be allowed under privacy laws to demand that a veil of fictionalization be placed over both Rashid's protocol and my commentary—or even that both be prohibited entirely—for life is, of course, *not* a literary event. This dialogue, so unusually and uncomfortably open for all participants, myself and Rashid included, has only become possible through the generosity and equanimity of third parties.

The real "Daniel" had no misgivings about his character after reading through the text, but indeed about the form of a dialogue in which I have the last word: whereas Rashid often relativizes his own alphabet, I oppose him with universalistic claims without appreciating the values possibly contained in Rashid's alphabet. "It's not *that* cool here in the West, after all!" he writes. On this point I truly do not wish to contradict him.

In defense of the structure I can only point out that Rashid has already published his protocol in Beirut without my commentary (under the title *How the German Came to His Senses*) and that it is currently uncertain whether a new edition containing my comments can be released there—not because of the costs of the translation into

Arabic, which the Goethe Institute would gladly cover, but precisely because of those differences in culture and mentality that the dialogue seeks to identify.

If I come across as a know-it-all, I can regret this but not change it. Yes, I believe in the universal value of individual freedom and responsibility, in the inviolability of the dignity of every single human being, everywhere in the world. Neither do I doubt that one day even in Arabia and Iran no lovers of any kind will be persecuted—moreover that same-sex couples will be recognized—nor do I doubt that this will represent progress for all of inseparable humankind.

p. s.: My daughter was born in October 2005; I was allowed to be present and to cut her umbilical cord in Berlin, where she lives with her mother. In my arms, she sometimes complains that she finds no breasts on me, but when she is full and has burped she likes to sleep on my stomach. Daniel has already applied for the job of babysitter, and even my partner finds her quite charming, for a girl . . .

RASHID AL-DAIF: EPILOGUE

It was in November of 2005 and this book was in publication when I met Thomas Hartmann, who gave me news that Ingrid had given birth to a baby girl. I was aware that Ingrid would have a girl because I'd met Joachim the previous September during an invitation to Berlin to participate in the activities of the International Literature Festival. Joachim officially introduced me with great kindness and invited me, on the evening of my arrival, to dine at the Einstein Restaurant near the hotel where I was staying (the Esplanade Grand Hotel Berlin) next to the former Berlin Wall. With him was Ingrid, in the middle of her ninth month of pregnancy. They told me they had chosen an Arab name for their daughter. I didn't ask them why, but perhaps they wanted the name to carry the history of her origin and a reminder that this coincidence happened in Lebanon. Thomas Hartmann mentioned that the baby was given the family name of her mother and not that of her father, and also that Joachim remained with his partner but spent his time between both his partner and Ingrid—and his daughter, of course—in something of a ménage à trois, as the French would say.

Thomas advised me to publish this epilogue to complete the account, and he informed me Joachim had no objection to it.

IRONY AND COUNTER-IRONY IN RASHID AL-DAIF'S
HOW THE GERMAN CAME TO HIS SENSES

KEN SEIGNEURIE
SIMON FRASER UNIVERSITY

While numerous studies of homosexuality in the Arab world exist
within the thriving academic discipline of gay studies, almost nothing
exists by way of opening an intercultural dialogue over the question.[1]
Attitudes toward homosexuality are apparently so widely divergent as
to be almost paradigmatic of a more generalized great cultural divide
between the West and the Arab world. In the Arab world, discussion
of homosexuality tends toward formulaic rejection:

> Homosexuality is a subject that Arabs, even reform-minded
> Arabs, are generally reluctant to discuss. If mentioned at all,

1. See however al-Bab, accessed March 1, 2014, http://www.al-bab.com/arab/
background/gay.htm. The following is a sample of the numerous studies of sexuality
in the Arab world: Roger Allen, Hilary Kilpatrick, and Ed de Moor, eds., *Love and
Sexuality in Modern Arabic Literature* (London: Saqi, 1995); Mai Ghoussoub and Emma
Sinclair-Webb, eds., *Imagined Masculinities: Male Identity and Culture in the Modern Middle East*
(London: Saqi, 2000); Samar Habib, *Female Homosexuality in the Middle East: Histories
and Representations* (New York: Routledge, 2007); Samir Khalaf and John Gagnon,
eds., *Sexuality in the Arab World* (London: Saqi, 2006); Joseph Massad, "Re-Orienting
Desire: The Gay International and the Arab World," *Public Culture* 14, no. 2 (2002):
361–385 along with Arno Schmitt's commentary and Massad's response, 15, no.
3 (2003): 587–594; Samira Aghacy, *Masculine Identity in the Fiction of the Arab East Since
1967* (New York: Syracuse University Press, 2009); Nabil Matar, "Homosexuality
in the Early Novels of Nageeb Mahfouz," *Journal of Homosexuality* 26, no. 4 (1994):
77–90; Garay Menicucci, "Unlocking the Arab Celluloid Closet: Homosexuality
in Egyptian Film," *Middle East Report* 206 (1998): 32–36; Arno Schmitt, *Sexuality
and Eroticism Among Males in Moslem Societies* (New York: Harrington Park Press, 1991);
Stephen O. Murray and Will Roscoe, eds., *Islamic Homosexualities: Culture, History, and
Literature* (New York: New York University Press, 1997); Helen Rizzo, Abdel-Hamid
Abdel-Latif, and Katherine Meyer, "The Relationship Between Gender Equality
and Democracy: A Comparison of Arab Versus Non-Arab Muslim Societies,"
Sociology 41 (2007): 1151–1170; Brian Whitaker, *Unspeakable Love: Gay and Lesbian Life
in the Middle East* (London: Saqi, 2006); J. W. Wright and Everett K. Rowson, eds.,
Homoeroticism in Classical Arabic Literature (New York: Columbia University Press, 1997).

it's treated as a subject for ribald laughter or (more often) as a foul, unnatural, repulsive, un-Islamic, Western perversion.[2]

In the West, while many also reject homosexuality for reasons not all that different from those commonly adduced in the Arab world, the weight of educated opinion in favor of gay rights can also be dogmatic. Joseph Massad has argued compellingly that a powerful "Gay International" assumes for itself a "missionary role" that seeks to impose its own "sexual epistemology" on the rest of the world, and in particular, on the Muslim Arab world.[3] In such a discursive impasse, any text that would so much as dare to establish an intercultural dialogue within the whirl of social issues surrounding homosexuality deserves attention. If, moreover, it can offer a rhetoric that actually makes understanding alien viewpoints easier, then it probably deserves a place in the early twenty-first-century literary canon.

The origin of *'Awdat al-almani ila rushdih* (*How the German Came to His Senses*) and its rhetoric of irony and counter-irony in the service of promoting intercultural dialogue can be traced to Fall 2003, when the Lebanese novelist Rashid al-Daif visited Germany for six weeks under the auspices of the prestigious German West-Eastern Divan program sponsored by the Berlin-based Wissenschaftskolleg. There he met and worked closely with a German writer, Joachim Helfer.[4] In Spring 2004, Helfer returned the visit to Beirut for a further three weeks of joint lecturing and collaborative work. The aim of this sensible and well-organized program is to improve mutual awareness of German and Middle Eastern literatures through face-to-face meetings, joint cultural activities, and the writings that emerge from these encounters. Such exchanges usually feature a common interest or identity among participants in order to ensure a minimum of common ground. Not this one. Al-Daif is from a working-class background; Helfer from the haute bourgeoisie. Al-Daif was in his fifties at the time of the exchange; Helfer was

---

2. Whitaker, *Unspeakable Love*, 9.

3. Massad, "Re-Orienting Desire," 361, 363.

4. See "Westöstlicherdiwan: Literarische Begegnungen," accessed March 1, 2014, http://www.west-oestlicherdiwan.de/projekt-en.html.

in his thirties. Al-Daif survived the fifteen-year Lebanese Civil War (1975–1990) and its aftermath of Israeli and Syrian military occupations; Helfer acquired a vast cosmopolitan culture through study and travel. Al-Daif obtained his PhD in France in the early 1970s, is a former member of the Lebanese Communist Party, and spent his career as a university professor; Helfer lives from his writing and independent means. Any complete study of their encounter would have to take into account these factors. For the purposes of this narrowly focused essay, the salient facts are that al-Daif is a straight Arab male and Helfer is a gay German.

Throughout the term of the program, al-Daif and Helfer enjoyed a good rapport, and afterwards they discussed the writings they would produce as the fruit of their experience. With Helfer's blessing, al-Daif chose to write about Helfer's homosexuality, that aspect of his colleague that he found both most interesting and most alienating. To ensure that this text would be received as a contribution to actual dialogue, al-Daif took advantage of Helfer's offer to use his real name and used his own as well. The text, however, is a "novelized biography" of what al-Daif regarded to some extent as Helfer's real-life *bildung*, so in the interest of thematic unity he added and modified some material. Thus, despite the text's close correspondence with actual events, it is crucial to avoid conflating characters and actual persons. For the purposes of this essay, "Rashid" and "Joachim" refer to the textual creations, and "al-Daif" and "Helfer" to the persons upon whom these characters are based. When he had finished writing, al-Daif submitted the original Arabic manuscript for translation into German and for Helfer's approval before publishing it. Helfer read the translation and approved its publication in Arabic, but for the German edition, he interpolated lengthy responses into al-Daif's text, swelling the original ninety pages to more than twice that length. The German publisher, Suhrkamp, brought out the longer product in Fall 2006 under the title of *Die Verschwulung der Welt* (*The Queering of the World*). The scope of this essay, however, is limited to studying al-Daif's opening gesture of intercultural dialogue in the original Arabic version and makes no attempt to deal with the al-Daif–Helfer exchange as a whole.

Judging by *How the German Came to His Senses*, it would not be too much to say that the nine weeks these writers spent in each other's company changed their lives. Al-Daif's close observation of the everyday life of an openly gay couple in Berlin provoked a thorough reassessment of gender norms and sexuality on his part, as revealed in the development of his character Rashid. For Helfer, who at the time was in a twenty-year-long relationship with a man thirty-seven years his senior, the experience provided the opportunity, perhaps the catalyst, for one of life's momentous decisions. *How the German Came to His Senses* traces these transformative processes, and the present essay explores their discursive mediations. The first section will focus on the character Joachim's development, the second on the character Rashid's. As striking as these developments are, the fundamental claim being made here is that there exists in the diegesis an identifiable rhetoric that Rashid employs, wittingly or no, to convey his views to Joachim and to interiorize those of Joachim. This rhetoric and its role in promoting intercultural dialogue is the focus here, not its ostensible efficacy.

A RHETORIC OF INTEREST AND SELF-INVESTMENT

Al-Daif's contribution to intercultural communication springs, with no little irony, from a miscommunication. On the first page of *How the German Came to His Senses*, he writes that he sees the aim of the West-Eastern Divan program to be "dialogue" (*al-ḥiwār*). His understanding of this term consists of the articulating of one's point of view and the interiorizing of another without necessarily adopting it as one's own. He sees dialogue as process-oriented and superior to "debate" and "negotiation," both of which are end-oriented.[5] Al-Daif doubtless failed to see, however, that dialogue could mean something else. The West-Eastern Divan program's self-description does indeed mention the word "scholarly dialogue" at one point and the term "divan" certainly suggests dialogue, but the website's introductory paragraph emphasizes a slightly different priority:

---

5. Al-Daif explained his understanding of "dialogue" to me in conversation, Beirut, November 2006.

In autumn 2000, the "West-Eastern Divan" project initiated new forms of literary encounters aimed at *improving the mutual awareness* of German and Middle Eastern literature. The core concept envisages German authors travelling to Arab countries, Turkey or Iran, to meet fellow-writers there and then those writers being invited back to Germany to return the visit. This kind of exchange visit gives the writers a chance to get to know each other in their own environment, take trips together through the country, give joint readings, and write about each other's literature and each other's world each in their own language.[6] (emphasis added)

To improve "awareness" is not the same thing as to engage in dialogue. Like dialogue, it is distinct from debate and negotiation, but it is also a lesser interpellation. To improve awareness of the other indicates a mere velleity to direct attention. Dialogue, by contrast, rubs two consciousnesses together in discursive exchange and bears the potential to spark disagreement as well as concord.[7] If one seeks only to improve awareness, as the introduction to the West-Eastern Divan states, dialogue such as al-Daif conceives it may seem intrusive. This fundamental misunderstanding about the purpose of the exchange may explain much of the umbrage Helfer takes in his response to al-Daif's text.

---

6. "Westöstlicherdiwan: Literarische Begegnungen."

7. With respect to the statement that dialogue "rubs two consciousnesses together," it is important to note that the discursive category of dialogue, unlike for example that of critique, must assume the sovereign subjectivity of each participant. If from the outset one party considers the other in thrall to unconscious illusions, the discussion will take place on nonintersecting planes. For example, Frédéric Lagrange's otherwise excellent article argues that the generally impoverished representation of homosexuality in modern Arabic literature is symptomatic of a displacement of "the shock of encounter with the West." While this claim is thoroughly plausible and insightful to the literary analysis of al-Daif's novels, it would not be a good point of departure for dialogue, for in presuming to know the "real" reason for the consciously held views of another person one commits the "orientalist" error of knowing the other better than the other knows him- or herself. "Male Homosexuality in Modern Arabic Literature," *Imagined Masculinities*, 187.

The slippage from awareness to dialogue means that the narrator, Rashid, does not simply bring things to Joachim's attention. He affirms viewpoints and convictions with the aim of eliciting responses, which from the standpoint of one who seeks only awareness, could tax tolerance. This section of the essay concentrates on how al-Daif's notion of dialogue jars a communicative contract based on promoting mutual awareness. It will also be important to identify whether al-Daif's use of persuasive discourse—his rhetoric—tips into the agon of debate, negotiation, or proselytization. After all, if his notion of dialogue is ultimately coercive, it will not be much good as a means of dealing with difference.

While the aim here is to identify the distinctiveness of al-Daif's rhetoric, it is first necessary to concede that in numerous ways it does not depart all that much from a Western humanist discourse that prioritizes individual autonomy, equality, solidarity, and human fulfillment. Thus, the narrator stresses the prerogatives of the individual free conscience, noting, for example, that if his son were gay it would distress him profoundly, but that in the end he would support him (4, 66). Likewise, he claims: "As a matter of principle, I am completely on the side of those who suffer on earth and of oppressed minorities, including gay men and lesbians" (26, 120). Moreover, he believes in the human capacity for change and development, striving to free himself from the prejudices of his own culture:

> As a rule, I exercise constant vigilance to keep at a distance from the behavior and ideology of the society I belong to and count myself among those who reexamine at every turn society's convictions—and indeed my own personal convictions—yet many of my society's ideas have penetrated me and do their work in me without my realizing it. (3, 60)

These principles raise the bar on Rashid's brand of dialogue by accepting universalist moral norms and refusing any appeal to culturalism. In effect, he invites the reader to evaluate his rhetoric according to a strict criterion of respect for individual autonomy.

Other elements of Rashid's discourse apparently contradict Western progressive norms. He reports, for example, what many in the Arab world actually believe about homosexuality: "For us, the homosexual act is disgraceful, shameful, and must be suppressed. It's a crime punishable by law. Homosexuals are called perverts and their practices are considered sex acts against nature" (3, 60). Rashid states these sentiments without endorsing them, but characteristically in this text, he also refuses to distance himself from them. By employing recognizably progressist and socially conservative discourses, the narrator runs the risk of self-contradiction and alienating all audiences. At the same time, this ambiguous positioning opens the discursive field wide enough to contain the positions that people actually hold as opposed to those that one side or the other believe they are supposed to hold.

Rashid even seems at times to revel in what may come across as pandering or provocation depending on the reader's standpoint toward homosexuality. Especially early in the narrative, he voices matter-of-fact prejudices about gays with no apparent diegetic motivation for it, declaring for example, "I'm from an environment that honors and celebrates procreative masculinity; one that revels in it every chance it gets" (2, 60).[8] Like many of Rashid's statements, his unreflective association of homosexuality with submissive femininity may be seen as a dual gambit directed toward two readerships. To those hostile toward homosexuality, it apparently establishes Rashid as a kindred spirit by engaging their basest convictions. To readers sympathetic to homosexual rights, it is a test of their willingness to engage with actually existing heteronormative attitudes, effectively daring them to slam the book shut as the narrator glumly mutters: "Well, you said you wanted dialogue with the other. . . ." The onus, however, as I shall argue, is moveable.

Rashid's departures from progressive norms can often be traced to the way he frames questions according to values prevalent in Arab culture. In trying to understand Joachim's attraction to men in their late teens, he makes the nuanced distinction between

---

8. For an analysis of Lebanon's "penis-centered masculinity," see Ghassan Hage, "Migration, Marginalized Masculinity and Dephallicization: A Lebanese Villager's Experience," *Sexuality in the Arab World*, 107–129.

pedophilia and pederasty that one might not expect from a narrator who conflates homosexuality and femininity. Yet he avoids framing Joachim's desire according to either of these concepts, favoring instead the norms of a family-centered affective economy. He asks Joachim whether by enjoying the body of a young man, he does not feel he is profiting from the fruit of another family's labor without himself contributing through fatherhood to someone else's enjoyment (10, 86). Typically, he opens the question but does not plump for one response or another, apparently content to stretch the terms of the dialogue to include the family-centered priority along with that of sexual autonomy.

In his own life, too, Rashid keeps judgment in abeyance as long as possible for himself and for others. On the topic of some Arab men's attitudes toward Western women, he writes:

> The Western woman is not as cautious in her dealings with men as an Arab woman is, and the Arab man reads this as availability. My wife would go out from time to time to shop, taking our son with her in his stroller. Some workers in the supermarket showed a special interest in our son, and when my wife returned and told me how kind and attentive they were, I listened without offering an opinion or remark of any kind. I knew at the time that two wives of friends lived in the neighborhood and did their shopping at the same supermarket. No workers were "interested" in their children or showed any special kindness toward them. The wives were Lebanese. Then my wife came along one day and said to me the supermarket workers' interest in the boy went a little too far. (28, 122)

To explain to his wife the workers' behavior according to the cultural codes he knows would have meant reducing her freedom to respond according to her own lights. The scene thus dramatizes the narrator's commitment to the reader's freedom to experience, evaluate, and respond without tutelage.

Yet neither this text's departure from humanist norms nor its framing of questions according to Arab family values fundamentally tax Joachim's tolerance—after all, tolerance means putting up with different, even odious, views. The most jarring element of Rashid's rhetoric is his relentless interest and investment in his colleague's life. Rashid's priority on dialogue means that questions flood his mind about Joachim's personal life choices. He respects Joachim's autonomy but refuses the corollary that discussion of private life is off-limits. Indeed, Rashid treats Joachim's private life as if it were his own. Even though Joachim is exceptionally forthcoming and Helfer himself expressly approved publication of the text, the foray into Joachim's intimate life often seems to go too far—especially since Joachim, in keeping with the task of simply promoting awareness, asks very few questions of his own. When Rashid learns that Joachim last made love with a woman twenty years previously—already no mean revelation—he follows up by inquiring whether Joachim doesn't yearn to be a father. His colleague responds that he might have fathered children in two cases, and Rashid asks him about the first one:

> "Did you ever see the child?"
> "No!"
> "You don't want to see it?"
> "No!"
> "Would you like to know some day whether you're the father?"
> "No!" (II, 87)

About the second case of presumed fatherhood, Rashid is surprised that Joachim again did not care to know whether the child was really his own:

> Joachim didn't ask her what made her think her eldest was his!
> I conveyed my puzzlement at his total absence of curiosity, as
> if the matter had to do with another person and not him.
> (12, 88)

Ironically, Joachim treats his life as if it belonged to another, whereas Rashid treats Joachim's life as if it were his own. He continues:

He was surprised by my confusion and reflected for a
moment like someone who is searching for a response but
can't come up with anything. When I asked him whether the
child was male or female, he said he didn't know. I asked
him if it was important for him to know, but he raised his
hand and his head in a gesture I couldn't understand. I
didn't know if it was a gesture unique to him or one of
the gestures Germans use to accompany their speech—or to
take the place of speech—as a slight nod for us means "no"
and a brief shake of the head left and right means "what?"
(12, 88)

After a moment's reflection, Joachim breaks the silence as
if recovering a lost memory: "She slept with me to acquire some
experience! Women in Germany today decide, as I've mentioned
to you on numerous occasions. She determines what she wants
from a man. We are nothing to them" (12, 88). Rashid's interest
and investment are arguably intrusive, and Joachim's willingness
to speak and answer questions with good grace suggests the latter's
exceptional cooperation. His palpable impatience, however,
also implies that Rashid has exceeded the bounds of acquiring
awareness. Nevertheless, Rashid's emphasis on family and
fatherhood and his investment in his colleague's life as if it were his
own encourage Joachim to think about long-since settled affairs.
Indeed, his interest uncovers levels of complexity in Joachim and
perhaps in contemporary gender relations in Germany. Joachim,
somewhat surprisingly, demonstrates continued willingness and,
if anything, a greater inclination to discuss these issues as the
exchange unfolds.

The discussion about fatherhood foreshadows a great
turning point in Joachim's life. When Joachim visits Beirut,
Rashid, in keeping with both his interest in his colleague and his
heteronormative convictions, decides to arrange for Joachim to
meet a woman whom he hopes will attract his colleague's attention.
In all fairness, he also helps arrange for Joachim to meet a gay
man, but Rashid clearly hopes to turn Joachim on to the charms
of heterosexuality. The attempt is not without humor as Rashid

contrives at a party to bring his colleague into the proximity of a woman who, Rashid fancies, resembles a young man (33, 131). The would-be matchmaker is never coercive but he does seek to persuade, which certainly exceeds the program's brief of promoting mutual awareness and arguably that of dialogue as al-Daif himself defines it. Predictably enough, these good offices come to nothing, but they do lead to more discussion, more self-examination. At least from the reader's standpoint, Rashid's affective investment goes a long way toward redeeming what might appear as an intrusive interest in his colleague. It doubtless exceeds the purview of the exchange program, but is also the transformative element in Rashid's notion of dialogue.

Eventually, Joachim meets Ingrid, a Beirut-based German, independently of Rashid's ministrations. No cause-effect relation exists between the colleagues' discussions of desire, sexuality, and family on the one hand, and Joachim's meeting Ingrid one day, going home with her, and deciding—in the span of minutes after twenty years of life as a gay man—to join with her in parenthood. Yet in the text as a literary work, it is hard to ignore that we are reading about a process—a *bildung*—in which decisions are part of a web of experiences, which would include Joachim's dialogue with his colleague Rashid. Thus, Joachim's self-fulfillment unfolds in unpredictable ways and from unpredictable causes, but these are not implausibly conditioned by what is termed here Rashid's rhetoric of interest and self-investment. Rashid's questioning assumptions, keeping inference in abeyance, and taking a personal interest in his interlocutor as if he were the self emerge as elements of this rhetoric.

A RHETORIC OF OTHERING THE SELF

It is one thing to display interest in another's life; it is quite another to interiorize an alien standpoint and to undergo change oneself. This section is devoted to identifying how, if at all, Rashid himself undergoes change as a result of the dialogue with Joachim. Numerous obstacles stand in his way. For one thing, his avowed prejudice against homosexuality is overdetermined by a literary and popular tradition that most often derides homosexuality or depicts it as shameful.[9] In the aim of clearing a discursive space to deal with the issue, al-Daif could have pretended this reality does not exist by emphasizing the small haven of alternative lifestyles that exists in Beirut.[10] This threadbare topos of Vanguard Beirut, Paris of the Orient, would take for granted the validity of a pro-gay social telos when this is precisely the question at hand. Instead, al-Daif's narrator assumes a position close to popular opinion even at the cost of alienating Joachim.

Rashid's effort to understand the gay German on the gay German's terms unfolds according to a recognizable rhetoric. It may not look like much of a rhetoric, or like much of an effort either, since the narrative opens with what some might consider a manifesto of homophobia. From the heteronormative title, *How the [Gay] German Came to His Senses,* and throughout the first dozen pages, the narrator affirms in numerous ways that gay men are essentially other: effeminate, lascivious, unhygienic, and prone to pederasty. He allies himself with the law and popular attitudes, noting that homosexuality in Lebanon remains illegal, and he refuses to fudge the issue by claiming that the laws are outdated or ignored (3, 60). He stresses that he sees homosexuality as a threat to young people and admits that he worried constantly about his son's sexual orientation while the latter lived in France, a country ostensibly more tolerant than Lebanon of homosexuality (3, 65).

The narrator, having established his solidarity with commonly held beliefs at the cost of maximizing his alienation from Joachim, might be expected to soften these hard edges before meeting his colleague. Instead, he goes so far as to exaggerate his anxiety, fretting over his first meeting with Joachim:

> I must be cautious from the beginning, clear from the beginning, dissuasive from the beginning in such a way that

9. See Whitaker, *Unspeakable Love,* 9. Whitaker's book is a helpful account of the everyday lives of gay men and lesbians in the Arab world. In addition to a wealth of anecdotal accounts, the book surveys the depiction of homosexuality in contemporary Arabic literature and cinema, as well as reviewing legal, popular, and religious attitudes toward homosexual practices in the Arab world.

10. For a profile of Beirut's gay subculture, see Sofian Merabet, "Creating Queer Space in Beirut," *Sexuality in the Arab World,* 199–242.

boundaries are drawn from our very first meeting and that each of us stays within them! Because some gay men don't remain within their limits and don't hesitate to disturb others, especially when you consider I'm a hairy man—even if I don't have a mustache to show for it. I say this in all candor and without a qualm. (4, 70)

The narrator has stated his opposition toward homosexuality in the name of candor, but the anxiety displayed in this passage seems just a bit much. The narrator's manic determination to quarantine Joachim also contrasts strikingly with what he affirms previously in the same paragraph:

When Thomas Hartmann informed me about my colleague's homosexuality, I said, "Why not?" This would be an opportunity to become closely acquainted with openly lived homosexuality—and in Berlin to boot, the city where the largest gay pride demonstration takes place every year. (4, 70)

The contradiction between a desire to witness the everyday life of a gay man and the paranoiac assumption that body hair drives gay men wild vehicles no little irony, but the object of the irony is unclear: is the narrator's receptivity toward "openly lived homosexuality" a hypocritical gesture toward political correctness, or is his wild irrationality toward homosexuality an authorial wink over the head of his homophobic narrator? To be sure, the same paragraph suggests both openness and anxiety toward homosexuality. Rather than to opt for one side or the other, it is more fruitful to be attentive to the effect of this ambiguity. If neither the openness nor the homophobia are completely on the level, irony defamiliarizes each pole without denying anything.

During the first face-to-face encounter alone with Joachim, Rashid's exaggerated defense against gay depredations further denaturalizes his homophobia:

In any case, I'm hairy even if I don't have a mustache. I was conscious of this when I met Joachim alone, face-to-face, for the first time. It was in Berlin in the apartment the Wissenschaftskolleg gave me for my six-week stay. At one point he rose from the sofa and sat next to me as I explained to him an Arabic expression written on a gift I had given him. I was somewhat surprised when he sat next to me. I got up to examine the gift and reflect on the inscription. I made a point of sitting on another sofa and told him my girlfriend in Beirut had chosen this gift for him, but the truth was I had chosen it, not my girlfriend. I claimed this to create a pretext that permitted me to talk about my girlfriend, and from there I proceeded to talk about my relations with women in general. (5, 75)

Of course, some readers will see no irony or humor in this passage, just prudence before the gay menace, while others will condemn the narrator for homophobia. Those on the lookout for litmus tests will find what they seek. Still others will see the narrator set himself up without being able to determine to what extent he is the butt of irony. Thanks to the narrative convention of reader identification with the narrator, such passages lead the reader to unmoor convictions from the realm of self-evident truth. From whatever ideological harbor the reader may hail, the text appeals for a placing in abeyance of convictions in order to leave open a range of interpretive possibilities. Thus, having no sooner established in the opening pages of the narrative maximal distance from homosexuality, Rashid's ironic exaggerations transform this distance from a gap to a discursive field.

The fact that some readers fail to detect ambiguity is not all that surprising. Al-Daif never telegraphs his irony by polarizing an issue or erecting laughingstocks. Counter-irony keeps interpretative closure in abeyance, leaving the reader to wonder whether the narrator is serious.[11] This delicate equivocation between candor and self-irony is a hallmark of al-Daif's writing dating back to his war novels. In *Nahiyat al-bara'a* (*This Side of Innocence*), the narrator—

---

11. Linda Hutcheon notes that irony and counter-irony open "dynamic and plural relations among the text or utterance (and its context), the so-called ironist, the interpreter, and the circumstances surrounding the discursive situation." *Irony's Edge: The Theory and Politics of Irony* (New York: Routledge, 1994), 11.

again "Rashid"—obstinately insists on understanding his torturers' point of view to such an extent that one feels half entitled to wonder whether he is not a masochist. In *How the German Came to His Senses*, even when Rashid admits to tugging his sleeves to conceal the hair on his wrists in front of Joachim as a woman would tug her skirt to avoid exciting unwanted interest, the downright campy impression is again just barely plausible (6, 76). The shred of plausibility within this absurdity is due to the way the text disappoints interpretive expectations habitually brought to irony. After such a send-up of homophobia, one might expect some clear signal to the reader that the narrator has been unfairly prejudiced. This never happens. Instead, an ironic vignette about gay men and body hair suddenly veers into the counter-irony of tragedy as the narrator mentions the 1980s AIDS epidemic and its prevalence in the promiscuous gay community (4–5, 71). The narrator thus quickly reframes a question from irrational fear to historical context for it. Or again, when Rashid meets an esteemed Arab colleague in Berlin, a near-pun in Arabic between the word for "gay" (*mithlī*) and "like me" (*mithli*) leads the colleague to believe momentarily that Rashid "is like" Joachim. Predictably enough, Rashid hastily disavows any nonprofessional link whatsoever to Joachim, but the comic irony of the situation is countered by the narrator's churlish comment: "Mine was the haste of a man soiled by impurity as I disavowed any connection and clarified the matter. I wanted not a trace of doubt to linger in his mind" (7, 80). The self-irony again exposes Rashid's irrational opposition toward homosexuality, but it stops short of defanging his conviction. This rhetoric of irony and counter-irony keeps readers off-balance as long as possible. Neither those who identify with the narrator's homophobia nor those who condemn it can achieve closure over the question at hand, and the longer the reader suspends judgment, the more natural suspension feels, and the more plausible frank dialogue becomes.

With the reader's judgment of Rashid in abeyance, the depiction of Joachim is crucial to whether Rashid and his engaged reader will be able to interiorize the alien subject position. In contrast to Rashid's effusive displays of heterosexuality and boorish behavior (such as refusing to sit next to Joachim while the latter throws his

arm over a seat back on a city bus), Joachim is depicted as winsomely
unconcerned (6, 76). He is patient and understanding even as Rashid
frankly expresses views on homosexuality that he must find offensive.
His quiet confidence and the good-faith explicator role he assumes
contrast positively with the narrator's anxiety to square stereotypes
with his observations of Joachim's life. Indeed, much of the text's
humor springs from the contrast between Rashid's anxiety and
Joachim's rational calm. As a result, notwithstanding his reservations
about homosexuality, Rashid soon comes to admire many things
about his colleague and by the same token so does the engaged reader.

Rashid's opposition to homosexuality boils down to a half-dozen
claims: the gay obsession with sex, the ephemerality and mere titillation
of gay relations, the absence of female tenderness, the filth and
insalubriousness of a wholly masculine environment, and its sterility
as a social norm. Rashid, however, is a good listener and is attentive
to his surroundings. It is not lost on him when events contradict
these convictions and even expose an element of self-projection in
them. Thus, Joachim is never depicted as being obsessive about sex
whereas Rashid is made to feel like a lecher when he eyes women
appreciatively in Berlin (8–9, 81). Chastened, he listens closely as
Joachim explains that sex is not generally the uppermost thing for
people—gay or straight—in Europe (27, 121). Likewise, Rashid must
revise his belief that gay relations are essentially ephemeral in light of
Joachim's twenty-year relationship with his partner, "N." As for gay
hygiene, Rashid's initial opinion is clear:

> Somewhere in my consciousness, the relationship between
> two men meant quite simply sexual relations. Asswork. This
> relation is reflected on things, leaving its traces everywhere:
> on household wares, door handles, plates, spoons, and in
> the bathroom . . . especially in the bathroom, where sin
> hides and grows. And in the kitchen sink where the food of
> two "bachelors" remains on spoons and plates and where
> traces of their lips remain on coffee and tea cups, on wine
> and whiskey glasses, and on other kinds of liquor glasses.
> Two men living together equal dirt, negligence, and the
> absence of women! (14, 94)

When he visits Joachim and his partner's apartment in Berlin, Rashid is again forced to revise his ideas:

> My friend and his partner's house was very clean and well lighted. Its wide glass façade loomed in the sky above the roofs of East Berlin. It was a surprise, and a good one. . . . I'd never before seen anything like this house, save to a limited extent among the delicate and highly cultured wealthy. (14, 94–95)

Rashid even has to revise his view about the lack of female tenderness in gay relations, as the relationship between Joachim and his partner, N., is depicted as exceptionally gentle and generous.[12] By midway in the narrative, only the sterility of institutionalized homosexuality remains for Rashid to examine. In this way, Rashid's expression of disobliging opinions is balanced by his honesty in recording his own misapprehensions and errors. Yet even though Rashid's convictions are exposed as parochial and prejudiced, he never admits this fact. The absence of signposting functions as a counter-irony as the reader wonders whether the narrator is aware of being contradicted.

In effectively learning to appreciate the human as opposed to specifically gay passions, frustrations, and yearnings in Joachim, Rashid comes to concede that Joachim's relationship with N. is a lot like that of a straight couple, complete with commitments, obligations, temptations, and infidelities:

> It also dawned on me that I was dealing with a person in a relationship and that this was something I hadn't before fathomed. I noticed the relationship between two men had its obligations. The man had to return in the evening to the other man in this relationship just as a man in a marriage has to return to his wife. I noticed I didn't ask him about his

---

12. For the difference between same-sex sexual relations, which may be as common in the Arab world as elsewhere, and a "gay lifestyle," which is uncommon in the Arab world, see Jared McCormick, "Transition Beirut: Gay Identities, Lived Realities: The Balancing Act in the Middle East," *Sexuality in the Arab World*, 243–260.

partner as I would ask any other married man about his wife.
I noticed I behaved with him as if his conjugal commitment
had no existence, as if he were a bachelor and not attached.
Such concerns didn't exist in my culture. The intimate
relationship between two men in my "spontaneous" culture
was secret, not public. I realized I now had to take into
consideration this relationship, not to forget to ask about
N. from time to time and to suggest he accompany us when
I invited Joachim someplace, or when we decided to do an
activity, just as I would with a married man. (34–35, 135)

By this point in the narrative, the heteronormative reader's
easy engagement with the narrator's earlier convictions undergoes a
challenge. Rashid's changing views serve to deflect this reader's desire
toward acceptance of homosexuality, failing which the narrator would
be entitled to mutter: "I thought you and I saw eye to eye. . . ."[13]

I have tried to show how Rashid's success—apparently despite
himself—in accepting a homosexual union to the point of considering
it on the same level as a heterosexual union is the result of a rhetoric,
a patterned use of discourse for persuasive effect. In this case,
Rashid's rhetoric is self-oriented and consists of exaggerating the
difference between self and other in order to unmoor convictions
from their harbor in self-evident truth and to make them available
for discussion and, eventually, reevaluation. Identification with the
narrator tends to encourage a similar process on the part of the
reader. Engaged readers follow Rashid as he evaluates his convictions
as if they belonged to someone else. The process surprises Rashid
himself as he comes to see even Joachim's yearning for a young man
as not incongruous with the "sacred" cedars of Lebanon:

I asked myself if I felt a sort of contradiction between the
sacredness of the place and the worldliness of the subject.
In the holy atmosphere replete with "Gibranic" charm,
romanticism, and mysticism, I felt sympathy with Joachim . . .

13. For a theorization of "deflection of desire," see Ross Chambers, *Room for
Maneuver: Reading (the) Oppositional (in) Narrative* (Chicago: University of Chicago Press,
1991), 235.

The sincerity that emerged from Joachim's conversation put him in harmony with this place in spite of the peculiarity I mentioned or maybe (why not?) because of it. Joachim displayed his desire for a man twenty years his junior as if it were of a mystical nature because he deeply and fervently believed in a kind of providence, which believers would call God, that shepherds this world and would not forsake one who dreams of giving all. It had not forsaken his roommate, N., who also had a great desire to give. He gave and was given. (32, 127–128)

The terror of triggering a gay mania for body hair is well behind the narrator, but the degree of empathy Rashid feels for Joachim does not mean that he has resolved all questions about the otherness of homosexuality.

COMPARISON AND CATACHRESIS

If discussion, observation, and the visit to the gay couple's apartment lead Rashid to revise his ideas about some things, these same experiences also pique his abiding interest in the social implications of institutionalized homosexuality, which Rashid distinguishes from the right to gay self-expression:

I told him legalizing gay marriage was something different from legalizing gay rights to self-realization. . . . I mean, quite apart from the question of morality, all societies that genuinely legalize homosexual relations make them equal to those of man and wife. These are societies that somehow accept annihilation and disappearance, which is particularly applicable to German society. (16, 99)

Thus while he eventually comes to terms with homosexuality as a legitimate mode of private self-realization, here Rashid frankly expresses his misgivings about public policy in favor of homosexuality. Rhetorically, his claim that to legalize gay rights is "somehow [to] accept annihilation and disappearance" is again a way of affirming maximal alienation from his interlocutor to the point of exaggeration. Again, it is impossible to determine to what extent the statement is ironic, but indicators elsewhere such as the narrator's oft-repeated praise of fecundity suggest that this conviction will not be easy to unmoor.

From this point, Rashid engages a desultory and characteristically frank discussion of various public policy aspects of homosexuality. His method here is to contrast current practices in Germany with those in Lebanon and the Arab world without obviously juxtaposing them. Some comparisons redound to the credit of social legislation in favor of homosexuality in Germany. He relates Joachim's account of a young gay German who committed suicide in despair at his plight prior to the adoption of gay rights legislation in Germany (17, 100). The shame this young man felt is implicitly recapitulated in the story of a similar fate suffered by a young Lebanese man much more recently:

> When one gay youth told his family about his sexual orientation, a pall of unbearable sadness fell over the home. The mother isolated herself, the father isolated himself, and they were no longer able to speak to each other or to their son. A deep depression afflicted the youth, forcing him into the hospital where, after several days of treatment and during a guard's moment of inattention, he jumped from the window into the street below and died. Tragedy! (25, 118)

Such comparisons inch Rashid toward conceding the necessity of changing social policy toward homosexuality, although it is never clear to what extent he wishes for change.

Other implicit comparisons lead the narrator to contextualize homosexuality within broader questions of changing gender roles. From memory, he recalls a couple of exceptionally warm and affectionate German women from his childhood (20–21, 106). He avoids any explicit contrast with contemporary women's roles, but it is clear that he is exercised by some women today who want from men "only that drop of semen and nothing else":

This phenomenon is becoming well known in Europe and
the West, generally, where women have relations with men
in order to become pregnant on purpose, telling the men
only after becoming pregnant, or telling them after the
baby is born, or not telling them at all. They want the men
to stay out of their lives, informing them only because they
should know. (47, 158)

Between his childhood and adult images of German
womanhood came the sexual revolution, toward which Rashid
is ambivalent. This broader phenomenon has been Rashid's
principal concern from the outset, which is why his acceptance of
homosexuality as a personal practice does little to allay his fear of
institutionalized homosexuality:

Of course, I'm not saying the decline in Germany's
birthrate is due to homosexuality; rather that the
legalization of homosexuality goes hand in hand with this
situation. It goes along with the decline in the birthrate,
with the rise in living standards and cultural levels, with
the priority on the individual and on individual freedoms,
with the respect for women's rights, with their presence in
society, and especially with their right to work and their
right to promotion and other such things. It's a reason, a
cause, and a part of everything. (17, 99)

In such an overdetermined struggle between, as Rashid sees it,
a modernizing West and a recalcitrant Arab world, "the bed is a
frontline" (2, 58).[14] From this standpoint, Joachim's homosexuality
is also a casualty of the gender wars. His desire for a "Greek
relationship" with a young man appears to Rashid as both a fruit of
the sexual revolution and a flight from prevailing relations between
the sexes. Thus even though Rashid eventually accepts Joachim's

---

14. For sexuality and modernity in the Arab world, see Lagrange, "Male
Homosexuality in Modern Arabic Literature," and Mai Ghoussoub, "Chewing
Gum, Insatiable Women and Foreign Enemies: Male Fears and the Arab Media,"
Imagined Masculinities, 169–198; 227–235.

personal sexual orientation, at the same time he sees his colleague as a closet heterosexual who would realize this potential if only social conditions permitted it.

In Rashid's struggle with change, he invokes as a foil scenes from traditional Arab life. Having recounted Joachim's point of view that German women today take the initiative in sexual relations, Rashid muses parenthetically:

> I remembered, while we were discussing this subject, how a polite girl from home must be moderate in eating when invited to others' homes. Among her qualities is moderation in eating even if she's plump and her moderation wouldn't fool anyone. I often heard the saying: "The amount a girl eats is inversely proportional to her good education." This was a truism in the past and remains so to this day, even if to different degrees and depending on social milieu. (19, 105)

These demure girls whose restrained appetite supposedly betokens their sexual restraint are also the implicit backdrop for the scene from Rashid's young manhood when a French girl takes it for granted that he, freshly arrived from Lebanon, will make love to her in her parents' home with her brother in the next room (29, 123). Rashid invokes these contrasting scenes not as a way of demonstrating the superiority of one practice over the other but rather as a means of setting out the parameters of dialogue between patriarchal and liberated social values just as earlier he creates a discursive field stretching from homophobia to gay rights.[15]

The same technique of comparing what he witnesses in Germany with what happens in the Arab world allows Rashid to gauge and ultimately question his own society. In a Berlin restaurant with his son and the German director of the West-Eastern Divan program, Rashid notices at the adjacent table:

---

15. For the representation of women in *How the German Came to His Senses*, see Nicola Liscutin, "West-East Divan or Procrustean Bed?," *al-Kalimah* [*The Word*] 1, no. 2 (2007).

a young man in his early twenties and another in his late thirties. From time to time, they would kiss each other as if they couldn't swallow a bite without kissing. Facing them were a man and his wife. Thomas, who heard them easily, mentioned to us that the younger man called them Mom and Dad. I began observing; the scene preoccupied me to such an extent I couldn't tear my eyes away. I can safely say the parents were not delighted, especially when their son kissed his partner. Theirs was not the situation of parents in the presence of their son and his beloved girlfriend. If he were to kiss her, they'd be glad for him and happy for the love that joined them. (29–30, 123–124)

This is one of the more difficult scenes for Rashid to fathom, perhaps because, from his standpoint, it is stranger than all his ironic exaggerations hitherto. He notes that it would be impossible to see such a thing in the Arab world, but this very fact also convinces him that it is impossible to assume the normativity of his own social codes. As such it is off Rashid's cognitive map and he muses: "Respect for the rights of others means you have to accept what you don't like and don't wish for" (30, 124).

Back in Lebanon, a different scene almost juxtaposed with this one has Rashid and Joachim attending a traditional family dinner. Nobody besides Rashid knows about Joachim's sexual orientation, and nobody else notices Joachim pay attention to the sixteen-year-old son at dinner. Tension builds as Rashid imagines the scandal that would erupt if the boy's father knew his son was the object of a homosexual gaze. Rashid envisions catastrophe, but Joachim's regard for the young man turns out to be no more prurient than a heterosexual's regard for a young woman would be. Nor does the boy's fascination with Joachim bespeak more than his interest in Joachim's conversation. This anticlimactic conclusion to the dinner emblematizes the general result of Rashid's anxieties throughout the narrative. As with his concern over body hair, the "gay menace" fails to materialize. Yet again, however, Rashid's concerns are not simply dismissed. Throughout the dinner the boy's mother bustling about him in a flurry of maternal attention underscores the strong conditioning influence of the Arab family over the lives of young people, as if to suggest that she stands as a firewall between her son and any behavior she would deem untoward, including, presumably, homosexual desire (27, 121).

Juxtaposed to the meal in the German restaurant, the family dinner also reveals a cultural catachresis in Gayatri Spivak's sense of a concept-metaphor with no adequate referent between cultures. To say that the Arab family pictured in this scene—or for that matter, Rashid's interest in Joachim—is "intrusive," "oppressive," or even just "doting" is to speak from a standpoint outside the culture of which it is a part and therefore to misapprehend it in context. Likewise, it would also be catachrestic for Rashid to condemn from the standpoint of the Arab family the German institutionalization of homosexuality as revealed in the Berlin restaurant. This impasse is metaphorized in the difference in table manners between Germany and Lebanon:

> Many things passed over Joachim's head by virtue of his being German. . . . I saw Joachim was always confused when he was invited to lunch or dinner. How to begin? With what? We put all courses out on the table at the same time and there is no starter or main course; instead, we put everything out and everybody serves himself. You begin with whatever you wish and reach out to take seconds as much as you want without having to ask permission. A person at the table with us doesn't have to wait for others in order to finish his plate, or to wait for the lady of the house to ask if anyone wants seconds or to pass to the next course. In France, I found it burdensome when I was invited to lunch or dinner to be prevented the pleasure of finishing my meal without waiting for others. It took me some time to get used to this, and I still wait, when I have to, out of politeness. (28–29, 122)

Of course, social policies toward homosexuality and table manners are not comparable, but the scene does underscore a degree of noncommensurability between German and Arab contexts.

Afterward, Rashid stresses: "The issue is not one of intentions but of culture," reckoning more fully the difficulty of understanding German culture on its own terms (29, 123). Yet, as difficult as communication may be, he does not see the differences between Germany and the Arab world as insurmountable. In the latter third of his narrative, a mantra emerges: a culture must be read according to its own "alphabet" and not be the object of projected cultural codes.

Thus Rashid has not jettisoned his heteronormative convictions regarding institutionalized homosexuality, but he does try to understand it on its own terms. Through discussion, comparison, and recognition of catachreses, Rashid has made strides toward understanding the gay German and his social context. Yet nothing seen or heard during his encounter has shaken his conviction expressed early on that institutionalized homosexuality is a sign of a sterile, exhausted society (16, 99). Here again, just as with his fear of ostensibly homosexual prurience, lack of hygiene, and promiscuity, events "speak" and it is up to him to adequately read and frame them.

When the activities of the exchange program bring Joachim to Beirut, a city "chock-full of young men," Rashid feels compelled to put him in contact with women, preferably those who resemble boys. For his part, Joachim is happy to meet numerous people—gay and straight—and discovers a particular affinity with Sader, a gay man. Again, just when irony begins to make Rashid's effort to wean Joachim from desiring young men look almost ridiculous, events supervene in counter-irony. Joachim's meeting Ingrid, making love with her, and deciding to parent a child with her astounds Rashid—who reads life's plot twist as a vindication of his views on homosexuality. Rashid's exultation in his colleague's capacity to assume a heterosexual subject position as if it were a meritorious accomplishment reintroduces irony. He banters with Joachim, asking according to his candid and self-revealing wont, "Germany has returned to its senses, then?" and Joachim diplomatically declines to respond (41, 147). When Joachim mentions a name for the baby, Rashid urges him to name the child "Rashid," taking for granted that his intervention was instrumental in Joachim's decision but also because in Arabic *rashīd* means "the right way," "rational," and "mature," as opposed to the wrong, perverse, and immature way Joachim had been behaving for the previous two decades of his life (42, 148). The self-irony that makes Rashid look like an insufferable busybody peaks when he implies that his mediation can spark the salubrious transformation of Germany as a whole: "Has Germany been restored overnight?" (40, 147). In the same spirit, he then suggests that they name the child "Lebanon," the nation that mediated Joachim's heterosexual activity and Germany's reembrace of fecundity. The irony here is just a little too much and functions again to defamiliarize Rashid's convictions.

Just as Rashid had to modify his prejudices about homosexual practices early in the text as a result of observing events, here they force him to reframe his beliefs. He rashly assumes that Joachim's fatherhood would displace his homosexual proclivities, but at a going-away party he throws for Joachim upon the latter's departure from Beirut, Rashid is surprised to see Joachim's gay friend, Sader, in attendance. He is even more surprised at his own response:

> Of course, I wasn't naïve to the point of claiming I expected him to change his behavior after his friend's pregnancy. But I surprised myself that I behaved as if I aimed for this, or as if I were driven by this desire without being conscious of it. (46–47, 157)

Rashid's confusion is redoubled when he learns that Joachim will continue to live with N. but will return to Beirut where he and Ingrid, who did not conceive on their first meeting, will meet in order to try again. He wonders what kind of couple they are forming and how he should respond. Casting around to understand the new reality, he discusses the matter with a friend, a recovering cancer patient who has no time for dogmatic distinctions. Through this friend, Rashid comes to realize that whether Joachim and Ingrid get married or not, whether Joachim remains gay or not, and whether Ingrid wants only Joachim's drop of semen or not, they are going to have a child. He lights therefore on the notion of throwing the couple a wedding celebration, letting the new practice fill the old social structure as it will (49–50, 162).

The example of Joachim, Ingrid, and their daughter gives Rashid his response to the demographic consequences of homosexuality. Theirs is a family redefined as Ingrid moves back to Berlin to raise the baby in proximity to her parents and to Joachim, while the latter remains committed to N., seeing his child and her mother frequently. Joachim, therefore, "comes to his senses," not by embracing heteronormativity—which by continuing his life as a gay man he manifestly refuses—but by expanding his capacity for human fulfillment beyond a homo-heterosexual binary. Within the context of this narrative, Rashid's rhetoric of interest and self-investment clearly mediates this transformation, though not in a way anyone, least of all Rashid, could have predicted. Rashid, too, comes to his senses through a rhetoric of othering the self that leads him to cease projecting a heteronormative framework on individuals and cultures. Key to these rhetorics is a play of irony and counter-irony that puts convictions into abeyance in order to expand the field of discourse. The upshot is, as Rashid realizes when he takes final leave of Joachim and Ingrid in the last lines of the main narrative, "that much discussion must take place in order to achieve a clear understanding between Arabs and Germans. Much discussion—and a fervent desire for discussion" (53, 168).

COLONIAL DISCOURSE AND DISSENT IN RASHID AL-DAIF'S AND JOACHIM HELFER'S CONTRIBUTIONS TO THE WEST-EASTERN DIVAN

REBECCA DYER

ROSE-HULMAN INSTITUTE OF TECHNOLOGY

In addition to focusing on the alternating cultural explanation and dissent in Rashid al-Daif's *How the German Came to His Senses*, I examine Joachim Helfer's use of colonial discourse in *The Queering of the World*, an unfortunate rhetorical choice given his position as a European visitor depicting a region formerly controlled by Europe—Lebanon having been part of the French Mandate for Syria and Lebanon from the end of World War I until its independence in 1946. Although Germany did not directly administer colonies in the Middle East or North Africa, it is noteworthy that Germany's first chancellor, Otto von Bismarck, proposed and then hosted a watershed event in colonial history: the 1884–1885 Berlin Conference, during which the outlines of Africa's colonized territories were drawn. By 1912, after the European nations' "Scramble for Africa" that the Berlin Conference had formalized, Germany had enlarged its empire by claiming more of the interior adjacent to its coastal holdings. Although recent interactions between a German writer and his Lebanese counterpart may seem far removed from nineteenth- and early twentieth-century colonial ambitions and policies, my analysis demonstrates that aspects of Helfer's text and the conflicts and misunderstandings between him and al-Daif borrow from and build on European colonial discourse that dehumanized the colonized "native" and imposed a hierarchy on global cultures— deeming those of colonized people inferior, even savage—in order to justify European conquest.

The inequities of Germany's well-intentioned cultural program called the West-Eastern Divan are important considerations, not because they explain away any tactless humor or tongue-in-cheek homophobia evident in al-Daif's text, but rather because they illuminate the historical and economic factors that undergird Helfer's representation of Arabs. Helfer's response essay contains explicit commentary on international financial disparities and their effect on the cultural exchange: the funding was too low to interest a German writer of al-Daif's reputation, Helfer writes, in an effort to explain his pairing with a more established and widely translated author. Although neither remarks much on the difference in the length of each author's visit, it is noteworthy that al-Daif was required to live in Berlin for six weeks while Helfer was in Beirut for half that time. It is noteworthy as well given the colonial history of Lebanon that Helfer and al-Daif's interactions took place in French, their only common language, rather than in either author's native tongue. In what follows, I consider al-Daif's blurring of genre conventions, point out the necessity of distinguishing between the author and narrator in this instance, and delve into his self-representation as a critic of his culture and—drawing on Tayeb Salih's *Season of Migration to the North* (1969)—as the (imagined) object of the desiring Western gaze. In addition to examining al-Daif's depiction of earlier German visitors, including a significant reference to Kaiser Wilhelm II's visit to Lebanon's Bekaa Valley, I analyze al-Daif's implicit critique of Europeans' presumption of cultural superiority, both authors' designated audiences, and the written "conversation" that took place after their visits concluded.

REPRESENTATIONS OF "NATIVES," GENRE, AND NARRATIVE VOICE

There are important resonances between the texts that comprise the West-Eastern Divan exchange and *Heart of Darkness* and other European literary works of the colonial period. Chinua Achebe argues in his 1975 critique of *Heart of Darkness* that fictional characters' prejudices and political perspectives cannot be neatly separated from those of their authors. Labeling Joseph Conrad "a thoroughgoing racist," Achebe insists that Marlow's ideas about race are Conrad's own, and backs up his case by quoting from Conrad's journals, in which the author approvingly describes the "twinkl[ing]" whiteness and superior bearing of an Englishman while reducing the Africans he encounters to swaying, black limbs.[1] Achebe acknowledges that "[i]t might be contended, of course, that the attitude to the African in *Heart of Darkness* is not Conrad's but that of his fictional narrator, Marlow, and that far from endorsing it Conrad might indeed be holding it up to irony and criticism. Certainly, Conrad appears to go to considerable pains to set up layers of insulation between himself and the moral universe of his story."[2] Could al-Daif have been holding up his narrator's thoughts "to irony and criticism" as Achebe imagines Conrad's apologists would have it in that much earlier case of a narrator being perceived by some critics, Achebe among them, as speaking for the author? In this regard, it appears to be not Helfer but al-Daif who resembles Conrad—or who at least is borrowing a literary technique from him—if Conrad indeed meant to critique Marlow along with the other company men sent to the Congo region. Perhaps the negative reactions to al-Daif's portrayal of homosexuality in *How the German* have resulted in part from his having neglected to set up the expected "layers of insulation" between himself and his narrator; additionally, his playful blurring of literary genres appears to have contributed to misunderstandings.

In terms of genre, al-Daif has responded as a novelist might be expected to respond to his charge by the West-Eastern Divan organizers to describe his impressions of his cross-cultural encounter. However, his reliance on first-person narration and other essay conventions led readers, critics, and even his partner in the exchange to confront the text as a work of nonfiction and to assume that the narrator is al-Daif himself. By undermining the reader's idea that the traditional speaking/writing "I" is necessarily revealing his own thoughts, al-Daif enables his self-deprecating narrator to express (in comic parody) his culture's more provincial ideas about same-sex relationships—hinting at their hurtful consequences and at his own previous naïveté. He also performs, through the narrator, the realizations and recalibrations that result from conventional ideas being challenged by deepening personal knowledge of and mutual respect for a homosexual peer.

---

1. Chinua Achebe, "An Image of Africa: Racism in Conrad's *Heart of Darkness*," in *Hopes and Impediments: Selected Essays* (New York: Doubleday, 1988), 11, 14.
2. Ibid., 9.

Written after the publication of al-Daif's text in Arabic, *The Queering of the World* highlights the younger German writer's confusion regarding al-Daif's behavior during the exchange as well as uncertainty regarding al-Daif's narrative voice. Early on, Helfer seems to answer thoughtfully his questions about al-Daif's objectives, noting that "it would be naïve to take [the text's] unabashed naïveté, which is typical for Rashid's entire oeuvre, to be authentic. In fact, I believe it to be an attempt, through the creation of ironic distance from the self using a literary mask called 'Rashid,' to speak of things about which one usually remains silent in his society" (72). For other readers of al-Daif's *How the German* as well, the "authentic" voice of the author is difficult to pinpoint, indicating how important it is in this case to avoid conflating author and narrator. Helfer's familiarity with al-Daif's other works of fiction, particularly *Dear Mr. Kawabata*, which is similarly narrated by a misguided character named Rashid,[3] clearly helped him to recognize al-Daif's signature humor and use of irony. Nevertheless, whether *How the German* is a work of fiction or nonfiction remained a prime source of confusion for Helfer, who states that "Rashid is by all means a master of the novelist's craft: the tweaking and deleting that first make one of life's contingencies into an event worthy of literature" (149). Helfer apparently expected an accurate retelling but detected aspects of shared experiences that had been "tweak[ed] and delet[ed]," suggesting that this description of al-Daif as "a master of the novelist's craft" is not meant in this context solely as praise. Helfer later brings up the writer's obligation "to bear witness" while raising inadvertently the question of genre once more: "We are both aware of the fact that this dialogue [. . .] violates the boundaries of good taste; it can be felt to be obscene, monstrous, because it lifts the curtain on living human beings rather than characters" (168). Here, Helfer appears certain that al-Daif had produced a work of nonfiction and deems the textual dialogue between the two "obscene, monstrous" precisely because it is about actual people. Helfer's confusion about al-Daif's choice of genre is also evident in his many factual corrections to al-Daif's text.

---

3. Rashid al-Daif, *Dear Mr. Kawabata*, trans. Paul Starkey (London: Quartet, 2000).

Early in *How the German*, al-Daif introduces readers to his culture
and its ideas about masculinity and homosexuality, indicating that
he had a non-Arab audience in mind, perhaps as a result of the
West-Eastern Divan context and his expectation that the text would
be translated:

> I'm from an environment that honors and celebrates
> procreative masculinity; one that revels in it every chance
> it gets. The father in our culture is called "Abu" followed
> by the name of his eldest son, and the eldest son is named
> after his grandfather. The ancient Arab critics described
> the greatest and most creative poets as stallions. For us,
> the homosexual act is disgraceful, shameful, and must be
> suppressed. It's a crime punishable by law. Homosexuals
> are called perverts and their practices are considered sex
> acts against nature. (2–3, 60)

This is a significant passage not only because the Western-educated,
transcultural narrator is using first-person plural to describe
attitudes seen by many in the West as inhumane and atavistic but
also because it introduces outsiders to other, uncontroversial
aspects of al-Daif's native culture and language, such as naming
customs. Passages like this—overly homogeneous primers on Arab
culture—suggest that al-Daif differs from Helfer in his conception
of the primary audience for his text.

Helfer had stated in his prickly response that "[i]t should be
clear to both of us that even—and especially—in such a dialogue,
our statements are directed first and foremost at our own societies.
Neither of us is, after all, a typical representative of his respective
society [. . .]" (57). The fact that Helfer was targeting fellow Germans
compounds problems with his word choice, tone, and even with the
formatting of his essay. As Nicola Liscutin argues, Helfer's editing
of al-Daif's text (his insertion of breaks in the German publication
where none appeared in the Arabic publication) and his attempts
at correcting and enlightening al-Daif following the performance

of homophobia in his text contain a troubling Orientalist aspect.[4]
The demeaning terminology used to describe Arab men is jarring
too—especially given Helfer's evident erudition and skill as a writer.
His portrayal of young men making "simian gestures" and sporting
"a lot of gold chain on their black-haired brown chests" alongside
men of al-Daif's generation ogling women with "pure animalistic
gallantry" indicates that he is revisiting colonial-era tropes and
approaching Lebanese men through a filter of negative ethnic
stereotypes (62–63, 84).

As Edward Said has written, "a very large mass of writers [. . .] have
accepted the basic distinction between East and West as the starting
point for elaborate theories, epics, novels, social descriptions, and
political accounts concerning the Orient, its people, customs,
'mind,' destiny, and so on. [. . .] European culture gained in
strength and identity by setting itself off against the Orient as a sort
of surrogate and even underground self."[5] To the "surrogate" and
the "underground self," I would add (pace Achebe) the primordial
self in that Helfer repeatedly refers to al-Daif's beliefs and customs
as atavistic. For example, Helfer describes al-Daif as being frozen
in an earlier, less tolerant age. Instead of accurately capturing
contemporary Beirut, Helfer writes, al-Daif portrays "perhaps
the Beirut of his youth, probably his home village, and certainly
the bizarre reality of the Gulf States, where the Middle Ages are
alive and well" (61). Like Marlow in *Heart of Darkness*, who heard in
Africans' supposedly savage cries and drumming a discomforting
reminder to Europeans of their origins, Helfer responds to
Rashid's descriptions of Arab sexual mores not only by reminding
readers of extremes such as "honor killings" and the stoning of
adulterers and the like but also by bringing in anecdotes from his
own nation's history (including Nazi castration and extermination
of homosexuals), suggesting that Lebanese culture—or at least al-
Daif's representation of it—is similarly atavistic, even barbaric. It is
noteworthy that even in the context of a formal cultural exchange,
Helfer makes the point repeatedly to al-Daif that what he is describing

4. Nicola Liscutin, "West-East Divan or Procrustean Bed?," *Al-Kalimah [The Word]* 1,
no. 2 (2007): http://www.alkalimah.net/en/article.aspx?aid=13.
5. Edward W. Said, *Orientalism* (New York: Vintage, [1978] 2004), 2–3.

as Lebanese or Arab culture is actually not foreign to Germans, who
had just a generation or two before held similar beliefs:

> When the avant-garde of the Gay Pride Parade points the
> way to the future with a wink of the eye, it is also pointing
> back to the past at the same time: here, too, homosexuality
> was considered a scandal and was illegal until just a few
> decades ago. This difference, like many of the other ones
> alleged to be rooted deep in our cultural background,
> proves on closer examination to be simply an example of
> noncontemporaneity (*Ungleichzeitigkeit*). (64)

Likewise, in response to al-Daif's description of young Christian
Arab men and women's caution when choosing a "proper" café
to visit and beverage to order when on a date, Helfer relays to his
German audience that he had insisted to al-Daif that this was nothing
new: such careful choices and dating rituals were in place during his
mother's upbringing in the Lower Rhine after World War II.

Of course, Helfer makes a valid point that in traditional societies
gay men are often persecuted, sometimes brutally (an actual point
of agreement with al-Daif, as it happens), and he appears to be
tracing commonalities across cultures and centuries, as Conrad had
done through Marlow's description of the vaunted River Thames as
having been a place of "utter savagery" to its Roman conquerors.[6]
Nevertheless, Helfer's suggestion to his German audience that
al-Daif is describing "noncontemporane[ous]" rather than distinct
cultural practices—with the Lebanese trailing behind the Germans
by at least "a few decades"—reinforces Said's point that "the residue
of imperialism" is evident "not only in what is said but also in how
it is said, by whom, where, and *for whom*."[7]

The "residue of imperialism" is also evident in the comparative
lack of auto-critique in Helfer's text. While al-Daif acknowledges
that some of his nation's customs are in need of revision,
Helfer does not respond in kind by critically analyzing aspects

6. Joseph Conrad, *Heart of Darkness* (New York: Norton, [1902] 1988), 10.
7. Edward W. Said, *Culture and Imperialism* (New York: Vintage, 1993), 21
(emphasis added).

of contemporary German culture or even his own choices or understanding of events. Instead, after a short visit, he judged harshly many aspects of Lebanese beliefs and behavior, as is evident in his description of the "often quite grotesque exaggeration of the differences between men and women" visible on the streets of Beirut (62). Additionally, despite al-Daif's expertise in Arabic literature, Helfer suggests that he would know better how to introduce Lebanese students to the work of Abu Nuwas, a court poet who sang about pederasty. Helfer writes that when he had asked about Abu Nuwas's poetry, he was disappointed that al-Daif evasively "relegated the explosive content to the ivory-towered, ineffectual realm of classical art" (65). As these examples indicate, Helfer critiques al-Daif's oblique manner of broaching potentially volatile topics and finds fault with a culture that is conflicted about homosexuality—even if German culture, too, remains conflicted, as Liscutin has noted.[8]

DESIRE AND THE WESTERN GAZE

The critical attitudes Helfer expresses toward Lebanese displays of manliness in dress and manner contrast with and yet oddly echo the rather implausible scenario depicted by al-Daif in his text, in which the narrator describes himself as hairy and provides anecdotal evidence that gay men are titillated by mustaches and body hair. Although Helfer roundly criticizes this portion of the text for its implication that gay men are on the prowl for heterosexual men who bare their hairy wrists in public, al-Daif is reaching beyond categorizations of sexual preference in his depiction of Europeans—two out of his three anecdotes featuring Frenchmen—who desire the "exotic" hairiness of Arabs. Here, al-Daif seems to be using Europeans' preconceptions of Arab men for his own ends and is echoing, perhaps inadvertently, Tayeb Salih's *Season of Migration to the North.* A serial seducer of London women, Salih's Mustafa had turned Western ideas of Arab sensuality and virility to his advantage, and al-Daif in his novelized essay plays the same tune in a different

---

8. Liscutin, "West-East Divan."

key. Whereas Mustafa tells fanciful stories and recites the poetry of Abu Nuwas, counting on the smell of "rains in the deserts of Arabia" to seduce European women, the character Rashid playfully assumes the gay European's susceptibility to such sensual exoticism.[9]

It is possible that al-Daif, a professor of Arabic literature, intentionally incorporated elements of Salih's iconic, anticolonial novel into his conversations with Helfer and ultimately into *How the German*. Just as the narrator of Salih's novel is a double for Mustafa (evident in their similar colonial-era Western educations as well as their appearance, which led the narrator to see his "adversary" Mustafa in a mirror), al-Daif's narrator treats personal details of Helfer's life as his to share. Ken Seigneurie has noted in his detailed analysis of irony in al-Daif's text that Rashid as narrator is remarkable in that he takes "a personal interest in his interlocutor as if he were the self," suggesting a complex type of representation that intermingles self and other as well as narrator and object of study.[10] In addition to mentioning the sensual poetry of Abu Nuwas (whom Salih quotes at length in his novel) and the doubling of the narrator and the man he investigates obsessively, al-Daif's representation of the Arab as an "exotic," sexually desired object of the Western gaze closely corresponds to Salih's. Most revealing of the dynamic between al-Daif and Helfer is the conversation about transcultural sex being the "theater of war," an idea found in both Salih's novel and al-Daif's novelized essay,[11] in which al-Daif calls the bed "a frontline between Arab 'tradition' and Western modernity" (2, 58).

To the section of al-Daif's text about Rashid's hairiness and ridiculous machinations to avoid being touched by a gay man, Helfer replies by insisting on his own lack of sexual interest: "as much as I fear hurting him with this unchivalrous statement," he writes, "it is indispensable for the understanding of our dialogue to state clearly that our encounter was free of erotic undertones, on my part in any case" (84). This disavowal of attraction is perhaps understandable

---

9. Tayeb Salih, *Season of Migration to the North*, trans. Denys Johnson-Davies (Portsmouth, NH: Heinemann, 1969), 142.

10. Ken Seigneurie, "Irony and Counter-Irony in Rashid al-Daif's *How the German Came to His Senses*," 181.

11. Salih, *Season of Migration to the North*, 34.

given his confusion about whether al-Daif's text is fictional or not. Yet, together, al-Daif's send up of Europeans desiring hirsute Arab men and Helfer's dismissal of al-Daif as an object of desire perform what Robert Young has called the "characteristic ambivalent movement of attraction and repulsion," in which "we encounter the sexual economy of desire in fantasies of race, and of race in fantasies of desire."[12] In addition to spoofing European "fantasies" of Arab sensuality and playing up his narrator's "repulsion" to gay bodies, al-Daif intentionally repulses both Helfer and the reader by playfully describing Rashid's filthy bachelor's apartment prior to it being set right by a woman, who, he stresses, is "by nature opposed to filth and decay, body odors, and forgotten corners" (14, 94). Here, al-Daif contrasts feminine "nature" with his narrator's supposedly less civilized and sanitized masculinity, comically expressing an essentialist idea of gender differences that Helfer and his partner's impeccable flat in Berlin would later undermine. Once again, al-Daif incorporates humor at his narrator's expense to illustrate Helfer's unsettling and transformative effect on Rashid's traditional notions of gender and sexuality.

DISSENTING AUTHORS

The early passage about procreative masculinity from al-Daif's text is also noteworthy because it is followed by a description of his narrator's complex critical position vis-à-vis his culture: "As a rule, I exercise constant vigilance to keep at a distance from the behavior and ideology of the society I belong to and count myself among those who reexamine at every turn society's convictions—and indeed my own personal convictions—yet many of my society's ideas have penetrated me and do their work in me without my realizing it" (3, 60). This statement indicates a keen awareness of the cultural subjectivity that escapes his "constant vigilance" and reveals a sophisticated idea of identity and influence, one that, I believe, Helfer does not give al-Daif sufficient credit for having expressed.

---

12. Robert J. C. Young, *Colonial Desire: Hybridity in Theory, Culture and Race* (London: Routledge, 1995), 90.

Despite the many differences in terms of their tone and approach, Helfer and al-Daif were nevertheless in agreement regarding their dissenting positions as writers within their respective societies. Helfer writes, for example, that "poets and thinkers must violate convention where it is the custom to make sweeping judgments about human beings and their actions on the basis of identity [. . .]. This is what Rashid does and this is what I do" (126). Based on biographical details drawn from his earlier reading of al-Daif's fictional oeuvre, Helfer makes a point to describe al-Daif as a man of political conviction who rejected his traditional Maronite background. Just a page later, however, he suggests that al-Daif has not thrown off the shackles of his religious upbringing as Helfer had earlier claimed, and in fact "is held prisoner perhaps less by the country in which he lives than the time, the old but certainly not eternal presence of the either/or logic" (130).

The cosmopolitan and often dissenting approach of al-Daif's narrator is evident in a number of intercultural vignettes in which he alternately explains and questions his society's norms. At times, he comes across as a keenly observant cultural ambassador, explaining to an imagined Western audience noteworthy differences in dining etiquette and the rationale behind them. He reveals, for instance, that he saw Helfer noticing a Lebanese hostess reaching in front of him for a bottle of oil and explains that etiquette in his country demands that the guest not be asked to pass anything or make any effort to serve him or herself. In anecdotes like this, al-Daif's narrator is no longer stressing his dissenting position relative to his culture. He is rather the sole participant in the exchange who can make sense of the differing ideas of proper conduct. In terms of sexuality, he seems less inclined to accept his culture's edicts without question but at the same time reluctant to reject tradition entirely. He appears in matters of sexuality similar to the narrator of al-Daif's 2007 novel, *Learning English*, another Rashid, who explains his frustration with his girlfriend's mother's meddling in the personal life of her divorced daughter by stating, "But this is our culture and there's no choice but to behave according to what the circumstances allow. Make do with what you've got, the saying goes."[13]

---

13. Rashid al-Daif, *Learning English*, trans. Paula Haydar and Adnan Haydar (Northampton, MA: Interlink, 2007), 12.

The narrator's willingness to "make do" perhaps explains why it is necessary for his namesake in *How the German* to have an emotional epiphany about the stigma attached to being gay in Lebanon. He explains that after Helfer spent time with Sader, an openly gay Beiruti, "he filled me in on how much homosexuals suffer in Lebanon and how they encounter insurmountable difficulties in affirming themselves. He told me what I already knew but without having been upset by it before" (25, 117). This passage, with its suggestion of the narrator finding himself for the first time "upset" at the mistreatment of gay people, is followed by a catalogue of psychological torments Lebanese gay men face, including attempted "cures," familial disowning, despair, and suicide. The passage is significant because it reveals through his narrator's portrayal al-Daif's openness to new and openly critical ways of understanding his society. Immediately afterward he contrasts Helfer's rebellion "only about matters that concern him" with "Romantic revolutionar[ies]," particularly those in the Arab world, who "nag and complain about 'issues' and proclaim their dissent every chance they get" (25–26, 118). Here, given his portrayal of "nagging" Romantics, he seems to side with Helfer's practical methods of dissent, while at the same time he hints that there is a selfish aspect to Helfer's focus on gay rights.

GERMAN VISITORS AND THEIR DEPARTURES

Al-Daif's own dissenting habits of mind are evident in his narrator's description of his previous encounters with Germans. He reminisces about a young German woman who had without asking taken a photo of his little sister who was "standing barefoot in the road, wiping her nose with her hand" (20, 106). He had been not yet ten years old, he writes, but had already internalized certain cultural norms, such as the idea that "photos were for special occasions and were taken of those who were wearing neat clothing" (20, 106). Although at the time he was upset and ashamed that his sister had been captured in disarray, the narrator admits that with time "A deep affection grew in me toward [the German woman] because she dared to make a gesture far beyond what was customary" (20, 106). But one might ask: Whose customs was she gesturing beyond? For the German photographer, presumably, no breach of customs had occurred. Although Rashid praises the German woman for her audacity, he implies that she was out of line in that cultural milieu—an overstepping tourist who takes a small child's photo without permission, perhaps in an effort to capture "authentic" Lebanese village life. In the blond woman's brazen act and the Lebanese family's strong but ultimately futile reaction, one can detect al-Daif's critique of international inequities, in this case the power imbalance between tourist and picturesque "native," who is unable to control her own representation. Even as Rashid claims to be impressed with the tourist's daring gesture, it is noteworthy that he ends his reminiscing with "Would that I had that photo!"— revealing his lingering sense that something was permanently stolen from his family (20, 106).

Similarly, Rashid mentions his brother's German girlfriend, who had been welcomed to his family "with incomparable deference, surely as much as Kaiser Wilhelm II enjoyed when he visited Baalbek at the beginning of the last century (in proportion to our means, of course). We served her the food of weddings and feasts and showed her the places in our region we loved and of which we were most proud" (20–21, 106). Although his attitude toward Helfer is not one of "incomparable deference," the narrator abides by the cultural and familial tradition of offering the "food of weddings and feasts" and providing a tour of favorite sites. Once again, al-Daif manages with this seemingly neutral portrayal of a German visitor to suggest an imbalance of power in the transcultural relationship. The reference to Kaiser Wilhelm II is significant in that the narrator is comparing more recent familial interactions with visiting Germans to the financial and cultural inequities of the past, when Wilhelm II signed an agreement with Lebanon's Ottoman rulers to enable German excavators to unearth the Roman ruins at Baalbek. That arrangement, too, was a cultural exchange solely funded and administered by Germany, and in that regard is comparable to the Federal Cultural Foundation-funded program that brought Helfer and al-Daif together.

In addition to resembling the "wedding" that Rashid would theatrically arrange for Helfer and Ingrid, the German woman of similar background with whom he would soon have a child, the second anecdote from Rashid's childhood anticipates the two authors' parting. About his brother's German friend, Rashid explains that despite his family's warm welcome and love for the woman (sealed by an attempted kiss on her lips by his little brother), "news from her stopped and news of us to her probably also stopped" (21, 106). Similarly, despite al-Daif's mentioning "a fervent desire for discussion" to continue between Arabs and Germans at the end of his text, the ending of Helfer's expresses no such desire: he describes the dialogue with al-Daif as "so unusually and uncomfortably open for all participants" (168), and ends with a postscript about his daughter's birth and about his partner's and Daniel's reactions to her. Given that this information is targeting the audience external to their exchange, al-Daif has presumably been left back at his "wedding" banquet, having been stunned into silence by Helfer's impassioned defense of those implicitly excluded from al-Daif's table: "I too love *The Thousand and One Nights* and have nothing against bringing poetry into life—on the contrary, I am all for it [. . .]. But no one should be unwelcome at this celebration of life [. . .]" (164). Helfer's direct address to al-Daif in this passage enables him to shrink his named audience to one while performing for his German-speaking audience his scolding and correcting of "Rashid, esteemed colleague" (165). By failing to include gay men like Sader or Helfer's long-term companion, N., at the table, he tells his partner in the cultural exchange, "You are not celebrating life but jeering at it; you are not bringing poetry into everyday life but driving humanity out of it" (165). Once again, Helfer brings in questions of genre and contrasts the literary with "reality," when he suggests that al-Daif's representation of events has now moved into the realm of "yarn": "When an Arab writer begins to spin a yarn, no one should contradict him—who wants reality (hummus, curd cheese, and kebabs with pita bread for the three of us) when you can have such a poem about a wedding banquet!" (164). Despite his alternatingly scoffing and lecturing tone, Helfer at last demonstrates his willingness to accept criticism of his methods by mentioning Daniel's concern about "the form of a dialogue in which I have the last word: whereas Rashid often relativizes his own alphabet,

I oppose him with universalistic claims without appreciating the values possibly contained in Rashid's alphabet" (168). The young man's insightful interpretation of the West-Eastern Divan's power dynamics—specifically his critique of the way that Helfer has responded to al-Daif once again—underscores Helfer's text's similarity to colonial discourse with its claims of universality and objectivity when interpreting the expressions of people considered less rational or evolved.

Complex and challenging to readers due to its blurring of novel and essay genres and its playful, self-deprecating narrator, al-Daif's text appears to reinforce heteronormative Lebanese society at times and to critique it at others. While critically examining his own society, al-Daif seems to anticipate Helfer's assumption of cultural superiority, and al-Daif's narrator's intercultural anecdotes hint at the personal and sociopolitical stakes of uneven exchanges while acknowledging that his and Helfer's differing sexual preferences, generations, and degrees of literary acclaim complicate considerations solely based on national status. Significantly, as I discuss above, al-Daif refers to earlier German visitors to Lebanon, including a visitor from 1898, Kaiser Wilhelm II (grandson of Britain's Queen Victoria), revealing that al-Daif was well aware of the colonial precedents of his and Helfer's exchange and hinting, I contend, that the colonial paradigm continues to influence intercultural relations, even a partnership as intimate and yet—paradoxically—as institutionally arranged and short-lived as al-Daif and Helfer's ultimately was. *How the German's* subtle reference to Salih's anticolonial novel indicates as well that al-Daif was aware of the literary precedents of his and Helfer's sexually and politically charged subject matter—unsurprisingly perhaps, given al-Daif's expertise in Arabic literature. Even if participation in the West-Eastern Divan, with its laudable objective of creating "new forms of literary encounters aimed at improving the mutual awareness of German and Middle Eastern literature," prompted Helfer to revisit demeaning tropes from the colonial era,[14] the epilogue that al-Daif added to his text in 2005 after the

---

14. "The Project: Idea, Aims and Realisation," Westöstlicherdiwan [West-Eastern Divan], accessed August 7, 2013, http://www.west-oestlicherdiwan.de/projekt-en.html.

birth of Helfer's daughter—in which he notes that she was given an Arabic name—provides a hopeful, forward-looking conclusion to their exchange.

THE HERMENEUTICS OF THE OTHER: INTERSUBJECTIVITY AND THE LIMITS OF NARRATION IN *THE QUEERING OF THE WORLD*

MICHAEL ALLAN

UNIVERSITY OF OREGON

The Queering of the World presents what could seem a classic tale of literary internationalism. Not only does the book offer a dialogue between two writers of different nationalities, it also directly engages the valences of translation, identity, and language through reflections on the experience of living in Germany and Lebanon. At first glance, the whole exchange seems to offer a path between Montesquieu's *Persian Letters*—with its reflections on cultural particularism—and Goethe's conception of *Weltliteratur*—with its emphasis on shared forms across national traditions.[1] There are even echoes of nineteenth-century writers such as Rifa'ah Raf'i al-Tahtawi, Ahmad Faris Shidyaq, Gustave Flaubert, and Gérard de Nerval, each of whom travels and comments upon the interplay between Europe and the Middle East.[2] And in both Rashid al-Daif's account and Joachim Helfer's response, the two writers reflexively consider the literary dimensions of transcultural observation, underscoring the framework through which observation occurs—in this case, the exchange facilitated by the West-Eastern Divan

Thank you to Sunayani Bhattacharya, Tadashi Dozono, Baran Germen, and Redouane Hadrane for comments and feedback on versions of this essay.

1. Montesquieu, *Persian Letters*, trans. C. J. Betts (New York: Penguin Books, 2004); for collected reflections on *Weltliteratur*, see Johann W. von Goethe in H. J. Schulz and P. H. Rhein, *Comparative Literature: The Early Years* (Chapel Hill: University of North Carolina Press, 1973).

2. Ahmad Faris Shidyaq, *al-Saq 'ala al-saq fi ma huwa al-faryaq: aw Ayyam wa-shuhur wa-a'wam fi 'ajam al-'Arab wa-al-a'jam*, ed. N. W. Khazin (Beirut: Dar Maktabat al-Hayah, 1966); Rifa'ah Raf'i al-Tahtawi, *An Imam in Paris: Account of a Stay in France by an Egyptian Cleric*, trans. Daniel Newman (London: Saqi, 2004); Gustave Flaubert, *Flaubert in Egypt: A Sensibility on Tour*, trans. Francis Steeqmuller (New York: Penguin Books, 1972); Gérard de Nerval, *Journey to the Orient*, trans. Norman Glass (New York: Moyer Bell, Ltd., 1982).

program. Consequently, it might seem that, on the pages of this quasi-fictionalized account, we encounter a twenty-first-century version of the classic tradition of travel writing with all of the potentials and limits this genre entails.[3]

There is, though, much more to the story. In the opening pages, we learn that Thomas Hartmann, who directs the West-Eastern Divan program, called Rashid to inform him of the writer with whom he had been paired for the six-week exchange.[4] "Naturally," Rashid writes, "he told me his name, Joachim Helfer, his age, thirty-nine, and summarized his works, activities, and other such things—but the remarkable thing was that he insisted on informing me that Joachim was gay [mithlī]" (1, 57). It is this "remarkable thing" that eventually propels the story forward. In fact, of all the items listed—age, publications, activities, and "other such things"—the detail regarding Joachim's sexuality is what most concerns Rashid, in spite of his claims to the contrary. "I told him," Rashid continues, "this was something personal that didn't concern me." And yet, as the story makes abundantly clear, Rashid takes the disclosure as an invitation to reflect on the category of homosexuality—all part of his quest to understand the mysteries of the intimate life of another. For the length of his account, Rashid takes this initial disclosure of Joachim's gay identity as the basis for his reflections, using sexuality as the groundwork from which to consider the distinction between Berlin and Beirut, Germany and Lebanon, and as he frames it, the East and the West.

Intriguingly, Rashid's professed indifference to Joachim's sexuality morphs into a suspicion as to why he would need to be

---

3. Here I'm thinking of figures such as Edward Said and Mary Louise Pratt. For a more recent generation of critically minded scholarship, see Shaden Tageldin, *Disarming Words: Empire and Seductions of Translation in Egypt* (Berkeley: University of California Press, 2011) and Tarek El-Ariss, *Trials of Arab Modernity: Literary Affects and the New Political* (New York: Fordham University Press, 2013).

4. In order to distinguish the author from the narrator, I will use the names Rashid and Joachim to refer to events outlined in the account. For extended analysis of the opening paragraphs of the account, see Ken Seigneurie's "Irony and Counter-Irony in Rashid al-Daif's *How the German Came to His Senses*" earlier in this book. Where Seigneurie emphasizes the potential the exchange offers for intercultural dialogue, I'll be focusing here primarily on the narrational limits that the exchange offers.

told. "I wondered," he writes, "whether this might have something to do with my being an Arab." This suspicion is repeated almost as a statement of fact in Joachim Helfer's response, which notes that had the exchange been with a French author, Thomas Hartmann "would undoubtedly have broached the topic less explicitly" (57). Already four paragraphs into his account, as though contradicting what he suggests a mere paragraph earlier, Rashid implies that the disclosure does matter: "But to be quite honest, despite my response to Thomas Hartmann that the whole matter was the writer's business and not mine, I was pleased he'd told me." He continues by qualifying, "Because, frankly, the whole thing preoccupied me somewhat." The preoccupation inflects not only how Rashid's account of the exchange transpires, but how the category of sexuality eventually plays out in the narrative—already evident in the dizzying set of reversals in the beginning of the book. These reversals, I will argue here, are part of the narrative performance that dissolves the legibility of identity categories. What transpires, in other words, is the dissolution of the opening disclosure in the narrative acrobatics that play out over the course of Rashid's account.

In a book ostensibly framed around intercultural exchange, sexuality might easily become just another distinguishing identity category akin to nationality, gender, or race. That the phone call from Thomas Hartmann takes age, gender, and nationality as key attributes worth mentioning already discloses a basic cultural logic—one shared in a paradigm of world literature that links writers across traditions, languages, and territories. In its formation, the West-Eastern Divan program facilitates exchanges between individual German writers and Turkish, Iranian, or Arab writers for visits to one another's home country, resulting not only in shared presentations and interviews, but also the production of a copublished set of essays. The program's goal of "mutual awareness" seems to embrace the common sense presumption that an author's identity impacts his or her literary production—or that somehow, an author carries the cultural, linguistic, and ethical frameworks of a home country.[5] And here, Rashid, the Lebanese straight author,

5. For a description of the project, see http://www.west-oestlicherdiwan.de/projekt-en.html. Accessed August 29, 2013.

and Joachim, the gay German author, stand in for who they are as writers and as narrated on the pages of the respective accounts. It is on this level that *The Queering of the World* appeals to a perceived literary multiculturalism—one that initially frames the terms of the exchange and ultimately inflects understanding of nationality, sensibility, and culture difference. In the multicultural logic by which we are all an amalgam of different identity categories, the West-Eastern Divan program might appear to deliver on the goal of dialogue across nationalities in a world republic of letters—or so it would seem.

That Rashid's account engages identity categories quite explicitly does not necessarily mean that it recapitulates the logic of multiculturalism. In fact, as I hope to suggest, it does something quite radically different by innovating formally on the narrative conventions of identity politics. Within this framework, confessing who you are is inseparable from the activity of being a subject— so that the most persuasive accounts stem from the first person testifying, as it were, to one's experience. Scholars have pointed to some of the limits of this presumption for years, especially as it pertains to the logic of cultural authenticity (in the case of Anthony Appiah's contribution to Amy Gutman and Charles Taylor's volume *Multiculturalism*), to experience (in the case of Joan Scott's contribution to historiography), or to the testimonial (in the debates surrounding Rigoberta Menchú and the anthropologist Elisabeth Burgos-Debray).[6] More recently, Adriana Cavarero's *Relating Narratives: Storytelling and Selfhood* considers the dimensions of a narratable self, and Judith Butler's *Giving an Account of Oneself* explores some of the valences of subject formation in the context of moral philosophy.[7] We tend to take as a given that to be a subject is to

---

6. Kwame Anthony Appiah, "Identity, Authenticity, Survival: Multicultural Societies and Social Reproduction" in *Multiculturalism: Examining the Politics of Recognition*, ed. Amy Gutman and Charles Taylor (Princeton: Princeton University Press, 1994), 149–164; Joan Scott, "The Evidence of Experience," *Critical Inquiry* 17, no. 4 (Summer 1991): 773–797; Rigoberta Menchú and Elisabeth Burgos-Debray, *I, Rigoberta Menchú: An Indian Woman in Guatemala* (London: Verso, 1983) and Arturo Arias, *The Rigoberta Menchú Controversy* (Minneapolis: University of Minnesota Press, 2001).

7. Adriana Cavarero, *Relating Narratives: Storytelling and Selfhood* (London: Routledge, 2000); Judith Butler, *Giving an Account of Oneself* (New York: Fordham University Press, 2005).

inhabit an identity that is confessed. Here, in the context of the literary exchange, it would seem that to be German, Arab, Lebanese, straight, or gay demarcates a horizon of what can be said on behalf of whom.

And yet, I hold out more hope for the sort of work the West-Eastern Divan exchange performs, as a sort of intersubjective confessional. Most curiously, it is the life of another person that is the subject of Rashid's account. The story we have emerges from Rashid's unrelenting desire to know more about Joachim's sexuality than about his nationality or age. In this intersubjective project, the disclosure of Joachim's status as a gay man prompts a scene of translation that enfolds Rashid, as the storyteller, into the life he aspires to narrate. This detail alone—the procedure by which the other is narrated—makes this exchange quite distinct. While Rashid's account reads at times as outright offensive to Joachim, it doesn't necessarily offer any sort of scientific exposition of what a homosexual is. It meditates instead on a set of affective responses to observations anchored in the struggle to understand the significance of the identity category. Here, on the pages of this narrated encounter, any knowledge of the other is refracted through the often-conflicted musings, sentiments, and responses of the observer.

If what Rashid offers, then, is neither a science of sexuality (with claims of neutral objectivity), nor an extended cultural explanation of behavior, how might we understand what his account performs? In this quest to understand Joachim's sexuality, we are ultimately led to a collision of two registers at play in classic travel writing: the struggle to delineate categories with which to understand the observed on the one hand, and the professed feelings, reactions, and responses of the observer on the other. Rashid's narrative flirts from start to finish with an inverted confessional, one whose progression reads as stream of consciousness and whose content reveals as much about the narrator as it does the subject upon whom he supposedly reflects. Knowledge is at stake, but the stability of the referent is shrouded in mystery, complicating the very structures through which the other is to be known. What Rashid offers the reader thus engages the logic of multiculturalism, but enfolds it

in the impossibility at the vanishing point of his narration—the
ever-elusive verification of the private life of Joachim.

THE SUBJECT OF SEXUALITY

Let us dwell here for a moment on the status of the disclosure as it
emerges initially in the phone call and as it reverberates throughout
Rashid's account.[8] We could begin by noting that Rashid's response
to Joachim's sexuality is itself the impetus for his reflections. We
might add, in turn, that Rashid's reaction mutates in the opening
pages—to the extent that his reflections offer much less a position
than they do a process. The indifference he initially professes is
performatively contradicted by the bulk of what we read, most all of
which stems from the bewilderment posed by Joachim's sexuality.
What begins as one attribute among many comes to dominate not
just the contents, but the very formal attributes of Rashid's account.
An accumulation of innuendos, inferences, and curiosities reveals
infinitely more about the perversity of Rashid's intrigue than
anything concrete about Joachim. Such is our starting point.

For readers of Rashid al-Daif—among whom Joachim Helfer
includes himself—it should come as little surprise that *The Queering of
the World/How the German Came to His Senses* proceeds as it does. Like most
of his work, this account engages on multiple levels with references
that span well beyond any one particular context—be it national,
linguistic, or literary. The narrator's associational reflections in
Azizi as-Sayyid Kawabata are echoed in what we read—as is the first-
person stream of consciousness narration that dominates a novel
like *Nahiyat al-Bara'a*.[9] And later, in *Tistifil Meryl Streep*, Rashid al-Daif
weaves pop culture references alongside citations of classical Arabic,
and he does so in a broader exploration of morality through
attitudes toward sex.[10] The ironic narrative twists, irreverent subject

8. It is worth noting that the disclosure, or references to the initial scene, occurs
both at the beginning and end of Rashid's account. Thomas Hartmann becomes,
in a curious way, almost a backdrop to the account itself.

9. Rashid al-Daif, *Azizi as-Sayyid Kawabata* (Beirut: Mukhtarat, 1995) and *Nahiyat al-
Bara'a* (Beirut: al-Masar, 1997).

10. Rashid al-Daif, *Tistifil Meryl Streep* (Beirut: Riad el-Rayyes, 2001).

matter, and associational thinking serve as a sort of signature across Rashid al-Daif's work.

We could say, then, that *The Queering of the World* plays with conflicting registers in a way that is characteristic of Rashid al-Daif's style, but it also performs some of the goals outlined in the West-Eastern Divan program. While the author's writing bears an obvious indebtedness to the Arabic literary tradition—with its remarkable Arabic prose, poetic inflections, and citations from the classical sources—it also demonstrates an outright irreverence of it in the incorporation of foreign terms, topics, and subject matter. Most important, though, is that there is no regard for the purity of one tradition over another. Rashid's account is much more concerned with what falls outside the ambit of his own experiences than it is with any affirmation of the position from which he speaks. His identification as Arab, drawn frequently as a point of contrast, reads almost as an ironic invocation of a civilizational discourse, which is itself undercut by the attributes of his writing, his choice of subject matter, and the lightness of his style.

But the novelty of the style derives in large part from how the narrative structures and limits what we read. To begin with, Rashid's account revolves around an exploration of an apparent statement of fact—that Joachim is gay. This simple detail is itself all the more telling when cast alongside discussions in queer theory. From the confessional in Michel Foucault's *History of Sexuality*, to the secret in Eve Kosofsky Sedgwick's *Epistemology of the Closet*, and the connotation in D. A. Miller's "Anal Rope," queer reading has tended to focus on a hermeneutics of suspicion: the paranoia of knowing or not knowing, the question as to who or what happened, the tension between the connotation of homosexuality and the denotative act or practice.[11] How does one recognize the homosexual in a text? In what ways can homosexuality ever be verifiable? Is witnessing a homosexual act a precondition for knowing the sexuality of a character? The open-ended questions animate, in many ways, the

---

11. Michel Foucault, *History of Sexuality*, trans. Robert Hurley (New York: Vintage, 1990); Eve Kosofsky Sedgwick, *Epistemology of the Closet* (Berkeley: University of California Press, 1990); and D. A. Miller, "Anal Rope," *Representations* 32 (Fall 1990): 114–133.

importance of queer theory when it comes to ways of reading with attention to sexuality. A queer reading, in these instances, is not so much the discovery of a homosexual in the text—it is, instead, an inquiry into the formations, recognitions, and subversions that texts make possible, especially when questions of sexuality, desire, and gender are brought to the fore.

Quite tellingly, in *The Queering of the World*, we begin in a most inverted manner—that is, with the initial disclosure of Joachim's sexuality. Already in the opening lines, we move away from a hermeneutics of suspicion, guessing the character's sexuality, and toward a suspicion as to how the category of homosexuality functions at all. As the story develops, what drives the narrative action is a sort of quest to discover more about the details of Joachim's private life as insight into what homosexuality might mean. And it is telling that these narrative events only further frustrate the narrator's efforts to make sense of Joachim. On one level, Rashid's account reads almost as a confessional on the other's behalf. Rashid draws the storyline from a detective-like inquiry into the details of Joachim's private life, tracing his interactions with N., Daniel, Sader, and Ingrid, but never quite knowing the intimate details of these encounters. Rashid thus draws us as readers to the limits of narration—to the horizon of what can be known and said about Joachim. We get, in turn, Rashid's associations with the category of the homosexual and his professed discomfort with what he understands it to mean. With allusions to Arab poets, fears for his son's sexuality in France, and reflections on two French friends, Rashid's account performs a confession of his own prejudice, revealing the clichés and stereotypes that he holds as the observer. And like the dizzying reversal in the first few paragraphs, these clichés and stereotypes are themselves complicated by the mere fact of his account, which reveals his struggle to make sense of Joachim without the burden of preexisting assumptions.

On another level, in addition to the narrator's personal associations, Rashid does flirt with a mode of observation intent upon broader generalizations about German life. Rashid begins his account by noting his investment in the bedroom as the site for social inquiry. He recalls his interest in morality, which he explores in detail in *Tistifil Meryl Streep*. "The bed," he writes almost axiomatically, "is a frontline between Arab 'tradition' and Western modernity" (2, 58). A sentence later, he reverses course: "Something in this expression is not fully precise . . . ," and later, "Sex is the 'moment' that defines and exposes controversies" (2, 59). In *Tistifil Meryl Streep*, these observations are filtered through Rashid's experiences with his wife, but in *The Queering of the World/How the German Came to His Senses*, he turns toward the sex life of another. We encounter a narrator in the mode of an ethnographer, one who confesses outright his lack of knowledge: "I admit," he tells us, "my understanding of homosexuality is not deep and my reading very limited" (5, 71). The bedroom may well be the site through which Rashid hopes to understand better the complexity of an encounter between the Middle East and Europe, and yet, in the end, it is the bedroom that is consistently foreclosed in his knowledge of Joachim. Much as Rashid is fascinated to know the homosexual, doing so would entail uncovering and witnessing the intimate acts in his life—a perversion of its own.

So even if we begin with the disclosure of Joachim's homosexuality, we ultimately become suspect of what the category might mean. Rather than a quest for knowledge, which would make the narrator a detective, the account ends up making a mockery of the narrator himself. He is confused, perplexed, and overwhelmed by the unintelligibility of the category. Whatever his suspicions are about Joachim's relation to N., Daniel, Sader, or Ingrid, Rashid's knowledge is itself absolutely and admittedly unreliable. What we have is a series of affective responses that filter the quest for knowledge through the confusion of his narration. Here, then, we have not the basis of the confessional structure (through which knowledge of the subject would be affirmed), but its vanishing point. We have, in the end, not so much an affirmation of the self, nor a celebration of the dialogical relationship set forth in the exchange, but a mockery of the terms of identity—or at the very least, a gesture to the impossibility of its realization.

ORIENTING NARRATION

There is, though, more to the story. After all, sexuality is by no means the only category at stake. In fact, sexuality is understood as it bears upon national distinctions between Lebanon and Germany, or as both Rashid and Joachim occasionally suggest, distinctions between the Arab world and the West. One could be tempted to read the exchange in terms of one gross reduction of intercultural complexity or a collision of misunderstandings: queer clichés, on the one hand, and Orientalist conflations, on the other. In addition to the attention that Rashid pays to Joachim's life, he also offers a not-so-subtle flirtation with practices of observation and deduction long explored in the Orientalist tradition—applied here to understanding homosexuality. His account transforms Joachim into the object of inquiry, and in turn, animates the frustration from which Joachim's response stems, even though Joachim himself often makes recourse to a cultural logic. Most amazingly, at the crossroads of queer theory and Orientalism, the whole encounter presents us with a framework in which identity politics exceed the boundaries of the self. Ultimately, the dialogical encounter ends up dissolving the distinctions that initially sustain the goals of the West-Eastern Divan program—and in this process, Lebanon, Beirut, Germany, and Berlin become as contested as the category of homosexuality.

If the declaration of homosexuality frames the beginning of Rashid's reflections, then it mirrors back differently in Joachim's response. Joachim's account dwells less on associations and responses to the identity categories than on the status of knowledge. Joachim reflects critically on the observations in Rashid's account: "While I did not expect to become an intercultural specimen as a person rather than as an author," and also notes, "This is acceptable to me as long as it serves the advancement of knowledge" (56). What is the status of the knowledge gained in the exchange? We seem to have exceeded the boundaries of generalization, questions of categories, and ways of life, and departed into mutual confessions of injury. There is injury that derives from not properly understanding the two frames within which the reading occurs, and incidentally, the frames lent to the whole event itself: nationality and sexuality. Rashid's account begins with the injury that the disclosure poses to him, refracted through his sense that, were he not Arab, it wouldn't have been mentioned. And Joachim's injury stems from the seeming objectification posed by Rashid's account.

It is thus all the more telling that, in a gesture of universalization, Joachim ends his response to Rashid with a classic turn to the conundrum of gay rights. "If I come across as a know-it-all," he writes, "I can regret this but not change it. Yes, I believe in the universal value of individual freedom and responsibility, in the inviolability of the dignity of every single human being, everywhere in the world." And then, turning back to the particularism not of Lebanon and German, but of Saudi Arabia and Iran, he continues, "Neither do I doubt that one day even in [Saudi] Arabia and Iran no lovers of any kind will be persecuted—moreover that same-sex couples will be recognized—nor do I doubt that this will represent progress for all of inseparable humankind" (169). He thus concludes his essay not with a reflection on Rashid, nor with a reflection on Germany, but with a projection onto two countries apparently outside of his model of progress: Saudi Arabia and Iran. The common denominator in this equation, it would seem, falls back on a dangerous civilizational cliché: the progressive Western gay man, on the one hand, and the supposedly repressive Orient, on the other.

Of the various instances when Rashid reflects explicitly on Joachim's approach to life, one seems especially important given how it eventually underscores both a philosophical and political distinction. Halfway through his account, Rashid notes, "Joachim, from what I could fathom, rebels only about matters that concern him" (26, 118). Rashid then goes on to qualify: "This doesn't mean he's selfish; rather that he is a very realistic person who dreams about what he can achieve." Even if relatively little is made of this almost parenthetical comment, it underscores a key distinction in the two narrative styles offered in the exchange. Quite simply: Rashid reflects on the status of his partner, his life, and those aspects of his intimate circle most difficult to ascertain, and Joachim, in response, reflects on the danger posed by Rashid's curious observational mode.

Against this backdrop, then, Rashid's suggestion takes on an interesting hue. What might it mean to think of a political position outside the framework of self-interest? By implication, what would a mode of narration be that speaks not so much from the self as from the other? Here, it seems that for all of its reversals,

contradictions, exaggerations, and irony, Rashid's account offers
us something that reflects back on a tradition of intercultural
communication. It does so not to triumph an underlying moral so
much as to question the very grounds for such inquiry. And it does
so not to turn back upon a motif of self-understanding, reaffirming
the importance of who he is, but instead to question implicitly
the framework for such inquiry, taking sexuality over nationality,
thinking morality alongside ethics, and making possible a different
mode of narration. Here we encounter the hermeneutics not of the
self, but of the other.

My title borrows and deviates from the famous lectures that
Michel Foucault delivered during the fall of 1980 entitled "About
the Beginning of the Hermeneutics of the Self."[12] Largely heralded
as a defining shift from his work as a historian of cultural systems
to a scholar of ethics, the lectures lay the groundwork for his
understanding of the confessional, as an attribute of Christian
subject formation, and a broader concern with "the critical ontology
of ourselves."[13] The importance Foucault's observations pose to
critical reflection on a generation of identity-based politics has been
paramount. And yet, here Rashid's account ushers us away from the
confessional and toward an alternate hermeneutic. It is precisely his
intrigue in stepping outside of the purview of his own experience and
his perverse fascination with Joachim's sexual life that drives forward
his narrative. The ultimate inversion, then, stems not from the life of
Joachim nor even that of Rashid, but from the inverted narrational
mode by which Rashid invests in the details of the other.

If the axes of the discussion bring us, first, to the consideration
of sexuality and in the second, to the consideration of Orientalism,
then here, in closing, I'd like to emphasize what this book raises at
the limits of narration. At the moment of the disclosure, outlined
in the opening pages, we are already welcomed into the narration
of a process of making sense of a statement—a translation in its own
right of an effort to come to terms with what homosexuality might

---

12. Michel Foucault, "About the Beginning of the Hermeneutics of the Self: Two
Lectures at Dartmouth," *Political Theory* 21, no. 2 (May 1993): 198–227.

13. See Michel Foucault, "What is Enlightenment?," in *The Foucault Reader*, ed. Paul
Rabinow (New York: Pantheon Books, 1984), 50.

mean, or more specifically still, how and why it would matter at all. As for Helfer's response, it too outlines an effort to make sense of Rashid's response, and in addition to puzzling over why the author would pay so much attention to one facet of his life, the response stems from a quest to understand how and why the story transpires. Beyond the underlying affect moving each writer to write, there is another level of engagement. Rashid's text works both due to the professed mediation of the narrator, whose interjections, observations, and confusion propel the writer, but also due to the narratological rendering of events—the relationships, meals, intimate contacts, and conditions presented in the story Rashid tells. Here, in spite of the initial disclosure, we are welcomed into the limits of what can be disclosed—that is, to what Rashid will and won't see in Joachim's life.

The point is not to gesture to the utter futility of such a project nor to the essential unknowability of the other, but instead, to highlight the process that this book underscores. After all, what we read is by no means a policy statement packaged and presented to the reader, but precisely the struggle to understand, analyze, and come to terms with the life of another. Life here is understood not as a ready-made biography, but as the twists, turns, and phenomena that make the initial disclosure ultimately the disintegration—rather than affirmation—of the identity category with which the book begins. The narrative dimensions introduced by Ingrid and the challenges posed to the category so prominently disclosed in the opening pages, the blindness and ignorance that underscore Rashid's limited account of what Joachim does, and the intersubjective dimension staged in the very effort to know the other, all make of the exchange something remarkable—not so much a hermeneutics of the self, in the sense elaborated through the theory of the subject in Foucault's work, but what we might call a hermeneutics of the other. And this hermeneutic struggle, we should note, does not simply resolve itself to intelligibility; instead, it is a procedure that ambiguates precisely what it sets out to know.

What, then, in ending, does this book offer to those of us working in literature across linguistic traditions? Far from presenting an exercise in immediate translation between Arabic, German, and

English and Beirut, Berlin, and the book market—as it certainly does—it also offers an inquiry into the limits of narration. On the one hand, as I've mentioned, it confesses the other, inverting the classic line of queer theory. On the other hand, it pushes against the conventional Orientalizing gesture that seeks a scientific and objective knowledge. But what it does most is point to some of the limits of the identity categories that, in effect, create our modern political grammar. In this story, the domain of propositions and philosophical axioms disentangles itself. We end as we begin—with the confusion over the category. The journey taken, however, is itself an insight into the limits of such an identitarian hermeneutic.

WRITING, READING, AND TALKING SEX: NEGOTIATING THE RULES OF AN INTERCULTURAL LANGUAGE GAME

GARY SCHMIDT
WESTERN ILLINOIS UNIVERSITY

To what degree is it possible for intercultural dialogue to occur when the participants are chosen for the express purpose of engaging in such a dialogue and are enjoined to do so? One might engage any number of discourses to argue that such a dialogue will be quite different from one conducted between the same individuals if they were to address similar topics in the context of a different task or, indeed, if no explicit task had motivated the exchange. The Hawthorne effect, ascertained and elaborated in the context of studies of worker productivity in industry, states that individuals being observed alter their behavior precisely because of this observation. This effect may not be entirely relevant to the encounter between Joachim Helfer and Rashid al-Daif, since we are not concerned with one-dimensional measures of worker productivity but rather with complex literary responses to equally complex experiences of reciprocal observation and self-observation. Nevertheless, one should not disregard the role played by both writers' conscious and subconscious desires to meet certain expectations, whether of the project organizers, their readers, or their own idealized notions regarding what constitutes a text that faithfully records an intercultural encounter.

The philosopher Ludwig Wittgenstein might be called upon to suggest that the two authors engage in particular "language games"—the rule-governed yet action-oriented deployment of specific utterances—in order to successfully (and possibly competitively) fulfill the task that has been imparted to them: discovering and expressing something meaningful regarding "cultural differences" and "intercultural communication."[1] The insight that academic

---

1. Ludwig Wittgenstein, *Philosophische Untersuchungen* (Frankfurt am Main: Suhrkamp, 2003).

discourse can be analyzed in terms of an "agonistics of language" is central to French philosopher Jean-François Lyotard's treatise, *The Postmodern Condition*:

> Wittgenstein, taking up the study of language again from scratch, focuses his attention on the effects of different modes of discourse; he calls the various types of utterances he identifies along the way (a few of which I have listed) *language games*. What he means by this term is that each of the various categories of utterance can be defined in terms of rules specifying their properties and the uses to which they can be put—in exactly the same way as the game of chess is defined by a set of rules determining the properties of each of the pieces, in other words, the proper way to move them. [2]

The rules of this particular literary and academic language game are established within the particularities of the two authors' literary and academic cultures and their respective institutional frameworks, as well as through the parameters of the West-Eastern Divan project itself. Seen from this perspective, examples of alleged intercultural disagreement, misunderstanding, or even conflict might be understood as arising at least in part from the different sets of rules being followed by the two authors, as well as their different perceptions of the task. Following Wittgenstein, my concern here is less with identifying expressed or perceived substantive differences between cultures and their apparent manifestations in disagreements between two authors who are being read as representative of these cultures than with the linguistic choices that they make in order to fulfill their task. For the purpose of my analysis, the form is the substance.

The formal choices made by the two authors (as a Germanist I am qualified only to analyze Helfer's contribution) are not only responses to the injunction to engage in intercultural dialogue requiring the use of certain ways of talking about the polysemic

---

2. Jean-François Lyotard, *The Postmodern Condition: A Report on Knowledge*, trans. Geoff Bennington and Brian Massumi (Minneapolis: University of Minnesota Press, 1993).

and contested sign expressed in English as culture and German as *Kultur*; these choices also attest to a kind of Foucauldian incitement to talk sex initiated by program organizer Thomas Hartmann. The homosexual/heterosexual dichotomy identified with Helfer and al-Daif, once established through Hartmann's speech act (his outing of Helfer to al-Daif), ultimately compels first the Lebanese author and then his German counterpart to produce intelligible meaning regarding presumed cultural differences surrounding sex, gender, and sexuality using the linguistic resources available to them within their respective sociolinguistic spheres.

Rather than attesting to a "clash of civilizations," to borrow the controversial phrase used by political scientist Samuel Huntington to describe the new multipolar world order that emerged after the Cold War,[3] and a basic disagreement about fundamental values (such as human rights, particularly in relation to gender and sexual orientation), the textual divergences can be explained in part through different understandings of the task of intercultural dialogue and the rules of the language game that this dialogue entails. Such differences cannot be reduced to merely the personal or the cultural but arise out of a dynamic interplay between the two: Helfer and al-Daif make choices to utilize genres and forms that are embedded in their own cultures and interpreted through particular cultural traditions and usages not unique to them and hence also transcultural. In reading this document, we witness the process in which two well-educated authors attempt to fulfill the task of intercultural dialogue by making different choices that become visible to the reader in terms of genre and other literary devices, including irony, self-reflectivity, and metaphor. The authors' choices (their moves in the game) in turn have important implications for the way cultural difference is constructed and imbued with causal attributes (or not) concerning the misunderstandings and disagreements of the exchange.

For example, Helfer explains differences in sexual mores and courtship practices in terms of *Ungleichzeitigkeit* (noncontemporaneity or nonsimultaneity), rather than by invoking deep cultural roots. *Ungleichzeitigkeit*, literally meaning "the quality of not being at the

---

3. Samuel P. Huntington, *The Clash of Civilizations and the Remaking of World Order* (New York: Simon and Schuster, 2011).

same time," has philosophical resonances in German, being used specifically by Ernst Bloch to refer to a divergence in developmental paths within different spheres *of a single society*, namely Germany on the eve of the Nazi party's rise to power.[4] Hence, Helfer's use of this loaded term rhetorically counters Huntington's claims that Western Civilization is unique rather than universal, for it places Germany and Lebanon both on a single linear path of development but merely at different positions. This might be considered to express an optimistic attitude regarding the possibility of overcoming differences in the area of gender roles and sexuality between the two societies in question, and indeed Helfer uses the term to counter al-Daif's claim that no one in the West can understand the courtship difficulties that he describes in one of his novels. In addition, Helfer's appeal to *Ungleichzeitigkeit* implicitly rejects the notion of Germany's superiority by calling attention to the oppressiveness of its recent past.

From another perspective, one identified by Huntington and elaborated on by Joseph A. Massad in regard to gender, sexuality, and LGBT rights,[5] Helfer's invocation of *Ungleichzeitigkeit* can be read as a rejection of cultural particularity and an insistence on one model of civilizational progress that is parochially Western yet masquerades as universal. Not only does *Ungleichzeitigkeit* suggest that there is only one possible trajectory of development—a single timeline—it also allows Helfer to position al-Daif as lagging behind the West in his understanding of homosexuality, for he considers the perceived equation of male homosexuality with effeminacy in al-Daif's remarks to reflect a paradigm of sexuality developed in Europe at the end of the nineteenth century: specifically, he refers to the notion of the "third sex" associated with German sexologist Magnus Hirschfeld, who viewed homosexuality as a congenital deviation and "inversion" of the normal sexual sensibility.[6]

---

4. Ernst Bloch, "Non-Contemporaneity and Intoxication," in *Heritage of Our Times*, trans. Neville Plaice and Stephen Plaice (Berkeley and Los Angeles: University of California Press, 1990), 37–183.

5. Joseph A. Massad, *Desiring Arabs* (Chicago: University of Chicago Press, 2007).

6. See, for example, Manfred Herzer, *Magnus Hirschfeld: Leben und Werk eines jüdischen, schwulen und sozialistischen Sexologen* (Hamburg: Männerschwarm Skript Verlag, 2001).

Hirschfeld's ideas are largely rejected by contemporary North American and European queer theorists, who in the tradition of poststructuralism emphasize fluidity, incongruity, and alterity over stability, coherence, and identity.

All this is significant because not only is the defense of LGBT rights important for Helfer but he is also concerned with *how* such rights are defended. His plea for homosexuality is not based on congenital disposition but rather on personal fulfilment and autonomy. He chose his partner not just because he was a man but also because he was the *person* he could envision spending his life with, and refers to himself as "the defender of my own happiness—like Rashid and every other human being" (91). Even more strongly, he writes: "Respect for individual freedom in the framework of boundaries drawn only in respect for the freedom of others is for me not only a nonnegotiable cultural achievement of the West, but also nothing other than its prevailing morality" (92–93). This is a clear statement of the telos of the timeline upon which Helfer has placed al-Daif and Lebanon in a lagging position. Since in this description it is the West that has "achieved" this morality by first reaching the goal, it is possible through such a formulation to describe sexual self-determination as *both* universal *and* a product of Western Civilization.

Helfer's insistence on sexual self-determination is consistent with his implicit invocation of poststructural paradigms of identity—although not consistent with the political discourse emphasizing congenital minority status for homosexuals often used by gay rights activists in another country classified as part of the West: namely the United States. By deploying the idiom of feminism and queer theory currently in vogue in European and North American universities, Helfer establishes a kind of academic legitimacy but also produces a jarring discordance with the more personal and confessional tone of al-Daif's text. In a manner of speaking, Helfer's approach deploys different rules associated with a different language game; a game associated with a different textual genre.

The German publishing industry is highly invested in genre designations, which appear to operate as important indicators for situating texts in terms of markets, readers, etc. Such labels may or may not be the result of an author's choice for a particular designation and may be more or less valuable for literary scholars as accurate categorizations of the text in question. For example, a compendium of texts resulting from the West-Eastern Divan project published by C. H. Beck in 2007 groups its texts into three categories: *Reportagen* (reports), *Gedichte* (poems), and *Dialoge* (dialogues); an excerpt from *Die Verschwulung der Welt* [*The Queering of the World*] is included in the third grouping. [7] One can certainly object to the naming of this unique text as a dialogue, given the fact that it consists of what was written originally by al-Daif as a unified whole and Helfer's asynchronous commentary, interjected after the fact without the opportunity for al-Daif to respond. The version of *Die Verschwulung der Welt* published by Suhrkamp, which, unlike the present English translation, includes al-Daif's text *only* with Helfer's commentary inserted, does not include a genre designation on the cover; however, it does refer to a "dialogue" in the cover blurb and carries the subtitle *Rede gegen Rede Beirut-Berlin*. The German *Rede gegen Rede* suggests a parity or equality on the playing field between the two authors that does not exist, although the designation does call attention to the competitive aspect of the exchange. Further, the inclusion of Beirut-Berlin can be interpreted as a language gesture that encourages the reader to interpret the remarks less as expressions of individuals than as representatives of cities and their respective national cultures and is vaguely reminiscent of the description of a soccer match insofar as the hyphen placed between the two capitals takes the place of the *gegen* (against). Indeed, the formulation *Rede gegen Rede* is a kind of play on words suggesting the phrase *Rede Gegenrede* (discourse counter-discourse) that when written as *Rede gegen Rede* (pronounced the same except for an emphasis on the third word rather than the second) further underscores the idea of an athletic competition.

The Suhrkamp cover blurb also refers to al-Daif's text as *eine Art anthropologische Studie* (a kind of anthropological study), and in his commentary Helfer concurs by describing himself as an

---

7. Joachim Sartorius, ed., *Zwischen Berlin und Beirut: West-östliche Geschichten* (Munich: Beck, 2007).

interkulturellen Anschauungsobjekt (object of intercultural observation). Whereas Helfer and his German publisher have redefined al-Daif's text for a German readership as an anthropological study and the combined text as a dialogue between cultures, they might have drawn upon another, transcultural genre of writing that is well-rehearsed and much analyzed in the German-speaking world in order to build a bridge between al-Daif's writing and a textual genre familiar to educated German readers: the novella. The novella as a form spans diverse canonical literary traditions and is identified with Boccaccio, Chaucer, and Cervantes, in addition to more recent German-language authors such as Thomas Mann (*Death in Venice*) and Franz Kafka (*The Metamorphosis*). None other than Goethe himself, building upon Cervantes, describes the genre as having the essential characteristic of narrating a *sich ereignete unerhörte Begebenheit* (unprecedented event that occurred).[8] Helfer's unexpected decision to father a child with a British-German journalist might be seen as precisely such an unprecedented occurrence, one that proves to be such an object of wonder for al-Daif that it explains "how the German came to his senses." Helfer reacts with considerable estrangement to al-Daif's description of the "wedding feast" that follows their decision to raise the child together while living separately: Would his alienation have been less had he read his Lebanese colleague's text as a novella rather than as an anthropological study?[9]

Thus we see less of a divergence between the two authors on the "nature of culture" (if I may) than in different choices for how one should *talk* about culture, or at the least, how one should perform an authorial response to the injunction to engage in intercultural dialogue. The different choices and responses of the two authors,

---

8. Winfried Freund, *Novelle* (Stuttgart: Reclam, 1998).

9. Andreas Pflitsch elaborates on the literary qualities of al-Daif's texts to argue against what he refers to as Helfer's "sacrilege": his intervention in a literary text and concomitant violation of its literariness. See Andreas Pflitsch, "'The Importance of Being Earnest': Anmerkungen zu einem Buch gewordenen Missverständnis zwischen Joachim Helfer und Rashid Al-Daif," in *Humor in der Arabischen Kultur: Humor in Arabic Culture*, ed. Georges Tamer (Berlin and New York: Walter de Gruyter, 2009), 347–366. One does wonder, however, how one might reconcile an injunction to intercultural dialogue with the drawing of sacred boundaries around a literary text? What would be the rules of a literary intercultural dialogue?

however, also must be viewed in the framework of the West-Eastern Divan project itself, which, Helfer rightly notes, manifests the power differential in the publishing industry between their respective societies. Helfer calls attention to this discrepancy but also uses it to his advantage in the context of the German publication, where he is able to subvert the genre chosen by al-Daif, transforming a literary response to the exchange into a pseudodialogue in which Helfer reserves the right to refute the false propositions set forth by al-Daif.

The two authors' different conceptions of their genre and the intercultural project are seen in a difference in register and tone, recognizable through the two authors' distinct rhetorical gestures and semantic choices from the very beginning of their texts. Whereas al-Daif begins with describing how he met Helfer for the first time as a direct expression of personal experience ("I met"), only vaguely referring to the goals of the Divan project and not wasting a single word on the form/genre that he has chosen, Helfer's first inserted comment uses the passive voice to refer to the specific nature of the task and the genre expectation of the textual product: an essay. More specifically, Helfer describes al-Daif's text (of which the German reader has only experienced a single paragraph) specifically as a *Protokoll* (protocol), a genre that is even less open to creativity and fictionalization than an essay. In German literature the protocol has primarily been associated with *Literatur der Arbeitswelt* (literature of the working world), which in postwar West Germany was practiced by socially progressive and politically engaged authors such as Erika Runge, Max von der Grün, and Günter Wallraff. These authors used documentary forms and journalistic techniques to investigate and record the conditions of workers in the Federal Republic of Germany with the aim of raising public awareness and inciting political action. Since a protocol is a documentation of which an accurate recounting of people, places, and events is expected, and since readers are encouraged or even expected to draw political conclusions based on the documentary record, it is not surprising that Helfer takes umbrage at certain inaccuracies in al-Daif's text, since he chooses to read it with the high standards of accuracy required for protocols and anthropological studies and since

GARY SCHMIDT

politically there remains much at stake worldwide for individuals
who do not conform to heteronormative expectations.

Helfer's opening commentary sets up not only genre
expectations but, in keeping with these, defines concepts that he
deems critical, such as "representativeness." His definitional efforts
bring to the fore how all attempts to read culture on the basis of an
individual's utterances—regardless of how educated and insightful
the individual is—are dependent on some rather giant leaps that at
any point can cause the leaper to plummet into an abyss. These leaps
are actually encouraged, perhaps even required, by the injunction
to engage in intercultural dialogue: one is caught in the paradox
of being tasked with overcoming cultural differences by identifying
cultural differences, thus running the risk of producing such
differences and reessentializing the notion of culture itself. Helfer
addresses this conundrum in his discussion of representativeness.
The assertion of representativeness, according to Helfer, requires
also the assertion of difference, and implicitly *différance*, the
neologism coined by French philosopher Jacques Derrida to
describe the process by which identity is created by constructing
binary oppositions that are permanently unstable and require the
endless deferral of meaning through the production of language.[10]
Helfer writes, "We can only represent our societies to the extent that
what we live and advocate can be lived and advocated in our respective
societies without scandal, while in the other's it would mean the
violation of a taboo" (57). In other words, a person, product, or
behavior cannot be at the same time representative of one culture
and of another: its possibility in one culture is juxtaposed with
its prohibition in the other—a binary distinction that sets up the
identity of one cultural group through disidentification with the
other. Logically, then, Helfer sets out to look for such taboos.

In keeping with the more academic (German: *wissenschaftlich*)
register of his commentary, Helfer presents us with a discussion
of masculinity and femininity implicitly grounded in the
deessentializing theories of feminism and queer theory, although
he never states this as such. His identification of al-Daif's "women"

10. Jacques Derrida, "From 'Différance'" in *A Derrida Reader: Between the Blinds*, ed.
Peggy Kamuf (New York: Columbia University Press, 1991), 59–79.

as simply a socially constructed category for the oppressed brings to mind Monique Wittig's cultural materialist analysis of women as a class of oppressed individuals that, rather than preexisting the oppressions of its members, bears a *"mark* imposed by the oppressor." Wittig references Simone de Beauvoir's famous claim that "one is not born a woman, but becomes a woman."[11] In a similar vein, Helfer's remarks on machismo play in Berlin's gay subculture as well as on historical links between male-male desire and warrior cults further reflect the notion of multiple masculinities, and, as Australian sociologist R. W. Connell reminds us, these are neither monolithic nor immutable but rather act as shifting sites of cultural contestation and social jockeying.[12] The assertions of Wittig, Connell, and many others not only reject a biological essentialism of "sex," but also a cultural essentialism of "gender"; just as it is true that the cultural meanings ascribed to an individual's biological sex vary across time and place, so too do they vary among individuals who attempt to describe, define, and hence—of necessity—limit their meanings within a particular cultural framework. By using the lexicon currently accepted in the field of gender and sexuality studies in Germany and North America, which emphasizes the social construction, performativity, multiplicity, and fluidity of genders and sexualities, Helfer establishes his credentials and marks his text as, at the very least, informed by these academic discourses.

Helfer's commentary also engages in the critical practices associated with contemporary gender and sexuality studies. Viewed from this perspective, al-Daif's "protocol" is a fiction masquerading as transparent representation and hence a fair target for deconstructive analysis. Thus, Helfer attempts to explode the frame of al-Daif's camera, for example when he excludes feminine display and homosexuality from his image of Beirut in favor of the "celebration and proud exhibition of masculinity" (61). Yet

11. Monique Wittig, "One Is Not Born a Woman," in *Feminist Theory Reader*, 3rd ed., ed. Carole R. McCann and Seung-Kyung Kim (New York and London: Routledge, 2013), 246–251. For discussions of the intellectual origins of queer theory in feminism, see Chapter 3 of William B. Turner, *A Genealogy of Queer Theory* (Philadelphia: Temple University Press, 2000), as well as Annamarie Jagose, *Queer Theory: An Introduction* (New York: NYU Press, 1997).

12. R. W. Connell, *Masculinities* (Berkeley: University of California Press, 1995).

this deconstruction is aimed not at Arab or Lebanese culture as a whole, but rather at al-Daif's portrayal of it, for as Helfer asserts, a culture is never being but always becoming, and is always in flux. Thus, attempts to link particular gender norms to the unchanging requirements of culture—for example, attributions of patriarchal structures or homophobic stereotypes to an Arab or Oriental worldview—ultimately fail, for as Helfer notes, Nazi Germany and the Islamic Republic of Iran arrived from very different cultural preconditions to similar homophobic and misogynistic policies. Through this linguistic move, culture seems to disappear as a meaningful explanation for sex-gender repression.

Problems arise when Helfer fails to grant autonomy to al-Daif as the author of his text and takes on an Orientalizing tone. This happens when he no longer believes in the "representativeness" of al-Daif's "protocol"—for example, in the Lebanese author's account of his son's first heterosexual experience. The German author alludes to broad general knowledge about the Middle East—"everything you can read" (67)—to suggest the improbability of al-Daif's story, and lapses into a didactic tone, lecturing the reader about what is typical for Arab society rather than allowing al-Daif's words to stand on their own. This gesture runs counter to the otherwise deconstructive trajectory followed by Helfer: rather than exploding the frame in order to make visible greater complexity and diversity, Western academic knowledge about the Middle East is invoked to exclude certain events from the realm of possibility and to challenge the faithfulness of al-Daif's "protocol."

Yet, Helfer also seeks to preserve his colleague's status and autonomy as an author, for example in his response to al-Daif's litany of stereotypes of homosexuals as effeminate, women-hating nymphomaniacs. Here, rather than read this as a genuine expression of personal belief, Helfer prefers to see it as a "literary mask" that reflects (i.e., is *representative* of) the values of al-Daif's Arab readership. The attribution of realism associated by Helfer with al-Daif's text is thus projected onto a different level, but one might ask if the recognition of this level of literariness and narratological complexity does not already require more complex reading strategies than those applied to a protocol or anthropological study, and indeed in spite of Helfer's reference to al-Daif's "literary mask" and his avowal of respect for his authorial autonomy, he continues to read his Lebanese counterpart's text as a protocol that must be corrected. Only this can account for the fact that he finds it necessary to contrast the reality of "hummus, curd cheese, and kebabs with pita bread for the three of us" to the large festive gathering in a restaurant described in al-Daif's narrative and then to attribute this discrepancy to an Arab writer's desire to "spin a yarn" (164). What constitutes the Orientalism of Helfer's linguistic move is the fact that he situates the fictionality of al-Daif's text in his belonging to a Middle Eastern literary culture, invoking *The Thousand and One Nights*, which represents the quintessential "Oriental" text for many German speakers, and offering even a corrective interpretation of it that he himself proclaims to be universal. Here, recourse to cultural difference becomes a last-ditch effort to explain discrepancies between the German author's lived experience of the events and the Lebanese author's stylization of these events in his narrative. It is understandable that an author whose writing has been almost entirely devoted to reflecting and stylizing his own biography would experience frustration when his life is appropriated by another author with very different results than he would wish for. The experience and representation of the new in a postmodern world in which so much appears to be a repetition of the past or a banalization of identity categories is one of Helfer's central themes: I argue elsewhere, for example, that specifically the threat of being perceived and pigeonholed as a gay author lurks behind the self-stylization of the protagonist of Helfer's second novel, *Cohn und König*.[13] Just as problematic, of course, is Helfer's apparent heterosexualization in al-Daif's account of "how the German came to his senses," which appears to omit a third option: an escape from the heterosexual/homosexual binarism.

But Helfer himself is also partly complicit in erasing or repressing fluidity in his observations of al-Daif and Lebanese society. A striking example of this occurs when Helfer expresses

13. Gary Schmidt, "Between Venice and West Hollywood: The Homosexual Text in Joachim Helfer's *Cohn Und König*," *Gegenwartsliteratur: A German Studies Yearbook* 4 (2005): 185–210.

an inability to understand why al-Daif interprets his behavior at a dinner party in a manner that, for the German author, is contradictory to how the Lebanese writer should have reacted based on the association of femininity with passivity/penetrability and masculinity with activity/penetration (Helfer refers to the Greek model of sexuality that he sees as the heritage of Lebanese and other Mediterranean cultures to build this argument). Helfer's comments are worth quoting in full:

> It is hard to comprehend [. . .] that the expectations and ideas that Rashid takes for granted, presumably representative of his society to some degree, are themselves so contradictory: if he considers me, as a homosexual, to be a woman rather than a man, why does he interpret it as an erotic sign and not as an attempt to avoid such a thing when I behave as a woman would in his society and sit next to a strange woman rather than a strange man? (132)

Such a standard of consistency regarding the "expectations and ideas" either of a culture or of its native informant—here al-Daif—is itself inconsistent with Helfer's statements explaining to al-Daif why his relationship with Ingrid does not mean he has become heterosexual; here he proclaims the logic of the "this but also that," championing the incongruity and fluidity of queer theory and practice. It appears that Helfer wants to embrace poststructural discourses on gender and sexuality for his own experience and his society, for himself and for Europe if you will, but precludes the possibility of the relevance of these discourses for al-Daif. Perhaps then, for Helfer, it is primarily academic discourse that in Lebanon lags behind the West, yet the question remains whether al-Daif's text should be read as academic discourse or as something entirely different.

THE TEMPLE OF HETERONORMATIVITY: RASHID AL-DAIF'S *HOW THE GERMAN CAME TO HIS SENSES*, JOACHIM HELFER'S *THE QUEERING OF THE WORLD*, AND NAVID KERMANI'S *THOU SHALT*—A COMPARATIVE READING

ANDREAS KRASS

HUMBOLDT UNIVERSITY OF BERLIN

THE SPECTER OF SODOMY

Jews, Christians, and Muslims share the same forefather, Abraham: "A father of many nations" (Genesis 17:5). Thus, Judaism, Christianity, and Islam are often referred to as "Abrahamic" religions. They have, of course, more in common than the highly esteemed patriarch that they trace themselves back to. Among many shared narratives they all tell of the destruction of Sodom, the city where Abraham's nephew Lot once lived. The legend is told in the Bible (Genesis 19:1–29) as well as in the Qur'an (sura 7:80–84). God burns Sodom to the ground since "the men of Sodom were wicked and sinners before the Lord exceedingly" (Genesis 13:13). As the story goes, Lot once received two guests—angels, in fact—and the inhabitants of Sodom called upon him to "bring them out unto us, that we may know them" (Genesis 19:5). In Hebrew (as in English), "to know" also means "to have sex with." What the Sodomites wanted to do with Lot's guests is understood today as homosexuality, a term coined in the nineteenth-century as part of medical discourse.[1] It thus carries with it still a strong pathological connotation and the bitter taste of discrimination. In premodern times, men practicing sexual acts with each other were named "sodomites" (referring to Sodom) in the Christian world and "*lūṭī*" (referring to Lot) in the Arab world. Both words are still in use—just as discrimination against and even prosecution of homosexuals are still present all over

---

1. Cf. Michel Foucault, *The History of Sexuality*, Volume 1: An Introduction (New York: Vintage Books, 1990).

the world, and are often justified by Christian, Jewish, and Islamic spiritual leaders.

The specter of sodomy is the subject of two German books published several years ago: Navid Kermani's collection of short stories titled *Du sollst* (*Thou Shalt*), published in 2005,[2] and Joachim Helfer's *Die Verschwulung der Welt* (*The Queering the World*), published in 2006.[3] While Kermani's book was unanimously well received,[4] Helfer's book caused a lively controversy in German newspapers and magazines.[5] Both Kermani's and Helfer's books appear in the contested and conflicted area between East and West: Kermani as a German-Iranian author and an expert in Islamic studies, Helfer as a German novelist responding to the book *'Awdat al-almani ila rushdih* (*How the German Came to His Senses*, 2005) by the Lebanese author Rashid al-Daif. Both Kermani and Helfer drew inspiration for their books from the renowned Wissenschaftskolleg (Institute for Advanced Studies) in Berlin. Kermani was a fellow at the Wissenschaftskolleg from 2000 to 2003, and he places the concluding story of his book in a fictitious institute whose parallel to its counterpart in the real world is more blatant than subtle. Helfer met his Lebanese colleague al-Daif as part of the West-Eastern Divan—an exchange program that was cosponsored by the Wissenschaftskolleg in order to promote cultural dialogue between Germany and the Middle East.

THE PLEASURES OF HOMOPHOBIA

All three books allow for disturbing insights into Eastern and Western discourses on male same-sex sexuality. Kermani's insight is rather voyeuristic and to some extent pornographic. The

---

2. Navid Kermani, *Du sollst* (Zürich: Amman, 2005). An English translation of some parts of the book is provided on the author's website: http://www. navidkermani.de/view.php?nid=106.

3. Joachim Helfer and Rashid al-Daif, *Die Verschwulung der Welt. Rede gegen Rede. Beirut—Berlin.* Aus dem Arabischen von Günther Orth. Mit einem Nachwort von Joachim Sartorius. (Frankfurt am Main: Suhrkamp, 2006).

4. Kermani lists two dozen reviews on his website: http://www.navidkermani.de/ view.php?nid=36.

5. The debate is documented on the website of the West-Eastern Divan: http:// www.westoestlicherdivan.de/.

concluding narrative of his book tells the story of a young male
chemist engaging in a sadomasochistic relationship with an older
male professor of religious studies. The narrative is preceded by
ten short stories alluding to the Ten Commandments (Exodus
20:1–17). Each evokes unsettling scenarios of heterosexual love
charged with violence and humiliation. In the first story ("I am thy
God") a man forces a woman to hail him as her sex god. In the
second story ("Thou shalt not make unto thee any graven image or
likeness") a man and a woman each indulge in sexual fantasies. In
the third story ("Thou shalt not take the name of thy God in vain")
a man forbids a woman to say that she loves him; and so forth.
Disturbingly, the narrator is complicit with the male characters'
misogynistic victimization of the female characters, which is made
all the more troubling by the fact that in some of the ten short
stories the female characters are presented as the guilty party. In
the sixth story ("Thou shalt not kill") the woman butchers the man
after the sex act like an animal. The tenfold horrors of heterosexual
love are followed by homophobic panic in an eleventh story, which,
significantly, takes up as much space as the ten preceding ones
put together. The aging professor—like Kermani an expert on the
Hebrew Bible and Iranian mysticism—repeatedly stresses the fact
that he is not gay, and moreover, that he could not be gay for the
reason that "sodomy was forbidden by God."[6] The narrator adopts
the perspective of the sadistic young scientist, who is increasingly
intrigued and aroused by exercising sexual power over the older
man. Eventually, he imagines himself as being as powerful as God.
Kermani does not spare his reader any detail in the depiction of
both sexual and religious humiliation: "I ordered him to jerk off
to the Scriptures."[7] Finally the younger man forces the older one
to deride his faith in front of the members of the institute: "God
himself has come and fucked mankind in the ass."[8] Again, Kermani
justifies the pornographic and blasphemous language with the
authority of the Bible. The title of the homosexual story quotes the

---

6. Cf. Kermani, *Du sollst*, 138.

7. Ibid., 145: "[. . .] als ich ihm befahl, es sich mit der Schrift zu machen."

8. Ibid., 151: "Gott selbst sei gekommen, er habe die Menschen in den Arsch
gefickt."

244   prophetic warning following the Decalogue: "Fear not: for God is come to prove you, and that his fear may be before your faces, that ye sin not" (Exodus 20:20).

QUEERING THE WORLD

The biographies of Joachim Helfer and Navid Kermani show some striking parallels. Both are renowned German writers. Both grew up in provincial towns in Germany. Both men are around fifty. Both are married and fathers of two daughters. Both live in gay-friendly cities (Kermani in Cologne, Helfer in Berlin). But there are also some significant differences. While Kermani is married to a woman, Helfer is married to a man. Kermani is openly straight, Helfer is openly gay. Kermani wrote a book of fiction that lustfully evokes homophobia with religious undertones. Helfer wrote a commentary on al-Daif's semifictitious reportage on his, Helfer's, life. In this riposte he eschews all mystification and demonization of homosexuality. The provocative title of Helfer's text—*The Queering of the World*—cites a phrase from the German author Hubert Fichte. Fichte once pleaded that the world could only be saved by becoming gay.[9] What both Fichte and Helfer mean by this bon mot is: the world can only be saved if heteronormative thinking is deconstructed. While the perspective of straight people is often restricted to the heteronormative world in which they grew up, the perspective of gay people is always twofold: though raised as straight and taught to see the world that way, from early on they also see it from a gay point of view. This gap between authentic and prescribed perspective, disturbing to the point of suicide for many a youngster, is only resolved by coming out. Once out, the gay person learns to express his or her non-straight point of view. By the same token, he or she learns to realize and express individual and cultural differences. In this respect, it may make sense to some extent to equate "gay" with "enlightened."

---

9. Hubert Fichte, *Alte Welt* (Frankfurt am Main: S. Fischer, 1992), 128: "Nur eine Verschwulung kann die Welt retten."

Two voices participated in the academic project that resulted in Helfer's book. First, al-Daif visited Helfer for several weeks in Berlin, and then Helfer repaid the visit and spent several weeks with his Lebanese colleague in Beirut. After the exchange, al-Daif wrote a report on his encounter with a gay man and published it in Arabic. The title of his book, *How the German Came to His Senses*, is a pun since the Arabic word for senses or reason is homonymous with the author's name: Rashid. The ironic subtext of the title is not so difficult to grasp: Helfer came to his senses by visiting Rashid al-Daif. With tongue-in-cheek humor al-Daif suggests that a man living in a same-sex relationship is insane, but his condition has a cure: "knowing" a woman and fathering a child. This kind of male heterosexual humor is well known with respect to lesbians: "She hasn't found the right man yet." Interestingly enough, the same logic seems not to apply to heterosexual men.

Helfer, rather than refusing to allow the publication in German of a book-length reportage on his private life, chose to respond to al-Daif's book by interspersing his own commentary. As he demonstrates, al-Daif reinterprets the actual events according to traditional Eastern prejudices about the character, desire, and lifestyle of Western homosexual men. Sometimes it is hard to tell whether or not the outrageous stereotypes presented by the narrator reflect the author's own beliefs. Many reviewers—such as the German writer Michael Kleeberg—think that the story told by al-Daif is self-deprecating and that he invented the role of the naïve narrator in order to ridicule homophobic anxiety in Arab societies, and to prompt a critical reflection.[10] Helfer, for his part, not only comments on the text, but gives his own account of the actual encounter with the real person al-Daif. It was the man al-Daif, not an ironic literary mask, who did and said what Helfer reports. If, for instance, making sure not to swallow any food at

---

10. A German and an Arabic version of his review can be found on the website of the West-Eastern Divan: http://www.westoestlicherdiwan.de/besprechungen_daif-helfer.pdf (German original), http://www.westoestlicherdiwan.de/3_rezensionen_arab_original.pdf (Arabic translation).

the dining table of a gay couple was an act of enlightened sarcasm, Helfer was definitely neither willing nor able to laugh about it.

CULTURAL JET LAG

Instead Helfer chooses to scrutinize the heteronormative stereotypes in both al-Daif's account and discourse, and to prove how absurd they are. He repeatedly states that such homophobic fantasies indicate a cultural anachronism rather than a fundamental cultural gap dividing the West and the East. Far from any Orientalist essentialism, Helfer interprets the level of homophobia in a culture as simply a reflection of the degree to which societies have become democratic and liberal. Germany introduced same-sex civil unions in 2001 and antidiscrimination laws that include sexual orientation in 2006. During this same time, a federal institution promoting equal rights and antidiscrimination practices was founded. In 2014, civil unions impart almost the same legal rights as traditional marriages—with the exception of full adoption rights. But, as Helfer reminds his readers, one must not forget that the repressive sodomy law of the Nazi regime—the infamous Paragraph 175—was adopted in full by the German postwar government. It was not until the late 1960s that West Germany began to relax the law little by little (East Germany already rendered it inoperative for all intents and purposes in 1959). Finally, in 1994 it was repealed— only twelve years before Kermani and Helfer wrote their books. After the repeal, the accelerating process of liberalization proved to be unstoppable.

It may be understandable if al-Daif—as benevolent reviewers of his book argue—plays the heteronormative fool in order to challenge and even expose Arab stereotypes on homosexuality. After all, the Lebanese author lives in a society still largely hostile toward homosexuality. Same-sex sexual acts are illegal in Lebanon (as they are in the entire Middle East), and punishable with fines or imprisonment. This, however, is not the case with the state and city where Kermani lives and works. In Germany, homosexuality is mostly accepted and at least fully legalized. In Cologne, the acceptance of gays is to the point that it has become part of local folklore and identity. (In this respect, Cologne is a sort of German San Francisco.) Why, then, did Kermani choose to create a story that presents homosexuality as a descent into hell? What good is the dark fog of homophobia wafting through the second half of his book? The cultural jet lag in Kermani's book is fabricated, but the headaches it causes are real. Paradoxically, *Thou Shalt* proves to be an Orientalizing book written by an expert in Islamic studies. By wrapping his story in mystic parables, biblical framings, and prophetic poses, the narrator resembles a scribe performing the Dance of the Seven Veils. In this book sex between men may not be just sex between men—it is made to signify the relationship between teacher and disciple, master and servant, God and people, science and religion, Occident and Orient, penis and anus. By overdetermining same-sex desire, the book attests to how learned and well-read the author is in both Eastern and Western literatures. But instead of illuminating how and why sexual phobias work, the book serves as a sound box in which they just resonate all the more.

DESTROYING THE TEMPLE

While Kermani worships in the temple of heteronormativity, al-Daif shakes it a little by performing an ironic, almost carnivalesque ritual of male heterosexuality. Helfer, however, is not willing to enter the temple of heteronormativity, not even in the tongue-in-cheek manner adopted by al-Daif. He prefers to demolish the sacred building, and he does so with the sort of furor that God showed when he destroyed Sodom. In a sense al-Daif is right in suggesting that Helfer came to his senses when he visited him in Lebanon. The cultural exchange program he participated in as well as his host's account of it inspired Helfer to write a commentary that relentlessly questions all the heteronormative biases al-Daif makes fun of. What may be funny in a straight man's world may be annoying in a gay man's world. Helfer stirs up traditional opinions about gender and sexuality. He tumbles the distinctions of sex and gender, male and female, and homosexuality and heterosexuality, until not one stone of the temple is left standing.

The difference between Kermani's holy earnestness and Helfer's witty analysis is even more evident when it comes to a motif that is crucial for both of them: the desire to have a child. In Kermani's dark book there is a scene in which the joy of parenthood is celebrated as the fulfillment of human existence. Significantly it is located in the context of the fourth or, depending on the version, fifth commandment: "Honor thy father and thy mother." It is the only episode in the book that deals with the mutual love between a man and a woman. It attempts to be prosaic by using language like "Make a baby with me,"[11] but then does not manage to escape the diction of religious conventions. There are priestlike phrases such as "deciding to preserve creation" (by procreation).[12] The children—the narrator calls them "little angels"[13]—are already burdened with patriarchal expectations before they are even born: "I owe them to my parents."[14]

For Helfer, the desire to have a child is also a crucial motif. However, the child is not presented as a heterosexual privilege or a heteronormative fetish but as the legitimate wish of all human beings, including gay men. Visiting al-Daif in Beirut, Helfer becomes acquainted with a German journalist working for an Anglophone newspaper published in Beirut. She is an expert on Arab culture and familiar with gender studies. They become friends and talk about their common interest in having a child. Finally, they decide to have a child together. While Helfer is not willing to give up his longtime relationship with his partner, she does not want to give up her career as a journalist. Al-Daif interprets this event as an unexpected turning point, like a device in a novel. He transforms Helfer's life story into an Oriental fairytale about the miraculous conversion of a gay European to heterosexuality. Helfer, on the contrary, vividly pleads for the warmth and security of a queer family that consists of a single straight mother, a partnered gay father, the gay father's partner in

---

11. Kermani, *Du sollst*, 47: "Mach mir Kinder."
12. Ibid.: "Entscheidung zur Schöpfung."
13. Ibid.: "Engelchen."
14. Ibid., 50: "Ich schulde sie meinen Eltern."

the role of the child's grandfather, the gay father's younger lover as the nanny, and a most welcome, tenderly loved, and happy daughter. According to Helfer, this family may be considered nontraditional, but it is nevertheless functional and intact.

DIALOGISM

The difference between Kermani's, al-Daif's, and Helfer's texts can be characterized with the term "monologic," which was introduced to the theory of the novel by the Russian literary historian Mikhail Bakhtin,[15] who differentiates between monologic and dialogic literature. Kermani's book is monologic to the extent that it reproduces heteronormative notions of gender subordination and homophobia. Although it attempts to scandalize the subject of sexuality by blending religious and pornographic discourses, it still reaffirms the ideology of reproductive patriarchal heterosexuality. In principle, the same applies for al-Daif's book since it also embraces a male, heterosexual point of view on gender difference and sexuality. In contrast to Kermani, however, it abstains from evoking grim fantasies of gender violence and sexual phobia. Rather, it reproduces and ridicules ordinary stereotypes of gay men. Al-Daif's book is dialogic to the extent that it implements irony and satire. However, the dialogic dimension is limited for two reasons. First, it cannot be taken for granted that readers of al-Daif's book will realize both its satirical character and the purported split between the sophisticated author and the picaresque narrator. Second, while irony and satire may be suited for questioning heteronormative stereotypes, they do not necessarily allow for establishing a reasonable and open-minded view on gay people and same-sex love. Tellingly, al-Daif refrains from analyzing or even mentioning the discrimination homosexual men and women still face in Arab as well as Western countries. His account of the gay men he has personally encountered in the Middle East simply skips the not-so-subtle facts of forced emigration or suicide, honor killings,

---

15. Mikhail M. Bakhtin, *The Dialogic Imagination: Four Essays*, ed. Michael Holquist, trans. Caryl Emerson and Michael Holquist (Austin: University of Texas Press, 1981).

fines, and imprisonment. Even the death penalty awaits gay men in some countries in the region. Helfer's text is truly dialogic, as its subtitle announces: "Rede gegen Rede"—literally "discourse versus discourse." While al-Daif wrote his book without giving Helfer the chance to comment on it, Helfer wrote a counterstatement that refers to al-Daif's depiction of their acquaintance point by point. Unlike al-Daif, Helfer does not claim to write an autonomous—and in this respect monologic—book. Several reviewers criticized the fact that Helfer fractured and fragmented al-Daif's text in order to respond to it. This objection does not make much sense since it is easy enough to read al-Daif's text separately by skipping the inserted passages written by Helfer. The publisher (Suhrkamp) has also provided a version of al-Daif's text without Helfer's annotations that can be easily accessed on its website. Helfer's text is also dialogic in a linguistic sense. By responding to and commenting upon al-Daif's account, it allows for two voices or two "alphabets" (to use al-Daif's term): a "heterosexual" and a "homosexual" one, an "Oriental" and an "Occidental" one. This form of dialogism results in a text that makes those binaries collapse. While al-Daif insists on the alterity of heterosexuality and homosexuality as if they were different languages, Helfer attempts to break the heteronormative binaries and bridge the supposed divide by offering an outspoken and unabashed counter-discourse.

As Helfer admits in his book, there may be many readers who are not susceptible to his point of view: "Ultimately, everyone hears what he himself can imagine" (89). It seems that he is right in this respect. Many reviewers enjoyed the humor of al-Daif's book and blamed Helfer for being a poor sport. However, sometimes it is not so easy for gay men to laugh at the funny, ironic jokes straight men like to crack about them. They are, though, still easier to stomach than those dark and repressive fantasies about "sodomites" and "*lūṭī*."

CONTRIBUTORS

MICHAEL ALLAN is an Assistant Professor and Director of Graduate Studies in Comparative Literature at the University of Oregon, where he also serves as Program Faculty in Cinema Studies and Arabic. His teaching and publications span the fields of world literature, postcolonial studies, as well as francophone and modern Arabic literature and film.

RASHID AL-DAIF is a Lebanese author of sixteen novels and three volumes of poetry. A number of his novels have been translated into several languages; six have appeared in English, including *Who's Afraid of Meryl Streep?* He earned a PhD in Arabic literature and linguistics in Paris and spent his career as a professor at Lebanese University. His work is diverse but often explores themes of war, the couple, and emigration. He currently lives in Beirut.

REBECCA DYER is Associate Professor of English at Rose-Hulman Institute of Technology, where she teaches contemporary British, transnational, and Middle Eastern literature and film. Her publications include articles in *Cultural Critique*, *PMLA*, *College Literature*, and *Cultural Politics* focusing on authors' and filmmakers' class commentary and anticolonial and antiwar advocacy. As a Fulbright scholar teaching and conducting research at Lebanese American University in Beirut in the fall of 2007, she had the opportunity to meet Rashid al-Daif and discuss his work.

JOACHIM HELFER was born in Bonn, West Germany, in 1964, where his family fled after partition. His father was a political prisoner in East Germany from 1948 to 1956. Joachim studied English linguistics and literature in Hamburg. Having met his life partner, Ralph Nash, early on, he shared in his occupation as a leading international dealer in African and Oceanic art. Writing poetry and fiction since childhood, he published his first novel in 1994. Today he lives with his two daughters and their mother in Berlin.

ANDREAS KRASS is Professor of German literature at the Humboldt University of Berlin. His fields of interest include medieval German literature, theory of translation, gender studies/queer studies, and the literary history of sexuality and intimacy. His most recent books are *Durchkreuzte Helden: Das "Nibelungenlied" und Fritz Langs Film "Die Nibelungen" im Licht der Intersektionalitätsforschung* (2014, coeditor); *Meine erste Geliebte: Magnus Hirschfeld und sein Verhältnis zur schönen Literatur* (2013); *Meerjungfrauen: Geschichten einer unmöglichen Liebe* (2010); and *Nur über seine Leiche: Literaturgeschichte der Männerfreundschaft* (forthcoming).

GARY SCHMIDT is Professor of German and Chair of the Department of Foreign Languages and Literatures at Western Illinois University. He is coeditor of the volume *Thomas Mann: Neue Kulturwissenschaftliche Lektüren* (2012) and author of the book *The Nazi Abduction of Ganymede* (2003). He has written numerous articles on gender and sexuality in contemporary German and Austrian literature and film that have appeared in such journals as *German Quarterly*, *Colloquia Germanica*, and *Gegenwartsliteratur*.

KEN SEIGNEURIE is Professor and Director of the Program in World Literature at Simon Fraser University. His most recent book is *Standing by the Ruins: Elegiac Humanism in Wartime and Postwar Lebanon* (2011). His previous book is an edited collection of essays on Arabic and Hebrew literatures of war, *Crisis and Memory: The Representation of Space in Modern Levantine Narrative* (2003). He is currently General Editor of the *Wiley–Blackwell Companion to World Literature*.